THE LIFE AND TIMES OF
SHAIKH NIZAM-U'D-DIN AULIYA

THE LIFE AND TIMES OF
SHAIKH NIZAM-U'D-DIN AULIYA

NEW EDITION

Khaliq Ahmad Nizami

OXFORD
UNIVERSITY PRESS

OXFORD
UNIVERSITY PRESS

Oxford University Press is a department of the University of Oxford.
It furthers the University's objective of excellence in research, scholarship,
and education by publishing worldwide. Oxford is a registered trademark of
Oxford University Press in the UK and in certain other countries

Published in India by
Oxford University Press
YMCA Library Building, 1 Jai Singh Road, New Delhi 110001, India

© F.A. Nizami 2007

The moral rights of the author have been asserted

First published 2007
Fourth impression 2012

ISBN-13: 978-0-19-567701-0
ISBN-10: 0-19-567701-3

Typeset in Stone Serif 9/12
by Star Compugraphics Pvt Ltd, Delhi
Printed in India by Ram Printograph, New Delhi 110 051

Dedicated
to
that noble spirit of human love and sympathy
which made
Shaikh Nizam-u'd-din Auliya's heart
ache with pain
when he prayed to God
to alleviate the misery of those in distress

شهنشاها باسم خدمتی در خدمت آوردم

زکانِ سینهء پر لعل شیرین چوں تو ایثاری

CONTENTS

FOREWORD

------•◦•◦•------

It would be difficult to exaggerate the importance of either the subject or the author of this work. Both stand as landmarks for the experience as well as the study of Islam in the Asian sub-continent. Shaikh Nizam-u'd-din Auliya is a thirteenth/fourteenth century Delhi saint who epitomizes the intense spiritual engagement of Muslims with the mystery and awe of the Unseen, and also its ethical consequence. Professor K. A. Nizami is the foremost scholar of premodern Indian Sufism, widely published and frequently cited in both English- and Urdu-language estimates of the major saints, the orders, and the contexts of the Delhi Sultanate and its successor, the Mughal Empire.

No saint stands higher than Shaikh Nizam-u'd-din Auliya in accounts of the Sufi impact on the first millennium of Muslim presence in South Asia. He is identified with the Chishtiyya, the premier Sufi order of India. He is himself the successor of the major saint of the Punjab, Shaikh Farid-u'd-din Ganj-i-Shakar, and the master of the last of the first cycle of Chishti saints in Delhi, Shaikh Nasir-u'd-din Chiragh-i Dehli. What remains astonishing after the passage of centuries is the singularity of Shaikh Nizam-u'd-din Auliya. He stands among, but he also stand apart from, his predecessors and successors in the Chishti order. In a tradition where humility and deference to one's ancestors and superiors is commonplace, it is doubly hard both to see how different Shaikh Nizam-u'd-din Auliya is and at the same time to relate him to the larger group—Sufis in general, Chishtis in particular—of which he is considered to be an exemplar.

The task of understanding Shaikh Nizam-u'd-din Auliya is made more difficult by the nature of source materials available about his life and times. The genuine is mixed with the spurious, the authentic with the inauthentic, the loftiest with the most banal. One of Professor Nizami's own teachers, Professor Muhammad Habib, has set the standard for weighing different kinds of historical evidence for all Chishti spiritual giants, including Shaikh Nizam-u'd-din Auliya. The best accounts are the early accounts. The best of the earliest accounts record the saint's own words (*malfuzat*), supplemented by biographical compilation (*tazkirat*) made either soon after the saint's lifetime or later by scrupulous scholars. All other evidence has to be invoked warily or else rejected outright. Pious error is no substitute for scholarly integrity.

K. A. Nizami has performed the task of making Shaikh Nizam-u'd-din Auliya come to life, despite the intervening centuries and the challenge of sifting and weighing disparate material. 'Reconstructing the life of a medieval mystic', he notes, 'is, by no means, an easy job because fact and fiction, chaff and grain, the genuine and the spurious get so mixed up in hagiological accounts that only a firm application of the principles of critique can help draw an authentic sketch.'

The merit of the present book is that Nizami follows his own admonition. He applies fairly and firmly the principles of criticism (*usul-i-asnad*) laid down by medieval scholars. In seventeen chapters he evokes the life of the major Chishti saint of Delhi: his birth into an immigrant Muslim family; his life as a fatherless child; his zest for knowledge that carried him, his mother, and sister to Delhi; his devotion to Shaikh Farid-u'd-din Ganj-i-Shakar; his work for sixty years (1265–1325) as the leader of the Chishti order in Delhi; and finally his influence on subsequent generations of Muslims, and non-Muslims—all are portrayed here with scrupulous attention to what is knowable and laudable, while rejecting, or calling into question, what is imputed but improbable and often regrettable.

Nizami's own account first appeared more than a decade ago, and it built on the landmark monograph of Shaikh Nizam-u'd-din's master that he himself had written thirty-six years earlier, *Life and Times of Shaikh Farid-u'd-din Ganj-i-Shakar* (1955). Both monographs measure up to the rigorous standards of modern as well as medieval scholarship. A recent book that attempted to assess the economic and social impact of Sufism on fourteenth-century South Asia (Riazul Islam, *Sufism in South Asia* (2002)) noted that, along with Habib's classic essay on source material stands Nizami's note, 'Evaluation of Source Material', which appeared as an appendix to his classic study, *Some Aspects of Religion and Politics in India during the Thirteenth Century* (1961/ 2002). And to this list must be added the compilation of Nizami's historical studies, volume one of which is *On Sources and Source Material* (1995). The latter includes a pioneering essay on a little-known collection of Shaikh Nizam-u'd-din's discourses, *Durar-i-Nizami* (first published in 1983).

It is attention to Nizami's use of *Durar-i-Nizami* that displays how scrupulous his forensic intelligence is and at the same time how broad his imaginative recapitulation of the life and mood, the teaching and legacy of Shaikh Nizam-u'd-din Auliya. Nizami is intent to site the saint at very different angles. On the one hand, he wants to show how court and hospice contrasted in the attitudes they had to the saint, so that the view of the historian Zia-u'd-din Barani, while sympathetic to the saint, makes a more pragmatic estimate of his legacy than does the poet Amir Hasan or 'Ali Jandar in their respective *malfuzat* of the saint. In other words, there is no single profile of the saint even from authentic sources, so that one must weigh between them in order to have a full appreciation of the saint. 'The life story of Shaikh Nizam-u'd-din Auliya', he observes, 'provides an alternative vision to the political intrigues of the period, just as the pomp and panoply of the court, the din and clatter of arms on the battlefield (as recorded by Barani), contrast with the meditative saint, now laughing, now crying, ever at prayer with the One, happiest in discourse with the poor (as recorded by Amir Hasan and also by 'Ali Jandar).'

Even though the account of 'Ali Jandar confirms the testimony and recollection of Amir Hasan, they do not represent the same views of their saintly subject. Like other followers of Shaikh Nizam-u'd-din, they saw the saint very differently according to their own interests, talents, and dispositions. 'The *Durar-i-Nizami*', notes Nizami, 'throws valuable light on the life, thought, and personality of Shaikh Nizam-u'd-din. It reflects his profound interest in the Hadith literature. 'Ali Jandar has presented the moral and religious teaching of the Shaikh in a very succinct manner. No doubt the *Fawa'id-u'l-Fu'ad* reflects greater understanding of the depth of the Shaikh's thought and combines brevity of expression with perspicacity of ideas, but as the arrangement is not thematic, it is only after a study of the entire text that a picture of the Shaikh's moral and spiritual teaching on any particular aspect can be formed. A reader of the *Durar* has before him systematized information on a number of vital topics connected with religious life.'

Consistent with this observation, Nizami uses data from 'Ali Shah Jandar to amplify both *Fawa'id-u'l-Fu'ad* and *Siyar-u'l-Auliya*, even though Amir Khurd, author of the latter, had incorporated most of *Durar-i-Nizami* into his own work. Nizami's *Life and Times* provides an account of the Shaikh that displays documentary history at its best and something more.

The something more is his own empathetic engagement with the Shaikh, with his spiritual quest, and with his legacy for all Muslims. It is a familiar trope in biblical scholarship to speak of the second naïveté. The second naïveté can occur only after one has applied the most critical standards to ascertain the likely core of historical evidence about a period, a person, or a movement. After the labour of making clear what did happen and what can be verified as likely to have happened, one still must ask: so what? What is it that makes this period or this person or this movement so important beyond a particular time or a specific region?

For Nizami that question opens up what he distills in the seventeenth and final chapter of his remarkable study of Shaikh Nizam-u'd-din. The saint was more than a scholar or a mystic. 'He was one of the most charismatic personalities of South Asia . . . [who] represented in his person the highest traditions of religion and morality.' Confirming that judgement requires examination of the one aspect of the Shaikh's life that has been the most controversial: the relationship between the saint as spiritual master and the sultan as political ruler of the Delhi Sultanate. For Shaikh Nizam-u'd-din it was his deference to Sultan 'Ala-u'd-din Khalji (the most prominent of the Delhi rulers during his lifetime) that allowed him the space to project his spiritual force within the confines of his own hospice. He never had direct contact with the Sultan but, through his lay disciples who were also courtiers, including the historian Barani and the poet Amir Khusrau, he did influence the tone of imperial rule.

Nizami captures the competing authorities and also the contradiction for the saint when he observes that 'the Sultan had muzzled freedom of action; the Shaikh concentrated on building independent and self-reliant personalities, capable of thinking and acting independent of the Sultan. He did not enter into conflict with the state but, on his part, never allowed the state to fetter his soul.'

Subsequent generations of Indian Muslims have tried to live the tension etched by Shaikh Nizam-u'd-din's life and legacy. At no time more than the present, at the dawn of the twenty-first century, is it crucial to rethink how politics and religion can ever be fully separate. They each make claims on the total allegiance of citizens, whether in South Asia or North America or Western Europe or East Asia, and yet the larger message of Shaikh Nizam-u'd-din is, in Nizami's words, that the state must never be allowed to fetter the soul. Nizami has marked his own life by the study of the lives of saints, and in his singular study of the most prominent saint of the Delhi Sultanate, he has provided a book which is at once timeless and timely. It deserves the widest possible readership and appreciation within and beyond South Asia.

Bruce B. Lawrence
Nancy and Jeffrey Marcus Professor of Islamic Studies,
Duke University

PREFACE

Few saints in the long and chequered history of medieval India had such impact on the life and thought of their contemporaries as Shaikh Nizam-u'd-din Auliya (1244–1325). For more than half a century, his *khanqah* in Delhi was a rendezvous for people drawn from different backgrounds—villagers and townsfolk, men and women, scholars and illiterates, rich and poor. The Shaikh had taken upon himself the stupendous task of showing people the way to God and inspiring them with that faith and confidence in Him which sustained them in their life struggles. Toynbee thought that 'the practical test of a religion, always and everywhere, is its success or failure in helping human souls to respond to the challenges of suffering and sin.'[1] By that measure, Shaikh Nizam-u'd-din Auliya's role in the religious history of South Asia was of immense significance. For him 'bringing happiness to the human heart' was the essence of religion. Amir Khusrau, one of his many famous students, and one who realized the measure of his achievement in reorienting religious attitudes in that period, called him 'healer of the heart' (*tabib-i-dil*). His life story, in fact, forms a fascinating chapter in the history of the philanthropic effort of man to reduce the woe and worry of his fellow human beings. Ibn Battuta has referred to a trust which was created in Damascus to bring solace to broken hearts.[2] Shaikh Nizam-u'd-din Auliya's own life became a trust of this type.

This work is based on an extensive critical study of the contemporary literature—both political and mystical. A select bibliography of the works used appears in Appendix X. The *Qiwam-u'l-'Aqa'id* of Jamal Qiwam-u'd-din, written in the Deccan in 755/1354 during

---

[1] Arnold Toynbee, *An Historian's Approach to Religion* (Edinburgh, 1953), p. 296.
[2] *Rihla*, I p. 63.

the reign of the Bahmanid ruler 'Ala-u'd-din Bahman Shah, barely twenty-nine years after the death of the Shaikh, has been used for the first time to reconstruct the life of Shaikh Nizam-u'd-din Auliya. In addition to other mystic works, *Nafa'is-u'l-Anfas*, *Ahsan-u'l-Aqwal*, *Shama'il-u'l-Atqiya*, and *Shawamil-u'l-Jumal dar Shama'il-Kumal* were also much referred to in the preparation of this study.

K. A. Nizami
Aligarh

INTRODUCTION

'How many scholars and learned men have flourished in the past,' Shaikh Nizam-u'd-din Auliya once told his audience, 'but nobody [now] knows who they were and where they lived. What really survives is [the memory of] living happily with people. This is real spiritual living (*hayat-i ma`nawi*).'[1] The Shaikh's own life illustrates the significance of this remark.

Shaikh Nizam-u'd-din Auliya's memory is enshrined in the hearts of men and his message of human love, goodwill, and tolerance echoes down the corridors of time. His life in Delhi was a continuous struggle to fulfil what he considered to be the divine purpose of creation: to show man the way to God and to make him realize the value of purposeful living devoted to the service of fellow human beings. He gave a revolutionary dimension to religious activity by identifying it with the service of man. He told his disciples that looking after the needy and the destitute was of greater value than formal performance of religious rites.[2] A contemporary saint once remarked that while God has given one power to mystics in general, He had bestowed two upon him: to pray to God and to bear the burden of caring for the people.[3] Both God and man thus formed the basis of his dynamic social value-system. His religious consciousness derived its sustenance from both. 'The fountain of all the nobler morality,' writes J. S. Blackie 'is moral inspiration from within; and the feeder of this fountain is God.'[4]

---

[1] *Fawa'id-u'l-Fu'ad*, p. 164; *Siyar-u'l-Auliya*, p. 539.
[2] *Fawa'id-u'l-Fu'ad*, pp. 13–14, 176; *Durar-i-Nizami*, MS; *Siyar-u'l-Auliya*, p. 128.
[3] *Tuhfat-u'l-Majalis*, *malfuz* of Shaikh Ahmad Maghribi, I.O.D.P. MS No. 977 f. 24ᵃ⁻ᵇ
[4] J. S. Blackie, *Self-Culture* (Edinburgh, 1886), p. 61.

Shaikh Nizam-u'd-din Auliya quoted with approval the saying of Shaikh Abu Sa'id Abu'l-Khair that, though there were as many ways leading to God as particles of sand, none was more effective and efficacious for attaining gnosis than bringing happiness to the human heart.[5] Whoever aspired to reach God had to seek His benevolence through service of His creatures.[6] This became the *élan* of Shaikh Nizam-u'd-din Auliya's life. Innumerable people brought their tales of affliction and misery to him and he prayed to God for them with his own heart aching in pain.[7] He not only helped his visitors to tide over their difficulties but created in them the self-confidence and self-discipline that gives dignity to human life and strengthens moral fibre. He believed that sincere faith in God and respect for moral values acted as a bulwark against the onslaught of material and mundane forces. A society which ignored moral and ethical ideals stood on quicksand.

Shaikh Nizam-u'd-din Auliya's family originally hailed from Bukhara. They were forced to leave their homeland under the pressure of Mongol invasions. Chingiz Khan reduced Bukhara, a flourishing city on the Zarafshan, to rubble: 'More than thirty thousand men were executed and the remainder were, with the exception of the very old people amongst them, reduced to slavery, without any distinction of rank whatever; and thus the inhabitants of Bukhara, lately so celebrated for their learning, their love of art, and their general refinement, were brought down to a dead level of misery and degradation and scattered to all quarters. But a few escaped the general ruin.'[8] Among the few who escaped were the father and grandfather of Shaikh Nizam-u'd-din Auliya. Ibn Athir informs us that it was a terrible day. 'Nothing was to be heard but the sobs and lamentations of husbands, wives and children who were being parted for ever.'[9]

Torn from their ancestral land and family ties, Shaikh Nizam-u'd-din's ancestors fled to India and eventually settled in Badaon—a quiet place where people who disdained political struggle and did not want to involve themselves in government service preferred to live away from

---

[5] *Siyar-u'l-Auliya*, p. 411; *Durar-i-Nizami*, MS.

[6] *Siyar-u'l-Auliya*, pp. 558–9.

[7] *Khair-u'l-Majalis*, pp. 104–5.

[8] Arminius Vambery, *History of Bokhara* (London, 1873), p. 130.

[9] As cited by Vambery, p. 130.

the hectic life of the capital. This refugee family, which had enjoyed such status and position in Bukhara, was now reduced to penury. The trauma served to deepen the sources of their faith in God, nurturing an attitude of resignation and contentment. After the early death of his father,[10] Shaikh Nizam-u'd-din was brought up by his mother, a lady of fervent piety and unshakeable faith. She did all that she could to help her son acquire the best possible education that Badaon could provide. In an age when pious and dedicated teachers looked upon imparting education as a sacred duty without expecting or accepting any remuneration, Shaikh Nizam-u'd-din Auliya applied himself with single-minded devotion to the acquisition of knowledge. Often, when he returned from school tired and exhausted, his widowed mother would say: 'We are the guests of God today.'[11] This meant that there was nothing in the house to eat. After a time, Shaikh Nizam-u'd-din persuaded his mother to accompany him to Delhi, where he could complete his education at the feet of eminent scholars of the capital. The early years of his stay in Delhi were extremely exacting and difficult. A *maund* of melons could be had in Delhi for two *jitals* but season after season passed away without his having tasted a single slice.[12] Attracted by the spiritual reputation of Shaikh Farid-u'd-din Ganj-i-Shakar (1175–1265), he decided to go to Ajodhan (now known as Pakpattan) and joined his discipline. The Shaikh, then about ninety years old, received his young visitor with warmth and affection, discerning in him signs of future greatness. He seemed to possess the requisite spiritual insight and flair to carry forward the work of the order (*silsilah*). After a brief period of training the Shaikh entrusted his spiritual heritage to the young man and appointed him as his chief successor (*khalifah*). In the beginning Nizam-u'd-din had to face the most severe hardships on account of lack of shelter and food. Later the circumstances of his life began to change. His *khanqah* (hospice) in Ghiyaspur, which was several miles away from the capital, began to attract visitors and disciples in large numbers. Enormous *futuh* (unsolicited gifts) flowed

---

[10] According to *Qiwam-u'l-'Aqa'id*, (MS, p. 12), he was a posthumous child. No other writer has mentioned this.

[11] *Siyar-u'l-Auliya*, p. 113.

[12] Ibid. p. 163.

into it as steadily as the Jumna flowed near his door.[13] From early morning till late into the night food was served to the visitors who thronged
the nearby roads like excited crowds proceeding to some fair.[14] The
Shaikh himself fasted all through the day and when *sahri* (a meal taken
a little before dawn when the fast begins) was served to him, he found
morsels sticking in his throat because some people in Delhi had gone
to sleep without their meals.[15] His concern for the weak and the destitute
endeared him to people who found spiritual solace in his company.
Inspired by the tradition of the Prophet.

الخلق عيال الله فأحب الخلق إلى الله من أحسن إلى عياله

(All God's creatures are His family; and he is most beloved of God
who does most good to His creatures.)
They called him *Mahbub-i-Ilahi* (Beloved of God).

The Shaikh was a teacher *par excellence*. He did not believe in
elaborating subtle ideas but expressed in his life the accumulated wisdom
of the mystic's way. There was such sincerity and compassion in his
words that whoever saw him received an inspiration to do something
noble in life. Even centuries later, a distinguished scholar of Delhi,
Shah 'Abd-u'l-'Aziz (d. 1823), used to say that the impact of the Shaikh's
personality was so profound that as soon as a visitor stepped into
Ghiyaspur his condition began to change.[16]
    The Shaikh was a sincere advocate of non-violence and rejected
revenge and retribution as laws of the jungle. He advised his followers
to be good even to their enemies. Some verses of Shaikh Abu Sa'id Abu'l-
Khair, which he recited often, embody the motto of his life:

He who is not my friend—may God be his friend,
And he who bears ill against me, may his joys increase
He who puts thorns in my way on account of enmity,

---

[13] *Khair-u'l-Majalis*, p. 257.
[14] Barani, *Tarikh-i-Firuz Shahi*, pp. 343–4.
[15] *Siyar-u'l-Auliya*, p. 128.
[16] *Malfuzat-i-Shah 'Abd-u'l-'Aziz*, p. 63.

May every flower that blossoms in the garden of his life,
Be without thorns.[17]

Born during the reign of Sultan 'Ala-u'd-din Mas'ud (1242–1246),
he died just after the accession of Muhammad bin Tughluq in 1325.
Thirteen rulers came to the throne of Delhi during this period. The
Shaikh never visited the court and never accepted any stipends, *idrar*
(allowances), or villages from the rulers of his time. The transient glamour
of political power never allured him. During his student days he had
once considered seeking appointment as qazi,[18] but this was a passing
feeling and it never occurred to him again. His aspirations were higher
and nobler. His ancestors had left Bukhara when the entire socio-political
fabric of Iran and Central Asia was torn up by the Mongols; he worked
in Delhi when the nascent Sultanate of Delhi was growing with new
hope and confidence. The need to sustain and refurbish moral and
spiritual values was as urgent in such times as in times of loss and
adversity. He could say in the words of Iqbal:

مرا فقر بهتر ہے اسکندری سے

یہ آدم گری ہے، وہ آئینہ سازی

(My poverty [stricken life]) is superior to the
[imperial] ways of Alexander;
Mine is [the job of] 'building man', he is
Simply [involved in] making the mirror.)

For years Shaikh Nizam-u'd-din Auliya himself remained rooted to
the soil of Delhi but sent several hundred of his senior disciples (*khalifahs*)
to different parts of the country to take his message of love and hope
to suffering humanity and work for a better social order in which the
material ego in man is subjugated to higher and nobler ideals. That is
a brief outline of Shaikh Nizam-u'd-din Auliya's life, told in some detail
in the following pages.

---

[17] *Fawa'id-u'l-Fu'ad*, pp. 86–7; *Durar-i-Nizami*, MS.
[18] *Fawa'id-u'l-Fu'ad*, p. 28.

II

Reconstructing the life of a medieval mystic is by no means an easy job because fact and fiction, the genuine and the spurious, get so mixed up in hagiological accounts that only the firmest application of the principles of criticism can lead towards an authentic sketch.

In the case of Shaikh Nizam-u'd-din Auliya, there is no dearth of reliable material for writing his biography. We have records of conversation (*malfuzat*), biographical accounts (*tazkirah*s), letters, etc. that throw light on his life and teachings. All this literature has been used carefully and critically in the preparation of this work.

The Shaikh did not himself compile any *malfuz* or biography of his spiritual master, Shaikh Farid-u'd-din Mas'ud Ganj-i-Shakar. Though he had collected some of his sayings, these were for his own personal use only.[19] He was fond of writing his comments on books; sometimes he would jot down memoranda on stray leaves of paper. These comments and random jottings were never consolidated into book form; nevertheless, some of them were available to Amir Khurd when he wrote his *Siyar-u'l-Auliya*.[20] His citations from these jottings throw much light on the Shaikh's views about some important issues of religion and morality.

The Shaikh had composed an Arabic *khutbah* (Friday sermon) which is still recited in many Indian mosques. M. G. Zubaid Ahmad has praised it for the sublimity and the elegance of the style, 'coupled with the heart burning expression of a lover's zeal and enthusiasm for the Divine love contained therein.'[21]

Thanks to the works of Amir Hasan Sijzi and Amir Khurd, Shaikh Nizam-u'd-din Auliya's life is known to us in the fullest detail. Hasan compiled a record of the Shaikh's conversations under the rubric *Fawa'id-u'l-Fu'ad*. The Shaikh himself glanced through it with approval.[22]

---

[19] *Fawa'id-u'l-Fu'ad*, pp. 30–1.

[20] See *Siyar-u'l-Auliya*, pp. 332, 392, 393, 496, *et passim*.

[21] *Contribution of India to Arabic Literature*, pp. 184–5. A few of the introductory sentences of this *khutbah* are presented in translation in Appendix II.

[22] *Fawa'id-u'l-Fu'ad*, p. 31. According to *Nafa'is-u'l-Anfas* (MS p. 13) Shaikh Nizam-u'd-din Auliya used to turn his face towards Hasan when he narrated any story, suggesting thereby that it could be noted.

The Chishtis looked upon it as their 'Manual of Guidance'.[23] If a disciple of the Shaikh, Maulana 'Ala-u'd-din Nili, kept himself busy in reading it day after day,[24] and Amir Khusrau offered to exchange all his works for it,[25] Hindu sentiments about it were no less reverential. A Hindu zamindar, Rao Umrao Singh of Kuchesar, had it transcribed because he believed that whoever had it copied for the fulfilment of any desire, his prayer was granted before the transcript was completed.[26] In the period of Sir Syed Ahmad *Fawa'id-u'l-Fu'ad* was part of the curriculum for Muslim students, girls included.[27]

Fawa'id-u'l-Fu'ad is an authentic and reliable record of the teachings of the Shaikh. Every discussion in it has relevance and embodies the reactions of the Shaikh to particular situations. If the dates of the conversations are correlated with actual changes in society, many historical events and developments come into focus.

Inspired by the tradition established by Hasan, a number of collections of the Shaikh's conversations were made by his disciples. Particularly noteworthy are the following:

(a) *Durar-i-Nizami*, by 'Ali Jandar

(b) *Khulasat al-Lata'if*,[28] by 'Ali Jandar (in Arabic)

(c) *Malfuzat*, by Khwaja Shams-u'd-din Vihari[29]

(d) *Anwar-u'l-Majalis*, by Khwaja Muhammad,[30] son of Maulana Badr-u'd-din Ishaq

(e) *Hasrat Namah*, by Zia-u'd-din Barani[31]

(f) *Tuhfat-u'l-Abrar wa Karamat-u'l-Akhyar*, by Khwaja 'Aziz-u'd-din Sufi[32]

---

[23] Barani, *Tarikh-i-Firuz Shahi*, p. 360; *Siyar-u'l-Auliya*, p. 308.

[24] Ibid. p. 278.

[25] Ibid. p. 308.

[26] Manuscript in author's personal collection.

[27] *Lakchuron Ka Majmu'a* (Lahore 1890), p. 270.

[28] *Siyar-u'l-Auliya*, p. 449. An extract from the work given by Amir Khurd refers to Shaikh's absorption in contemplation.

[29] Ibid. p. 318.

[30] Ibid. p. 200.

[31] An extract from *Hasrat Namah* appears in Ibid. pp. 346–8.

[32] Ibid. p. 202.

Excepting *Durar-i Nizami*[33] no other *malfuz* is available now. *Durar-i-Nizami* throws valuable light on the life, thought, and personality of Shaikh Nizam-u'd-din Auliya. It reflects his profound interest in the Hadith literature. 'Ali Jandar has presented the moral and ethical teachings of the Shaikh in a very succinct manner. No doubt *Fawa'id-u'l-Fu'ad* reflects greater understanding of the depth of the Shaikh's thought and combines brevity of expression with perspicacity of ideas, but, as the arrangement is not thematic, it is only after a study of the entire text that a view of the Shaikh's moral and spiritual teachings on any particular subject can be formed. However, a reader of the *Durar* has before him systematized information on a number of vital topics connected with religious life.

The earliest biography of Shaikh Nizam-u'd-din Auliya, entitled *Qiwam-u'l-'Aqa'id*,[34] was compiled in the Deccan in 755/1254 by Muhammad Jamal Qiwam-u'd-din, grandson of Shaikh Shams-u'l-'Arifin, and a disciple of the Shaikh.[35] Abu'l-Muzaffar Bahman Shah (1347–1348), the first Bahmanid Sultan, was on the throne when the book was compiled, and the author makes respectful reference to him. *Qiwam-u'l-'Aqa'id* supplies some interesting and important information not found elsewhere. This biography has not been used so far for details of Shaikh Nizam-u'd-din Auliya's life.

Qiwam-u'l-'Aqa'id is divided into nine chapters dealing with the birth of the Shaikh, his association with Shaikh Farid-u'd-din Ganj-i-Shakar, the respectful attitude of the 'Ulama and nobles towards the Shaikh, and the devotion that the saints and sultans had for him. It does not cover systematically every aspect of the Shaikh's life but records the recollections of the author's grandfather about the Shaikh under different headings.

---

[33] Manuscripts are available in; (i) my personal collection, (ii) Buhar collection, Calcutta; (iii) Salar Jang Museum, Hyderabad (61/5/99). An imperfect Urdu translation was published in Delhi by Sayyid Muhammad Yasin 'Ali Nizami in 1332/1913.

[34] The only MS is in Osmania University Library. It was transcribed in 791/1388. Perhaps this is the earliest available manuscript of any source on the life of the Shaikh. I have a photostat copy of the MS; page numbers are given by me.

[35] *Shama'il-u'l-Atqiya* refers to it as one of its sources. There is nothing surprising in the Shaikh's account being prepared first in the Deccan. With the exodus of the population from Delhi to the Deccan, people in the south were eager to preserve the Shaikh's teachings and act upon them in the new environment.

The most comprehensive and systematic biography of the Shaikh, along with his views on different topics, was prepared by Sayyid Muhammad bin Mubarak Kirmani, known as Amir Khurd. It was compiled between 752–90/1351–82 and called *Siyar-u'l-Auliya*.[36] Amir Khurd's ancestors were closely associated with Shaikh Farid-u'd-din Ganj-i-Shakar and Shaikh Nizam-u'd-din Auliya. The author himself was a disciple of the Shaikh and had close personal contact with almost all the principal *khalifah*s and relatives of the Shaikh. Though *Siyar-u'l-Auliya* also contains brief accounts of the elder saints of the Chishti order, it mainly provides the most reliable and authentic record of the life and thought of Shaikh Nizam-u'd-din Auliya and his spiritual descendants.

Some collections of conversations—like *Rahat-u'l-Qulub*, *Rahat-u'l-Muhibbin*, and *Afzal-u'l-Fawa'id*—are of doubtful authenticity. The apocryphal nature of this literature is too obvious, particularly in view of Shaikh Nizam-u'd-din Auliya's remarks in *Fawa'id-u'l-Fu'ad*[37] and the categorical repudiation by Shaikh Nasir-u'd-din Chiragh.[38] However, because this apocryphal literature came into circulation so early, it has some value in providing an insight into the teachings of the Shaikh as these were being interpreted by the common man. The compilers collected whatever they found floating down the stream of time. Naturally fact and fiction got mixed up. *Rahat-u'l-Muhibbin* and *Afzal-u'l-Fawa'id* reveal a better standard of scholarship but to attribute them to Amir Khusrau is incorrect. Had Khusrau compiled a *malfuz* of the Shaikh, it could hardly have remained unnoticed by generations of scholars and literary historians.

Some of the conversations of the spiritual successors of Shaikh Nizam-u'd-din Auliya also contain valuable information about him. Particular reference may be made here to *Khair-u'l-Majalis*,[39] conversations of Shaikh Nasir-u'd-din Chiragh, compiled by Hamid Qalandar. Shaikh Nasir-u'd-din was the principal successor of the Shaikh in Delhi

---

[36] Published by Chirangi Lal, Delhi, 1302/1885.
[37] *Fawa'id-u'l-Fu'ad*, p. 45.
[38] *Khair-u'l-Majalis*, p. 52.
[39] Edited by K. A. Nizami (Aligarh, 1959).

and stuck to the traditions of his master at a time when almost all the other disciples had been driven to the south by Muhammad bin Tughluq.

In the Deccan a family of three brothers—Hammad, Rukn-u'd-din, and Majd-u'd-din, sons of Maulana 'Imad Kashani—compiled several collections of the conversations of Shaikh Burhan-u'd-din Gharib, another *khalifah* of Shaikh Nizam-u'd-din. Hammad wrote *Ahsan-u'l-Aqwal.*[40] *Nafa'is-u'l-Anfas*[41] and *Shama'il-u'l-Atqiya*[42] were prepared by Rukn-u'd-din. *Ghara'ib-u'l-Karamat*[43] and *Baqiyat-u'l-Ghara'ib*[44] were the works of Majd-u'd-din. Since Shaikh Burhan-u'd-din Gharib had to work out the principles of his *silsilah* in a new milieu, he was nostalgic about Delhi and remembered with love and respect the traditions of Shaikh Nizam-u'd-din Auliya. Some pieces of information about the Shaikh found in this literature are extremely valuable and interesting. For instance, the Shaikh used to say that in his early life he was distracted by the possession of half a *tanka*, but in later life 'if treasures of the world' came to him he would not be disturbed'.[45]

Interesting snippets can be gleaned from other sources. *Jawami'-u'l-Kalim,*[46] conversations of Sayyid Muhammad Gisu Daraz of Gulbarga, compiled by his son Sayyid Muhammad Husaini, contains information about the features, habits, and routine of Shaikh Nizam-u'd-din Auliya. *Shawamil-u'l-Jumal dar Shama'il-u'l-Kumal*[47] of Abu'l-Faiz Minallah, compiled in 878/1473, also has interesting references to the Shaikh. The *Sarur-u's-Sudur*, conversations of Shaikh Hamid-u'd-din Nagauri, compiled by his grandson, informs us that Shaikh Nizam-u'd-din Auliya had a Kashmiri blanket (*galim-i-Kashmiri*).[48]

---

[40] MSS: personal collection; Aligarh Muslim University Library; Salar Jang Museum, MSS (478 and 1479).

[41] MS: Nadwat-u'l-'Ulama Library, Lucknow. That he was inspired by the tradition established by Hasan Sijzi is clear from this work (pp. 3–4).

[42] Lithographed Ashraf Press, Hyderabad 1347 AH; MS personal collection.

[43] MS in Salar Jung Museum 43/876.

[44] Azad, *Rauzat-u'l-Auliya*, p. 5.

[45] *Nafa'is-u'l-Anfas*, MS Nadwat-u'l-'Ulama Library, Lucknow, p. 51.

[46] Lithographed Intizami Press, Hyderabad.

[47] MS in Rauza-i-Shaikh Collection, Gulbarga.

[48] *Sarur-u's-Sudur*, MS personal copy, p. 82.

Among the later biographical accounts that contain some information about the Shaikh, and were referred to in the preparation of this study, the following may be noted:

1. *Siyar-u'l-'Arifin,* [49] by Hamid bin Fazlullah, known as Jamali
2. *Akhbar-u'l-Akhyar,* [50] by Shaikh 'Abd-u'l-Haqq Muhaddith Dihlawi
3. *Gulzar-i-Abrar,* [51] by Muhammad Ghauthi Shattari, compiled between 1014–1022/1605–1613
4. *Akhbar-u'l-Asfiya,* [52] by 'Abd-u's-Samad bin Afzal Muhammad, completed in 1014/1605–6
5. *Mir'at-u'l-Asrar,* [53] by 'Abd-u'r-Rahman Chishti, completed in 1065/1654
6. *Majma-u'l-Auliya,* [54] by Mir 'Ali Akbar Husaini Ardistani, compiled in 1043/1633–4
7. *Siyar-u'l-Aqtab,* [55] by Allah Diya Chishti, completed in 1056/ 1646
8. *Safinat-u'l-Auliya,* [56] by Dara Shukoh, completed in 1049/1640
9. *Ma'arij-u'l-Walayat,* [57] by Ghulam Mu'in-u'd-din 'Abdullah, completed in 1094/1682
10. *Matlub-u't-Talibin,* [58] by Muhammad Bulaq Chishti, completed in 1111/1699
11. *Rauza-i-Aqtab,* [59] by Muhammad Bulaq Chishti

---

[49] Lithographed Rizwi Press (Delhi 1311/1893).

[50] Lithographed Mujtaba'i Press (Delhi, 1309 AH).

[51] MSS in the libraries of the Asiatic Society of Bengal (dated 1155/1742–43), Lindensiana (dated 1078/1667–8), Asafiyah (Hyderabad), and Habibganj (Aligarh). An Urdu translation was published in Agra in 1326 AH.

[52] MSS in Peshawar (dated 1089/1678–9), India Office (dated 1098–9/1687–8), and Bankipur libraries.

[53] MSS in Asiatic Society (dated 1088/1677) and the British Museum (dated 1189/1775). References are to personal MS.

[54] Autographed copy in India Office Library.

[55] Lithographed Newal Kishore, Lucknow 1877.

[56] Published from Agra in 1269/1853. Shaikh Ja'far Sadiq of Gujarat (1084/1653) translated it into Arabic (MS in personal collection).

[57] MS in personal collection.

[58] MSS in India Office, Library, Aligarh Muslim University Library and personal collection.

[59] Lithographed Muhibb-i-Hind Press (Delhi 1887).

12. *Iqtibas-u'l-Anwar,*[60] by Muhammad Akram Baraswi, completed in 1142/1729
13. *Shajrat-u'l-Anwar,*[61] by Rahim Bakhsh Fakhri, compiled in the eighteenth century
14. *Anwar-u'l-'Arifin,*[62] by Hafiz Muhammad Husain
15. *Manaqib-u'l-Mahbubain,*[63] by Maulana Najm-u'd-din

Of these works, *Akbar-u'l-Akhyar* of Shaikh 'Abd-u'l-Haqq Muhaddith Dihlawi is decidedly the best, as the author has scrupulously applied the canons of criticism—*usul-i-asnad*—evolved by the medieval Muslim scholars which, according to Hitti, 'meet the most essential requirements of modern historiography'.[64] The author of *Siyar-u'l-'Arifin* occupied an important place as writer, poet, and Sufi. He was associated with the Suhrawardi order. Though his account of the earlier saints suffers from some historical inaccuracies, his sketch of Shaikh Nizam-u'd-din Auliya is, by and large, reliable and comprehensive. The *Gulzar-i Abrar,* though written in flowery language, contains some valuable and authentic information about the Shaikh and his principal *khalifah*s. The largest number of *tazkirah*s, as would be evident from the above list, appeared during the seventeenth century. The main sources of their information were *Siyar-u'l-Auliya* and *Siyar-u'l-'Arifin.*

Among the later works the *Matlub-u't-Talibin* of Muhammad Bulaq Chishti, who claims descent from a sister of Shaikh Nizam-u'd-din Auliya, is based on conscientious investigation.

---

[60] Published Lahore, 1896.
[61] MS in personal collection.
[62] Lithographed Newal Kinshore (Lucknow, 1876).
[63] Printed at Thamar-i-Hind Press (Lucknow, 1873).
[64] Abu-l'Abbas Ahmad ibn-jabir Al-Baladhuri, *The Origins of the Islamic State,* Introduction, p. 3.

1

BIRTH AND FAMILY

———◆———

Like many other distinguished families of the age that were uprooted
from their homelands by the Ghuzz and the Mongol invasions,[1] the
paternal and maternal grandfathers of Shaikh Nizam-u'd-din Auliya—
Khwaja 'Ali and Khwaja 'Arab[2]—left Bukhara[3] when the armies of
Chingiz Khan carried sword and fire into the flourishing cities of Central
Asia. Bukhara was a great cultural centre[4] where the *Silsilah-i-Khwajgan*,
precursor of the Naqshbandi order, had established numerous *khanqah*s
and *zawiyah*s. The use of the term *Khwaja* with the names of both
the ancestors of Shaikh Nizam-u'd-din was perhaps owed to their
association with the *Silsilah-i-Khwajgan*. Khwaja 'Arab[5] was a man of
means and possessed many slaves and considerable wealth. Both the

———

[1] *Tabaqat-i-Nasiri*, ed. Habibi, vol. i, pp. 440–1; *Futuh-u's-Salatin*, pp. 114–15.

[2] *Siyar-u'l-Auliya*, p. 94. The genealogical tables given in the printed edition of *Siyar-u'l-Auliya*
are interpolations. No earlier authority has given the family tree of Shaikh Nizam-u'd-din.
Jami calls him a *Khalidi* (*Nafahat-u'l-Uns*, p. 452), which may mean a descendant of Khalid
bin Walid, but some writers hold the view the *Khalidi* was a quarter of the city of Bukhara.
The author of *Siyar-u'l-Auliya* refers to a dream of Shaikh Nizam-u'd-din Auliya in which the
Prophet told him that he was among his sons (p. 210). See also *Matlub-u't-Talibin*, MS p. 40.

[3] *Siyar-u'l-Auliya*, p. 94; *Akbar-u'l-Akhyar*, p. 54. Jamali's statement that they came from
Ghazna is not correct (*Siyar-u'l-Auliya*, p. 59), unless he is referring to an intermediate station
between Bukhara and India where they stayed.

[4] For the history of Bukhara, R. N. Frye, *The History of Bukhara*, Cambridge 1954. According
to *Burhan-i-Qata'y* (as quoted by Dih Khuda) semantically the word *Bukhara* meant centre of
learning. Rumi calls it *ma'dan-i-danish*. Vamberry says that since Bukhara was built mostly of
wood, it was reduced to ashes in a few days (*History of Bokhara*, p. 129).

[5] His grave is outside the fort, near that of Miran Mulhim Shahid. Razi-u'd-din Bismil,
Tazkirat-u'l-Wasilin (Lahore, 1318 AH), p. 62.

grandparents of Shaikh Nizam-u'd-din first stayed at Lahore but later moved to Badaon, where many refugee families had settled, particularly those that eschewed government service and involvement in politics. It was here that Khwaja 'Arab gave his daughter—Bibi Zulaikha—in marriage to Khwaja Ahmad, son of Khwaja 'Ali. Nizam-u'd-din was born of this couple. His parents, deprived of all their material wealth and property, must have developed an otherworldly outlook and it was to run in the veins of their son also.

Badaon is one of those cities of northern India where Muslims had settled long before Ghurid armies reached there.[6] At Badaon was born Maulana Razi-u'd-din Hasan Saghani,[7] the famous author of *Mashariq-u'l-Anwar*,[8] at least ten years before the battle of Tara'in. Shaikh Nizam-u'd-din held him in high esteem both as a distinguished Traditionist and as a noble son of Badaon. The graves of Mir Mulhim Shahid, Haider Shahid, and a few others belong to the pre-Ghurid period.[9] Badaon attracted many scholars, poets, saints, and literati when the Mongols dispersed Central Asian families.[10] Due to its strategic position, the *iqta* of Badaon occupied an important place[11] in the administrative setup of the Sultanate. In fact, Badaon, where the Shaikh was born, enjoyed a political and cultural status second only to that of Delhi.

Shaikh Nizam-u'd-din was born on the last Wednesday of the month of Safar[12] in *circa* 642/1244.[13] He was given the name of Muhammad,[14] but became known as Nizam-u'd-din.

---

[6] K. A. Nizami, *Some Aspects of Religion and Politics in India during the Thirteenth Century* (Delhi, 1978), pp. 76–7.

[7] *Fawa'id-'l-Fu'ad*, p. 103.

[8] A collection of the traditions of the Prophet which was taught in *madrasah*s during the medieval period.

[9] *Tazkirat-u'l-Wasilin*, pp. 9–23.

[10] H. R. Nevill (*Budaun: A Gazetter*) has failed to catch or convey the cultural atmosphere of medieval Badaon. Razi-u'd-din Bismil's works—*Tazkirat-u'l-Wasilin* and *Kanz-u't-Tawarikh*—are a valuable contribution to the regional and cultural history of Badaon.

[11] Khusrau, *Wast-u'l-Hayat*, p. 78. For a brief account of Badaon during the early Sultanate period, see Nizami, *Tarikhi Maqalat*, pp. 39–44.

[12] *Siyar-u'l-Auliya*, p. 387. The Shaikh remembered the month but not the year of his birth.

[13] No early authority has given the year of his birth. It may, however, be worked out on the basis of some facts of his life. Shaikh Nizam-u'd-din went to Ajodhan to see Baba Farid when he was twenty years of age. He visited his spiritual mentor Baba Farid three times, once every year, before his death in 664/1265. Calculated on this basis the date of Shaikh Nizam-u'd-din's birth would be 642/1244.

[14] See Appendix I for a detailed discussion of his name and titles.

When was Nizam-u'd-din deprived of paternal love and care? According to Muhammad Jamal Qiwam-u'd-din[15] he was a posthumous child—a statement which is not corroborated by any other source. 'Ali Jandar says that his father died when Nizam-u'd-din was a suckling babe (*shir khwar*);[16] Amir Khurd, more vaguely, states that he was in his infancy;[17] according to Jamali, he was five years of age.[18] 'Ali Jandar's statement, coming straight from the mouth of the Shaikh, is more trustworthy. The Shaikh had heard about the circumstances in which his father died from his elder sister. According to her, their mother, Bibi Zulaikha, had dreamt that someone asked her to choose between her son and her husband as one of them was destined to die. Bibi Zulaikha chose the son. Soon afterwards Khwaja Ahmad fell ill and passed away.[19] His grave in Badaon, near the Sagar Tank, has been a popular place of pilgrimage[20] through the centuries. Hafiz Rahmat Khan built a mosque and an enclosure round it.[21] The grave of Khwaja 'Ali Bukhari is also in the same enclosure.

Deprived of paternal affection, Nizam-u'd-din grew up under the care of his mother, a lady of fervent piety, dedicated to higher moral and spiritual values. Like the mother of Baba Farid, it was she who inculcated in her son a deep and enduring love for religious devotion, and a spirit of resignation and contentment, which characterized the Shaikh's activities throughout his life. When Shaikh Nizam-u'd-din remarked in the context of Shaikh Farid's mother: 'a son is strongly influenced by the piety of his parents'[22] he perhaps had in his mind the influence of his own mother also.

---

[15] *Qiwam-u'l-'Aqa'id*, MS pp. 11–12.

[16] *Durar-i-Nizami*, MS fo. 113ª⁻ᵇ.

[17] *Siyar-u'l-Auliya*, p. 95.

[18] *Siyar-u'l-'Arifin*, p. 59.

[19] *Durar-i Nizami*, MS fo. 13ª⁻ᵇ; *Siyar-u'l-Auliya*, p. 95.

[20] *Tazkirat-u'l-Wasilin*, pp. 60–2.

[21] A village called Nizampur—comprising 20 *biswa* rent-free land—was given by early rulers for the maintenance of the tomb and expenses on the occasion of the '*urs* celebrations. *Tazkirat-u'l-Wasilin*, pp. 60–1.

[22] *Fawa'id-'l-Fu'ad*, p. 121.

2

LIFE IN BADAON: STRUGGLE OF AN ORPHAN

———————

It was really in Badaon that the ideas and sentiments of Shaikh Nizam-u'd-din Auliya were nurtured. Here were shaped the contours of his personality and his attitude towards God, man, and society.

Known for its geopolitical significance and cultural efflorescence, Badaon had a serene spiritual atmosphere. Thirty-seven times in the conversations recorded in *Fawa'id-u'l-Fu'ad* the name of Badaon came to the Shaikh's lips, and whenever he referred to it his mind fondly conjured up pictures of days gone by. Significantly enough, references to Badaon in his conversations increased as he advanced in years. Some time in 1319 Hasan Sijzi returned from Badaon with the army and reported to the Shaikh that he had visited the graves of his father, Maulana 'Ala-u'd-din Usuli, and others. The Shaikh remembered each one of them by their name and wept in silent homage to their memory. He loved Badaon—its flora and fauna, its fruits and gardens, its men and manners, its language and literature.[1]

A few incidents which his memory had preserved, and which he sometimes recalled with nostalgic emotion, may be mentioned here to illustrate his involvement with the culture of Badaon:

---

[1] The way he addressed Iqbal as *Lalla* (*Jawami'-u'l-Kalim*, p. 59), and liked the Purbi dialect shows the influence of Badaon on his expression. He used to say in moments of spiritual ecstasy: 'The promise and pledge that God had from me [on the Day of Creation] was in the Purbi rhyme.' 'Abd-u'l-Wahid Bilgrami, *Saba' Sanabil*, p. 63; Dara Shukoh, *Hasanat-u'l-'Arifin*, MS Nadwat-u'l-'Ulama Library, p. 21.

(a) Nasir, a young man from Badaon, once told the Shaikh that his father was a spiritually gifted person and had mysteriously disappeared.[2] Was there an analogy in this incident with the Shaikh's own life which made him remember this? Did his father not suddenly fall ill and die as if mysteriously taken away?

(b) Ahmad, a friend of the Shaikh in Badaon, was extremely pious and devoted. Though illiterate, he was always enquiring about matters of religious law (*Shari'ah*). He had come to Delhi with the Shaikh. When he heard about the death of the Shaikh's mother in Delhi, he wept bitterly.[3] Shaikh Nizam-u'd-din valued such affection and love.

(c) There was a preacher in Badaon who was so overpowered by emotion while delivering sermons that he jumped from pulpit to cornice.[4] Did such emotional exuberance have any lasting effect on the thought and character of the audience?

(d) One day the Shaikh noticed that some of his audience were not seated in the shade. 'They are sitting under the sun and I am burning', he said, and then suddenly his mind went back to Badaon and Shaikh Shahay Mui'tab. This Shaikh once went on a picnic with his friends and prepared a sweet dish with milk and rice. When the food was served Shaikh Shahay felt that something had been misappropriated from it. He was told that when the milk was boiling, an amount was taken off to prevent it spilling over. Shaikh Shahay was not satisfied. He asked his companions to stand under the sun till some perspiration flowed out of their bodies. A barber was then asked to take out from the Shaikh's body as much blood as perspiration had come out of the body of his friends. Nizam-u'd-din Auliya was deeply moved by the Shaikh's sense of justice.[5] He later commented on Shaikh Shahay's charismatic personality and how crowds flocked round him wherever he went.[6]

---

[2] *Fawa'id-u'l-Fu'ad*, p. 15.
[3] Ibid. p. 47.
[4] Ibid. p. 83.
[5] Ibid. pp. 90–1.
[6] Ibid. p. 176; *Durar-i-Nizami* MS.

(e) Shaikh Nizam-u'd-din Auliya had deep respect for Maulana
    Razi-u'd-din Hasan Saghani, the famous author of *Mashariq-
    u'l-Anwar*, who was born in Badaon. The Shaikh reported the
    following to his audience: Maulana Saghani went to Kol
    (Aligarh) from Badaon and became the assistant of the *Mushrif.*
    One day the *Mushrif* said something silly which brought a smile
    to the face of the Maulana. Irritated at this, the *Mushrif* threw
    his ink-pot at him. He escaped the ink but not the disgrace.
    He left the job, saying, 'We should have nothing to do with
    these illiterate (and uncultured) people.' Later the Maulana
    started coaching a son of the *Wali* of Kol at a salary of one
    hundred *tanka*s a month. From there he went for Hajj and
    thence to Baghdad. Subsequently he came to Delhi, which in
    those days had many distinguished scholars. Maulana Saghani
    was equal to them in every other branch of learning but in
    Hadith his position was supreme. Shaikh Nizam-u'd-din cited
    several stories about Maulana Saghani's insight in Hadith
    literature.[7] The Shaikh's own love of learning and reluctance
    to meet government officers was influenced by the experiences
    of the Maulana's early life.

(f) One day Maulana 'Ala-u'd-din Usuli and Shaikh Nizam-u'd-din
    Auliya were busy comparing and collating a manuscript. They
    came across a hemistich that neither rhymed properly nor made
    any sense. Both of them struggled unsuccessfully to put meaning
    into it. Maulana Malik Yar, who was not a very learned man,
    happened to come by. Maulana Usuli referred the matter to
    him. He recited the hemistich correctly so that its meaning
    became clear. The Maulana said that Malik Yar's correct recitation
    was due to his poetic sensitivity (*zauq*). Shaikh Nizam-u'd-din
    Auliya says that it was on that day that he came to know what
    zauq really meant.[8] When Maulana Malik Yar was appointed
    Imam of the Jama' Masjid of Badaon, some people objected
    to it as he lacked the requisite learning. On hearing about this
    objection, Maulana Usuli said that even if the Imamate of the

---

[7] *Fawa'id-u'l-Fu'ad*, pp. 103–5.
[8] Ibid. pp. 165–6.

Jama' Masjid of Baghdad was assigned to him, it would be nothing compared to his capabilities.[9] The Shaikh understood that it was not merely formal education but a developed and subtle taste which mattered.

(g) It was in Badaon that Shaikh Nizam-u'd-din Auliya developed respect for Qazi Hamid-u'd-din Nagauri. Many people of Badaon held him in high esteem. Khwaja Shahay Mui'tab had become his disciple and the saint had bestowed on him his *khirqah* (a cloak, symbolizing spiritual succession). Another saint of Badaon, 'Aziz Bashir, went to Delhi and wanted to get the *khirqah* from Maulana Nasah-u'd-din, son of Qazi Hamid-u'd-din Nagauri. But he did not oblige him as Aziz Bashir was found guilty of making exaggerated statements.[10]

(h) Khwaja 'Aziz, *Kotwal* of Badaon, had great respect for saints and dervishes. One day he was sitting in an orchard with a tablecloth spread out before him. Shaikh Nizam-u'd-din happened to pass by. The *Kotwal* saw him from a distance and requested him to come and join the meal. The *Kotwal* seated him next to himself and treated him with respect.[11] The Shaikh must have felt that those in authority could behave with grace and decorum if they so desired.

(i) A resident of Badaon used to fast regularly. At the time of breaking the fast (*iftar*) he used to sit at the door of his house and invite every passer-by to join him.[12] The influence of this practice may be read in the Shaikh's discourse that followed this reference.

(j) Iltutmish had left the mark of his religious thought and personality on the traditions of Badaon. Shaikh Nizam-u'd-din found innumerable stories about the Sultan circulating in Badaon and fondly narrated them to his audience in Delhi:[13] Iltutmish's mystical leanings, his respect for Shaikh Shihab-u'd-din Suhrawardi and Shaikh Auhad-u'd-din Kirmani, his fondness

---

[9] Ibid. pp. 166.
[10] Ibid. pp. 174.
[11] Ibid. pp. 174–5.
[12] Ibid. pp. 207.
[13] Ibid. pp. 211–12 *et seq.*

for mangoes, and his substitution of the word *naghzak* for *amba*, as the latter did not have a good meaning in the Turkish language. One day, as Iltutmish went out to play *chaugan* (an early form of polo), an old man stretched out his hand and begged for alms. Iltutmish did not give him anything and moved on. A few steps further the Sultan came across a stout young man and at once took gold pieces from his purse and handed them to him. Afterwards he turned to his companions and asked: 'Do you know why I did not give anything to that old beggar, while I gave unasked to this young man?' When the companions could not give any reply to the query, the Sultan said: 'Had it been left to my choice, I would have preferred that old beggar, but whatever is bestowed is bestowed by Him. I am helpless.' The Shaikh narrated this incident to his disciples when preaching 'faith in Divine action'.[14]

(k) Another saint of Badaon who seems to have made a deep impression on the mind of the Shaikh was Khwaja 'Aziz Karki.[15]

(l) Maulana Siraj-u'd-din Tirmizi of Badaon went to Makka with the intention of spending his last days and being buried there. One night he dreamt that corpses not worthy of being buried in the Holy City were being taken out of their graves, and the bodies of others who had died elsewhere but were spiritually gifted were put in their place.[16] He returned to Badaon. The Shaikh realized that sincere devotion is rewarded irrespective of time and place.

(m) Shaikh Nizam-u'd-din Auliya heard a number of stories about the spiritual qualities of Shaikh Jalal-u'd-din Tabrizi who had been in Badaon for some time.[17] He came to know here about the change brought about by Shaikh Jalal-u'd-din Tabrizi in the lives of sinners and vagabonds. Probably he developed respect for Shaikh Shihab-u'd-din Suhrawardi, spiritual mentor of Shaikh Tabrizi, during his stay in Badaon.

---

[14] Ibid. p. 212.

[15] Ibid. pp. 212–13.

[16] Ibid. pp. 216–17.

[17] He quotes Shaikh Jalaluddin's remark about Qazi Kamal-u'd-din Ja'fari of Badaon: 'Does the Qazi know how to offer his prayers?' Ibid. p. 236.

(n) A child was born in Badaon in an 'Alawi family at a time generally considered inauspicious. His parents handed him over to a sweeper-woman. After four or five years the woman brought the child to Badaon. He was now a fair-looking and attractive child. His parents took him back and arranged proper education for him. He turned out to be such an erudite scholar that many residents of Badaon learnt at his feet. Shaikh Nizam-u'd-din Auliya had seen him.[18] From this life story the Shaikh learnt to reject superstitious attitudes.

(o) The Shaikh once told his audience that a preacher of Badaon was asked about ecstasy in audition parties (*sama'*). He said: 'When gram is put in the oven, it shoots up and down.'[19]

(p) A dervish lived outside the city of Badaon. The Shaikh once asked him the reason for his living there. He replied that a travelling-companion of his had asked him to stay there till he returned. He had not returned so far, but he was staying there in order to keep his promise.[20]

The significance of these incidents and anecdotes pertaining to Badaon becomes clearer when the Shaikh appears to weave his thought round them and draw morals from them.

Nizam-u'd-din lived in Badaon for sixteen years and received his early education there.[21] These were days of poverty and struggle. His widowed mother was financially broken but spiritually impregnable. She provided emotional and moral support to her son. She made poverty itself look like a thing to be taken pride in. She never allowed the mind of her son to waver or to turn into channels not consistent with the life that was awaiting him. With quiet, single-minded determination Nizam-u'd-din spent his time and energy in acquiring knowledge. His mother and his sister were the only two other members of the family and all of them bore the pinch of poverty with courage, fortitude, and resignation to Divine Will.

---

[18] Ibid. p. 243.
[19] *Durar-i-Nizami*, MS.
[20] Ibid.
[21] *Siyar-u'l-Auliya*, p. 100. Jamali's statement that he left Badaon at the age of 25 is not correct. *Siyar-u'l-'Arifin*, p. 59.

Names of two of Nizam-u'd-din's early teachers have come down to us—Shadi Muqri and Maulana 'Ala-u'd-din Usuli. Both were men of distinction in their own fields.

Shadi Muqri knew the Qur'an by heart and could recite it according to its seven methods of recitation.[22] He was an experienced and able teacher, and developed in his pupils a liking for memorizing the Qur'an. He was originally the slave of a Hindu.[23] Perhaps on securing emancipation he became the pupil of a great scholar-saint of Lahore, Khwaja Muqri. It was generally believed that whoever received elementary instruction in the Qur'an from Shadi Muqri eventually succeeded in committing the Holy Book to memory. Though Nizam-u'd-din committed the Qur'an to memory in Delhi—many years after leaving Badaon—he ascribed it to the blessings of Shadi Muqri.

Maulana 'Ala-u'd-din Usuli was a pious, dedicated, and erudite scholar of his day. His life was spent in penitence and penury, holding fast to traditions of scholarship in extremely indigent circumstances. Often he starved for days but never disclosed it to anybody. He carried on his instructional work even though hunger and thirst made his mouth dry and choked.[24] He was reluctant to accept gifts. If people insisted, he accepted only to the extent of his immediate need. He ate very little at the time of *sahri*.[25] Sometimes he had to live on seeds from which oil had been extracted (*kanjara*). One day he kept the *kanjara* in his turban and forgot about it. When his barber came and offered to cut his hair, the Maulana allowed him to take off the *dastar*. The barber was shocked to find that the Maulana lived on *kanjara* and informed the well-to-do neighbours about the circumstances in which the great scholar was passing his days. A rich neighbour sent to him 1,000 *jitals*, a few *maunds* of grain, and some jars of purified butter (*ghee*). The Maulana refused this gift[26] and admonished the barber for revealing his circumstances to others. Young Nizam-u'd-din's mind was deeply influenced by this example. He learnt from him the value of dedication

---

[22] *Fawa'id-u'l-Fu'ad*, p. 154.
[23] Ibid.
[24] *Siyar-u'l-Auliya*, p. 419.
[25] Ibid.
[26] *Khair-u'l-Majalis*, p. 190.

to higher ideals, and in later life used to refer to him very affectionately as 'my teacher'.[27] Shaikh Nizam-u'd-din even narrated Traditions of the Prophet on the Maulana's authority and approvingly quoted his views about ablution. Abd-u'l-Faiz Minallah says that a distinction of Shaikh Nizam-u'd-din Auliya was that he had one spiritual mentor and one teacher, perhaps referring to Maulana 'Ala-u'd-din.

Maulana 'Ala-u'd-din Usuli had the humility of the true scholar. He never behaved as if he was the final authority on any subject. He would listen patiently to his pupils and not hesitate to tell them that, for further clarification of the point, they could consult other scholars also. He looked upon teaching as a cooperative work in which the teacher and the student both participated.[28]

Maulana Usuli's own life had known a particularly dramatic turn. In his youth, while once loitering on the streets of Badaon, he happened to pass by a house where Shaikh Jalal-u'd-din Tabrizi, the distinguished saint, was staying. Shaikh Tabrizi, who was sitting in the *dehliz* of the house, glanced at the wandering youth and saw in him signs of future greatness. He called him in and bestowed on him the robe that he was himself wearing. From then on 'Ala-u'd-din took to studies with all the enthusiasm of a reformed youth. In course of time he so distinguished himself that he came to be looked upon as the most learned man in Badaon.[29]

Bibi Zulaikha must have heard about the piety and erudition of Maulana 'Ala-u'd-din when she decided to put her son under his charge. When Nizam-u'd-din finished *Quduri*,[30] the Maulana declared him qualified to have 'the turban of scholarship' (*dastar-i-fazilah*) put on his head. In those days this declaration was usually made at a function which resembled present-day convocation ceremonies. Nizam-u'd-din reported this to his mother with a touch of concern because it was difficult for the family to arrange for the *dastar* and the feast. His mother mollified him by promising to arrange everything: the carder quickly

---

[27] *Fawa'id-u'l-Fu'ad*, p. 165.

[28] Ibid.

[29] Ibid. For his grave, see *Tazkirat-u'l-Wasilin*, p. 85.

[30] Abu'l-Hasan Ahmad bin Muhammad al-Quduri (972–1037) was a distinguished writer on Muslim jurisprudence. His two well known books are *al-Mukhtasar* and *Kitab al-Tajrid*.

cleaned the cotton, the mother and the slave-girl prepared the spindles, and the weaver who lived in the neighbourhood wove a sheet of four yards within two or three days. Having washed the cloth without starch, Bibi Zulaikha gave it to her son along with a little food, to take to Maulana 'Ala-u'd-din. The Maulana contributed something from his own pocket and arranged a feast to which scholars and saints of Badaon were invited. The ceremony began once the feast was over. Nizam-u'd-din placed the turban before his teacher, who stood up and, taking one end in his own hand while the other was held by the pupil, started tying it round the latter's head. At every winding of the turban Nizam-u'd-din bowed in token of his respect and gratitude to his teacher. A notable saint of Badaon, 'Ali Maula,[31] who was a guest of honour on this occasion, was deeply touched at this reverential bearing of Nizam-u'd-din and remarked in Hindivi: 'Aray Maulana! Yeh bada hausi.' ('Oh Maulana! He will be a great man'). Maulana 'Ala-u'd-din asked 'Ali Maula the reason for this prediction. The latter replied: 'Ju mundasa bandhay, wa pain pasray?' ('Who, after wearing the *dastar*, bows himself before a teacher?'). For 'Ali Maula, Nizam-u'd-din's humility and the simplicity of this turban, which had no thread of silk in it, were signs of future greatness.[32]

It appears that Maulana 'Ala-u'd-din Usuli was principally a teacher of *fiqh* (jurisprudence) and, though blessed by Shaikh Jalal-u'd-din Tabrizi, had not formally been initiated in any mystic discipline.[33] Shaikh Nizam-u'd-din Auliya used to say that Maulana Usuli would also have attained spiritual eminence had he become the disciple of a saint. His heart was full of human kindness and he could not see anybody in anguish. He had once acquired a slave-girl who wept remembering her son. Maulana Usuli asked her if she knew the way to her village, Kanbar, near Badaon. He took her in the morning to a tank on the outskirts of the city, which she had identified, and allowed her to go

---

[31] 'Ali Maula was also an interesting figure of Badaon. He belonged to a group of bandits and as a device of deception carried a pot of curd on his head to sell. Shaikh Jalal-u'd-din Tabrizi saw him in that deceptive posture and discovered him. Through the Shaikh's intervention his life was completely changed. For his grave, see *Tazkirat-u'l-Wasilin*, p. 51.

[32] *Khair-u'l-Majalis*, p. 191.

[33] *Fawa'id-u'l-Fu'ad*, p. 165.

back to her family. After narrating this incident, Shaikh Nizam-u'd-din Auliya remarked with tears in his eyes: 'The *'ulama-i-zahir* [externalist scholars] do not agree with this [returning her to her people would mean returning her to her religion]. But one should know what a [great] thing he had done by bringing happiness to a heart.'[34]

Two books mentioned in connection with Maulana Usuli's instruction to Shaikh Nizam-u'd-din Auliya are *Hidaya*[35] and *Quduri*.[36] Once, when receiving lessons from Maulana 'Ala-u'd-din Usuli in a mosque, Nizam-u'd-din saw, as if in a trance, golden snakes running about and hissing. He threw his turban over them and they turned into heaps of gold *tanka*s. He rejected them.[37] Later, worldly charm appeared to him in a dream in the form of a woman.[38] He rejected her also. Thus wealth and lust were rejected by him early in life. The family's time in Badaon was passed in extreme poverty. Later, Nizam-u'd-din requested his mother's permission to move the family to Delhi so as to benefit from its better academic opportunities.[39] She readily agreed and at the age of sixteen Nizam-u'd-din left Badaon for Delhi. Perhaps he never again returned to his home town.[40]

---

[34] Ibid.
[35] A famous book on Muslim law, compiled by Maulana Burhan-u'd-din Abu'l-Hasan 'Ali Marghinani (1135–97).
[36] See footnote 30, above.
[37] *Siyar-u'l-Auliya*, p. 132.
[38] Ibid.
[39] *Qiwam-u'l-Aqa'id*, MS p. 16.
[40] *Siyar-u'l-Auliya*, p. 100.

3

EARLY STRUGGLE IN DELHI:
ACADEMIC LAURELS AMID POVERTY

———————

Shaikh Nizam-u'd-din and his mother and sister[1] had to endure even greater poverty during the early years of his stay in Delhi than they had known in Badaon. They accepted it with resignation to the will of God. Circumstances forced him to change his residence from one quarter of the city to another. Homelessness combined with destitution made his life especially trying. Nevertheless, he pursued his studies with great equanimity and remarkable dedication. His mother was a pillar of strength to him during these years of struggle and hardship.

On their arrival in Delhi, Shaikh Nizam-u'd-din's mother and sister stayed at an inn known as *Sarai Namak* (or Sarai Miyan Bazaar),[2] which had accommodation for women only. Nizam-u'd-din had found a place for himself in *Bargah-i-Qawwas*, which stood in front of the Sarai. In this very locality lived Shaikh Najib-u'd-din Mutawakkil[3] and Amir Khusrau[4]—both of whom were destined to be closely associated with him, one as a senior guide and friend and the other as a disciple and devotee. His life in Delhi at this time was hard indeed. In those days two *seer*s of bread could be had for a *jital,* but often he did not have

———————

[1] The sister was older than Shaikh Nizam-u'd-din (*Durar-i-Nizami*, MS fo. 113ᵇ). Her name, however, is not mentioned by any of the earlier authorities. Later writers say that her name was Bibi Zainab.

[2] *Siyar-u'l-Auliya*, p. 108.

[3] Ibid. p. 100.

[4] Ibid. p. 108.

a single *jital* to buy the bread.[5] His mother and sister bore these privations without complaint. When there was nothing in the house to eat, his mother would say: 'Nizam-u'd-din! Today we are the guests of God.'[6] Young Nizam-u'd-din derived inexplicable spiritual solace from this remark and always longed to hear it from her. During the days when there was no shortage of food, he would become impatient for the day when his mother would speak those words.[7]

Bibi Zulaikha was a remarkable lady—pious, serene in suffering, and resigned to the will of God. Though born into comfort and plenty, her resources of patience and fortitude were equal to the change in circumstances. She moulded the thought and personality of her son and demonstrated by example that endurance and moral excellence are possible even in the face of adverse conditions. Her one great concern in life was to educate her son as well as possible. Continuous fasts and endless struggle shattered her health and she did not live long enough to see her son at the height of glory, when instead of himself being a 'guest of God', he played host to hundreds of His creatures every day. Whenever she happened to look at the feet of her son, she remarked, 'Nizam-u'd-din! I see signs of a bright future in you. You will be a man of destiny some day.' Once, on hearing this remark, the Shaikh asked: 'But when will this happen?' 'When I am dead', replied Bibi Zulaikha.[8]

Bibi Zulaikha had great faith in God,[9] and when she prayed it appeared as if she was in direct communion with Him. Once her maid-servant escaped from the house. She vowed: 'I will not put a *dupatta* on my head unless she returns.' Not long afterward she was back home.[10] Shaikh Nizam-u'd-din Auliya used to say that whenever she was approached to pray for something, her prayer was soon granted by God.[11] Every month when the Shaikh saw the new moon, he offered felicitations to her by placing his head at her feet. On one such occasion, she said: 'Nizam! At whose feet will you put your head next month?' The Shaikh

---

[5] Ibid. p. 113.

[6] Ibid.

[7] Ibid.

[8] *Durar-i-Nizami*, MS fo. 113ᵃ; *Siyar-u'l-Auliya*, p. 150.

[9] Ibid.

[10] Ibid.

[11] Ibid. p. 152.

burst into tears. 'To whose care will you entrust me?' he asked.
'Tomorrow I will tell you,' replied the mother. She then directed him
to go and sleep at the house of Shaikh Najib-u'd-din. In the small hours
of the morning the maidservant came rushing and said that his mother
had called him. Nizam-u'd-din hurried to the house. 'Where is your
right hand?' asked his dying mother. He stretched out his hand. She
took it in her hand and said: 'O God! I entrust him to You.' So saying
Bibi Zulaikha breathed her last. The Shaikh used to say that if she
had left a house full of gold and jewels, it would not have given him
the same pleasure and consolation that these words gave to his bereaved
heart.[12] Throughout his life he felt as if he was living under the protection
and care of God. Bibi Zulaikha lies buried a mile away from the
Qutb Minar in a small village known as Udhchini.[13] It was the practice
of Shaikh Nizam-u'd-din Auliya throughout his life that whenever he
had a problem he went to the grave of his mother and prayed to God
there.[14]

It appears that Bibi Zulaikha's stay at Delhi did not last more than
four years or so.[15] Shaikh Nizam-u'd-din had no satisfactory accommodation as yet. He moved to the house of Amir Khusrau's maternal
grandfather, who was the *Rawat Arz*.[16] This was a three-storey building,
situated adjacent to the *burj* of the Fort, near the Darwaza Manda
and the Bridge. Palatial buildings stood all round. On the first floor
lived Syed Muhammad Kirmani and his family; on the second, Nizam-
u'd-din; and on the third, his friends and associates. Food was served
on this floor. For two years Shaikh Nizam-u'd-din lived in this house.[17]
His stay here must have been some time after joining the discipline
of Shaikh Farid, because it was at Ajodhan that he came into contact
with the Kirmani family. Nizam-u'd-din also had a servant, Mubashshir,

---

[12] *Durar-i-Nizami*, MS fo. 113ᵃ; *Siyar-u'l-Auliya*, p. 152.

[13] On the Mehrauli Road. For an account of the graves in the complex, see Khwaja Hasan
Nizami, *Nizami Bansari* (Delhi, 4th edn 1984), pp. 497–8.

[14] *Siyar-u'l-Auliya*, p. 150.

[15] Shaikh Nizam-u'd-din was 16 years old when he reached Delhi; he was 20 when he went
to Ajodhan with the permission of his mother. She died thereafter.

[16] *Rawat* means a Hindu cavalryman in contemporary literature. See Qureshi, *Administration
of the Sultanate of Delhi* (Karachi, 4th edn 1958), p. 152.

[17] *Siyar-u'l-Auliya*, p. 108.

with him at this house. Syed Muhammad Kirmani and Mubashshir served him with great devotion. Once it happened that three days passed and he had nothing to eat. The third night somebody knocked at the door and gave him a dish of *khichri* (rice boiled with lentils). 'Nothing in life has ever been so tasty as that *khichri*,' he used to say.[18]

When the maternal uncles of Amir Khusrau returned from their assignments, they made the saint vacate the house without giving him time to find suitable alternative accommodation.[19] The Shaikh hurriedly moved to the Chappardar wali Masjid that stood in front of the shop of Siraj, a grocer (*baqqal*). With his bundles of books, which were his sole belongings,[20] he took shelter in this mosque. He stayed there for one night. The next day Sa'd Kaghzi, a disciple of Shaikh Sadr-u'd-din, who had heard about this incident, came to the Shaikh and took him to his house. He accommodated him in a big room on the upper storey of this house while he arranged separate quarters for the family of Syed Muhammad Kirmani. For about a month the saint lived there. Subsequently he found accommodation in a house in *Sarai Rakabdar*, which was adjacent to the Qaisar Bridge. The Kirmani family also came to live there in a small room of the Sarai. Later, the Shaikh moved to the house of Shadi Gulabi, and from there to the house of Shams-u'd-din Sharabdar.[21] At this last place he lived for a number of years with some peace of mind.[22]

These frequent changes of residence must have been a great strain on the nerves of the Shaikh, who was anxious to spend his time in studies, meditation, and prayer. One day, while sitting on the bank of Hauz-i-Qutlugh Khan, and memorizing the Qur'an, a dervish came to him and advised him to leave Delhi and settle elsewhere. A number of alternatives came to his mind: he could go to Patiali, the hometown of Amir Khusrau; he could settle at Basnala, near Delhi; he could go to Bihar to the *khanqah* of Shaikh Khizr Paradoz[23] and teach his children; and so on. He went to Basnala but could not find a house to rent or

---

[18] Ibid. p. 113.
[19] Ibid. p. 108.
[20] Ibid. p. 109.
[21] For Sharabdar, see Qureshi, *Administration of the Sultanate of Delhi*, pp. 64–5.
[22] *Siyar-u'l-Auliya*, p. 109.
[23] Ibid. p. 112.

lease despite three days of strenuous search, and returned to Delhi disappointed. According to Muhammad Jamal Qiwam-u'd-din, he wanted some place near the river where he could busy himself in meditation.[24] He now thought of seeking divine guidance in the matter. He went towards the Hauz-i-Rani, near which was a garden, known as Bagh-i-Jasrat.[25] Here he prayed to God: 'O my God! I must leave this city but I will not do so at my own discretion. I will go to the place You direct me to.' While meditating on the problem, he heard a voice directing him to go to Ghiyaspur,[26] a place unknown to him at the time. He went to a friend, Naqib Nishapuri, to enquire where the place was, only to discover that the latter had gone to Ghiyaspur.

Ghiyaspur was at that time a desolate village with little human habitation. It was only when Kaiqubad settled at Kilugarhi that Ghiyaspur came into prominence and big crowds began to throng there.[27] Shaikh Nizam-u'd-din then thought of moving elsewhere to a quieter place. His mind was involved in these problems when his teacher Maulana Amin-u'd-din died, and Nizam-u'd-din went to the city to attend his *siyum*. On that very day a man with extremely charming features— but lean and thin and with an otherworldly expression on his face— came to him and strongly protested against his desire to settle away from society and recited the verse:

اں روز که مه شدی نمی دانستی

کانگشت نمائیِ عالمے خواهی شد

(The day that you appeared like a moon, did you not know that the world would point its finger towards you!)

The stranger told the Shaikh to behave in a way that would not put him to shame before the Prophet on the Day of Judgement. He exhorted

---

[24] *Qiwam-u'l-'Aqa'id*, MS p. 20.

[25] In some texts wrongly given as Hairat or Hasrat. Bagh-i-Jasrat was a well-known place in medieval Delhi.

[26] *Fawa'id-u'l-Fu'ad*, p. 142.

[27] Ibid; *Siyar-u'l-Auliya*, p. 111; *Qiwam-u'l-'Aqa'id*, MS p. 21.

the Shaikh to have the courage to be busy with God and serve His creatures.[28] Shaikh Nizam-u'd-din was so impressed by what the visitor said that he made up his mind to remain at Ghiyaspur. The Shaikh brought something for the visitor to eat but he left without touching it.[29]

When starvation became continuous, a scrip (*zanbil*) was laid at the door. People could put in it anything to eat.[30] At *iftar* time the bowl was taken in and emptied on the dinner-cloth. A beggar once happened to pass by. He thought that the food on the cloth was the leftovers from a dinner. He collected everything and left. Shaikh Nizam-u'd-din smiled and said: 'It appears that there is still imperfection in our work and for that reason we are being kept in hunger.'[31]

Initially there were only two disciples in the service of the Shaikh. There was a pious, saintly woman in the neighbourhood who earned her livelihood by spinning thread. She purchased flour with what her labour fetched her and baked her bread at the time of *iftar*. Once when the Shaikh and his disciples had not eaten for four days in succession, the woman sent them a *seer* and a half of flour which she had saved. The Shaikh asked his disciple Kamal-u'd-din to mix it with water and put it in some vessel to boil. It had not been fully baked when a dervish suddenly appeared and shouted: 'If you have anything to eat, do not withhold it from me.' The Shaikh asked him to wait a little as the pot was boiling, but the visitor was impatient. The Shaikh got up and, winding his sleeves round his hands, picked up the boiling pot and brought it to the dervish. The dervish lifted the pot and smashed it on the ground with the words: 'Shaikh Farid had bestowed his spiritual blessings on Shaikh Nizam-u'd-din. I break the vessel of his material poverty.' After this, the Shaikh's circle of disciples widened and enormous *futuh* (unsolicited gifts) started pouring in.[32]

One more story in this context is given by Amir Khurd. Some persons started from Chanderi to meet Shaikh Nizam-u'd-din Auliya in Delhi.

---

[28] *Fawa'id-u'l-Fu'ad*, p. 142; *Siyar-u'l-Auliya*, p. 111; *Qiwam-u'l-'Aqa'id*, MS p. 22; *Siyar-u'l-'Arifin*, p. 66.

[29] *Fawa'id-u'l-Fu'ad*, p. 143.

[30] *Siyar-u'l-Auliya*, pp. 113–14.

[31] Ibid. p. 114.

[32] Ibid. pp. 69–70.

On the way they met one Maulana 'Umar, who enquired about their destination and then remarked: 'Has that poor fellow [referring to Shaikh Nizam-u'd-din] anything [to give you]? Take these twelve *jitals* and give them to him.'[33] It is said that thereafter considerable *futuh* started coming to him. Almost an identical incident is reported about his transport problem.[34] The fact is that whatever the trials of poverty could do by way of deepening and integrating a mystic's personality, had now been achieved: it was time that *futuh* should come to him, not to solve his problems, but to enable him to solve the problems of others. Nizam-u'd-din had reached Delhi some time during the reign of Sultan Nasir-u'd-din Mahmud. Scholars, poets, mystics, and craftsmen of distinction from distant parts of the Muslim world had sought asylum in Delhi at that time.[35] Apart from those at whose feet he received formal education, he had opportunities to meet many other scholars of repute. This contact accounts for his extensive knowledge of standard works on different branches of Muslim learning.[36]

Of his teachers in Delhi, the names of Khwaja Shams-u'l-Mulk[37] and Maulana Kamal-u'd-din Zahid have reached us. It may be that there were others also, but either the duration of his association with them was short or he was not so impressed by them as to mention them in his gatherings. One of his teachers who is referred to only once in *Durar-i-Nizami* was Maulana Amin-u'd-din Muhaddith.[38] He died just before Shaikh Nizam-u'd-din decided to settle in Ghiyaspur. Another teacher, whose name is not mentioned, lost the esteem of Shaikh Nizam-u'd-din when he saw him exceedingly elated and happy on his son's appointment as *qazi* of some village. When his son, donning the dress of a *qazi*, came to see him, Shaikh Nizam-u'd-din Auliya also happened to be there. The father said, 'God be praised! What I had

[33] Ibid. p. 116.
[34] See below.
[35] *Futuh-u's-Salatin*, pp. 114–15.
[36] See below.
[37] *Fawa'id-u'l-Fu'ad*, p. 16. Jamali (*Siyar-u'l-'Arifin*, p. 60) and following him Ferishta (Chapter XII, p. 30) gives his name as Shams-u'd-din Khwarazmi. Shaikh 'Abd-u'l-Haqq (*Akhbar-u'l-Akhyar*, p. 77) follows *Fawa'id-u'l-Fu'ad*.
[38] *Durar-i-Nizami*, MS; *Siyar-u'l-'Arifin*, p. 66.

for years longed for, God has bestowed on you today.' Nizam-u'd-din
felt that receiving education from a teacher with such materialistic ends
in mind was hardly worthwhile and he lost no time in leaving him.[39]
   Khwaja Shams-u'l-Mulk was known for his erudition and learning.
Nizam-u'd-din learnt the *Maqamat*[40] of Hariri with him and committed
its forty sections to memory. The Maulana had a sense of humour
and if any student absented himself from his lectures he would ask:
'What have I done to you that you did not come? Tell me, so that
I may do it again.' But he was particularly affectionate and considerate
towards Nizam-u'd-din. He insisted on seating him close to himself
on a *chajja* (small balcony) where only two other pupils were permitted
to sit—Qadi Fakhr-u'd-din Naqila and Maulana Burhan-u'd-din.[41] If
Nizam-u'd-din ever absented himself from his lectures, he recited a
couplet expressing his profound desire to see him in the lecture room.
Nizam-u'd-din was always full of praise for his distinguished teacher
but on one occasion could not help mentioning his excessive regard
for gold. Balban had appointed Khwaja Shams-u'l-Mulk as *Mustaufi-
i-Mumalik*.[42] It was perhaps in that capacity that he amassed huge wealth.
In his last years a severe misfortune overtook him when the Sultan
ordered the confiscation of all his property. When the government
officers reached his house to seize his wealth and property, Nizam-
u'd-din happened to be there. The Maulana was extremely grieved and
upset at the government order. The young pupil, who had developed
a different attitude towards worldly attractions, did not have the audacity
to advise his teacher that material wealth was an obstacle in the realization
of God. But he humbly submitted that his teacher accept it as a decree
of God and remain resigned to His will. The Maulana did not utter a
word in reply but when Nizam-u'd-din took leave of him, he said:
'You should pray for the return of my wealth to me lest being deprived

---

[39] *Durar-i-Nizami*, MS.

[40] A classical work on Arabic literature compiled by Abu Muhammad al-Qasim al-Hariri
(1054–1122). It was a textbook for those who wanted to obtain scientific knowledge of the
Arabic language.

[41] *Fawa'id-u'l-Fu'ad*, p. 68.

[42] The auditor-general. For his functions, see Qureshi, *Administration of the Sultanate of Delhi*,
pp. 84–5. His appointment as *Mustaufi* was lauded by the famous poet Taj Reza in a *qasidah*.

of it should torment me.' Nizam-u'd-din was sorry to see his teacher so deeply attached to material wealth.[43]

The other teacher who made a real impact on his mind was just the opposite of Khwaja Shams-u'l-Mulk. Maulana Kamal-u'd-din Zahid was a distinguished Traditionist of Delhi, pious, erudite, and unassuming. Originally a native cf Marigala,[44] he settled in Delhi. He was a pupil of Maulana Mahmud bin As'ad Abi'l-Hasan al-Balkhi,[45] a pupil of Maulana Razi-u'd-din Hasan Saghani. When Balban came to know about his piety and scholarship, he called him to his court and requested him to accept the duty of leading his prayers. 'Our prayer is all that is left to us,' replied the Maulana, 'does he want to take that from us also? Balban was dumbfounded and did not pursue his request further.[46] Maulana Kamal-u'd-din Zahid did not leave any literary work. The *Kashif al-Haqa'iq wa Qamus al-Daqa'iq*[47] has been wrongly ascribed to him. It is, in fact, the work of Abu Salih Muhammad bin Ahmad Miyanji bin Nasir-u'd-din (d. 982/1574).[48] Had it been Maulana Kamal-u'd-din Zahid's work, the fact could have hardly escaped the notice of Shaikh Nizam-u'd-din Auliya.

Nizam-u'd-din received instructions in *Mashariq-u'l-Anwar* from him and committed the whole book to memory.[49] Maulana Kamal-u'd-din autographed a certificate on a manuscript of the work when he completed his study of it on 22 Rabi-u'l-Awwal 679/1280. This certificate[50] is significant because it throws light on several important aspects of the Shaikh's life. It shows that (*a*) Nizam-u'd-din was looked upon as a first-rank scholar by the great Traditionist who speaks about his scholarship in eloquent terms; (*b*) his spiritiual qualities were recognized by Maulana Kamal-u'd-din Zahid in that he asks in this

---

[43] *Durar-i-Nizami*, MS.

[44] Marigala is situated some sixteen miles from Rawalpindi along the Grand Trunk Road, as one proceeds towards Peshawar. Barani (p. 353) has referred to another distinguished scholar of Marigala, Maulana Miran, as one of the celebrities of 'Ala-u'd-din's period.

[45] *Siyar-u'l-Auliya*, p. 105.

[46] Ibid. p. 106.

[47] MSS in India Office Library (Loth 103), Asiatic Society of Bengal (A.e.20), and Pir Muhammad Shah Library at Ahmadabad.

[48] See Zubaid Ahmad, *Contribution of India to Arabic Literature*, p. 236.

[49] *Siyar-u'l-Auliya*, p. 101, 'Yud giraft'.

[50] See Appendix V.

note for Nizam-u'd-din to pray for him and his descendants; and (c) if the date of the grant of this certificate is correctly recorded, Nizam-u'd-din must have been about 43 years old at the time and must already have completed his formal education.[51] Amongst Traditionists there is a convention that the most sought-after certificate is from scholars instructed by someone in the direct chain of narrators or compilers of *ahadith*. Since Maulana Kamal-u'd-din Zahid was a pupil of the pupil of the author of *Mashariq-u'l-Anwar*, Shaikh Nizam-u'd-din would have considered it a privilege to receive the *ijaza* from him, even at such an advanced age. The words of respect used for the Shaikh by Maulana Kamal-u'd-din Zahid make it abundantly clear that the recipient of the certificate was a fully mature person with an established reputation. Incidentally it shows that Shaikh Nizam-u'd-din's academic interests continued for at least two decades after his initiation in the discipline of Shaikh Farid.

Maulana Kamal-u'd-din Zahid inculcated in Shaikh Nizam-u'd-din Auliya deep love for the Traditions of the Prophet and initiated him in the intricacies and principles of critique relating to *'ilm-i-hadith*. Throughout Nizam-u'd-din's life, Hadith literature remained one of the most absorbing fields of study and he developed great insight in it. It appears from *Durar-i-Nizami* that some of the sessions of his assemblies were exclusively devoted to elucidation and explanation of *ahadith*, and Qazi Muhi-u'd-din Kashani particularly participated in these discussions.

Taken as a whole, the two teachers who moulded the life and thought of Nizam-u'd-din were Maulana 'Ala-u'd-din Usuli of Badaon and Maulana Kamal-u'd-din Zahid of Delhi. Both of them disdained material wealth and passed their days in penitence and poverty. Apart from mysticism, the two special fields of academic interest for Nizam-u'd-din were *fiqh* (jurisprudence) and Hadith, and in these two fields he was indebted to Maulana Usuli and Maulana Zahid.

---

[51] Fifteen years had passed since Baba Farid's death and Nizam-u'd-din had by then established his reputation as a mystic teacher. That Nizam-u'd-din had continued his education after he got initiated in the discipline of Shaikh Farid is clear from a remark of the great saint (*Siyar-u'l-Auliya*, p. 107). This happened when Shaikh Nizam-u'd-din was only 20. It appears from this certificate of Maulana Kamal-u'd-din Zahid that he had been pursuing his studies for 23 years.

An essential part of the method of instruction in those days was a system of seminars and debates which deepened the foundations of a student's scholarship and developed his power of expression. Nizam-u'd-din distinguished himself as an excellent debater and became known as Nizam-u'd-din *Bahash* (Debater) and Nizam-u'd-din *Mahfil Shikan* (Breaker of Assemblies). Whatever the academic value of this power of debate and discussion, Nizam-u'd-din did not have any occasion to deploy these aptitudes in his life. In fact, the Chishti mystic tradition was opposed to casuistry and discussion. If Nizam-u'd-din learnt anything from his experience of debates in his school, it was the realization that such an approach is futile in bringing about a change in the outlook and character of a person.

4

AT THE FEET OF SHAIKH FARID
GANJ-I-SHAKAR

It was in Badaon that Nizam-u'd-din heard the name of Shaikh
Farid-u'd-din Ganj-i-Shakar (1175–1265),[1] whose *Jama'at Khanah* at
Ajodhan was one of the most renowned centres of spiritual activity
in medieval India. Since Ajodhan (later known as Pakpattan)[2] was a
meeting place of roads from different directions, people from every
walk of life—kings, nobles, soldiers, scholars, and merchants—visited
him and sought his spiritual blessings. The following two incidents,
one from Ajodhan and the other from Delhi, give some idea of his
popularity and charisma:

First, when he visited Delhi after the death of his master, Shaikh
Qutb-u'd-din Bakhtiyar Kaki, he was deluged by visitors and friends.
From the small hours of the morning till late into the night he had to
attend to them, and accept their invitations for feasts. He had to start
for Friday prayer exceptionally early because it was difficult to reach
the mosque on time for prayer due to the large crowds of admirers
gathered on the way. As he stepped out of the house, people eagerly
rushed towards him, kissed his hands and encircled him. No sooner
did he manage to come out of one circle than he found himself in

---

[1] For details about his life and teachings, see Nizami, *The Life and Times of Shaikh
Farid-u'd-din Ganj-i-Shakar* (Aligarh, 1955).

[2] For Pakpattan, see, M. 'Abdullah Chaghtai, *Pakpattan and Baba Farid* (Lahore, 1968).

another, and this process went on until he reached the mosque worn out and wearied.[3]

Second, in the month of Shawwal 651/1251 Sultan Nasir-u'd-din Mahmud marched towards Uchch and Multan. On the way his soldiers decided to pay their respects to the great Shaikh. When the soldiers flocked to the city all the streets and bazaars of Ajodhan were blocked. How to meet and see the Shaikh? A sleeve of Baba Farid's shirt was hung up on a thoroughfare. An ocean of humanity began to surge forward. The sleeve was torn to pieces due to pressure of hands. The Shaikh himself was mobbed so painfully that he requested his *murids* to encircle him in order to save his person from a public eager to elbow its way to him.[4]

The Shaikh of Ajodhan was at this time at the height of his reputation as a mystic. More than half a century of dedicated spiritual work had raised his stature immensely in the religious circles of the region under his care.[5]

Nizam-u'd-din was about 12 years old when he first heard in Badaon the name of Shaikh Farid. He was reading a glossary[6] when a musician, Abu Bakr Kharrat, came to see his teacher and started narrating details of his visit to Multan and Ajodhan. He referred to the religious devotions and penitences of Shaikh Baha-u'd-din Zakariya and said that the atmosphere of his *khanqah* was so deeply religious that even his maidservants busied themselves in *zikr* while grinding the flour. He then gave an account of his visit to the *Jama'at Khanah* of Shaikh Farid. For no obvious reason Nizam-u'd-din felt attracted towards him. He developed feelings of love and respect for him and after every obligatory prayer uttered his name ten times. He felt a spiritual exhilaration in remembering him. His schoolmates came to know of his attachment for the saint whom he had not yet seen. Whenever they desired him to swear on oath, they insisted that he should swear by the name of Shaikh Farid.[7]

---

[3] *Fawa'id-u'l-Fu'ad*, p. 145.

[4] Ibid. pp. 145–6.

[5] *Tarikh-i-Firuz Shahi*, p. 112.

[6] Some editions of *Fawa'id-u'l-Fu'ad* have *na't* (poems in praise of the Prophet), others have *lughat* (glossary). A misplaced dot has created this confusion.

[7] *Fawa'id-u'l-Fu'ad*, pp. 148–9; *Siyar-u'l-Auliya*, p. 100.

The seed of Baba Farid's love thus sown in the youthful heart of Nizam-u'd-din blossomed with the passage of time. While he was on his way to Delhi, an old relation, 'Uz, was also accompanying him. Whenever there was danger of bandits or wild animals, 'Uz cried out, 'O Pir! Come. We are in your protection.' Nizam-u'd-din enquired from him who was his *pir* whose spiritual help he sought so often. 'Uz referred to Shaikh Farid-u'd-din. Nizam-u'd-din's love for the saint increased all the more.[8]

As destiny would have it, when Nizam-u'd-din reached Delhi, he stayed in the neighbourhood of Shaikh Najib-u'd-din Mutawakkil (younger brother of Shaikh Farid), who was a simple, pious, and sincere dervish and passed his days in poverty resigned to the will of God. Once in his early life he was engaged by a Turkish noble, Itmar, to look after a mosque constructed by him and was also provided with a house. Itmar spent two and a half lakh of *tanka*s on the marriage of his daughter, an extravagance criticized by Shaikh Najib-u'd-din. 'You should spend rather more for the public benefit,' he told the Turk, who was displeased at this remark and dismissed him from service. Thereafter, the life of Shaikh Najib was one of poverty. According to Shaikh Nizam-u'd-din, he lived in Delhi without means for seventy long years. His house had only one room where he lived with a wife and two sons. A broken *chappar* (thatched roof) over the room provided space for receiving visitors. His poverty had touched such a level that even on 'Eid days he had nothing to offer to his visitors other than a glass of water. A saintly and pious lady, Bibi Fatima Sam,[9] helped the family in times of hunger and starvation. She would cook bread and send it to Shaikh Najib, who treated her as his 'sister'.[10] It was in the

---

[8] *Fawa'id-u'l-Fu'ad*, p. 145; *Siyar-u'l-Auliya*, p. 100. Shaikh Nizam-u'd-din had some strange spiritual experiences on his way to Delhi. A man dressed in a black cloak and grimy headgear came to him in a state of ecstasy, embraced him, put his chest on his, smelled it and looking intently at his eyes said: 'I scent the fragrance of Islam in his chest.' Ibid. p. 115.

[9] For her life, see Nizami, *Hazrat Bibi Fatima Sam* (Delhi, 1982).

[10] *Fawa'id-u'l-Fu'ad*, p. 244; *Siyar-u'l-Auliya*, p. 168. Shaikh Najib died in Delhi and was buried outside the city near the Darwaza-i-Manda (*Siyar-u'l-Auliya*, p. 168). His grave is in the same area where Bibi Zulaikha lies buried. See also Muhammad Habibullah, *Zikr- Jami' Auliya-i-Dehli*, MS British Museum, or. 1746, fos. 20b–21b.

company of such a saint with an otherworldly attitude and the courage of his convictions that Nizam-u'd-din passed the most formative period of his life. On completing his formal education in Delhi he asked Shaikh Najib-u'd-din to pray for him to be appointed *qazi*, the highest ambition of a scholar in those days. The Shaikh gave no reply. When Nizam-u'd-din repeated his request, Shaikh Najib said, 'Don't be a *qazi*. Be something else.'[11] At the time he must have reacted with disappointment but later in life, when a more purposeful sphere of activity had opened up for him, he realized the wisdom of Shaikh Najib's remark. In fact it was he who made Shaikh Nizam-u'd-din realize for the first time that he was destined to have an entirely different pattern of life. Instead of striving for worldly success and government jobs, he turned to the *khanqah* of Shaikh Farid-u'd-din Ganj-i-Shakar.

The decision to proceed to Ajodhan was taken suddenly and under dramatic circumstances. According to Jami, one night he was busy in prayers in the Jama' Masjid of Delhi. In the early hours of the morning he heard a muezzin reciting the following verse from the Qur'an (57: 16):

Has not the time arrived
For the believers that they,
Their hearts in all humility,
Should engage in the remembrance of God.

The Shaikh felt an emotional storm surging within him. He left for Ajodhan without any provision for the journey.[12]

Shaikh Nizam-u'd-din was twenty[13] when, on a Wednesday,[14] he reached the tumble-down hut of Shaikh Farid at Ajodhan. When he was conducted to the presence of the Shaikh, now nearing his ninetieth year

---

[11] *Fawa'id-u'l-Fu'ad*, p. 28; *Siyar-u'l-Auliya*, p. 169.

[12] *Nafahat-u'l-Uns*, p. 452.

[13] *Siyar-u'l-Auliya*, p. 106.

[14] Ibid. Amir Khurd gives the day but not the year. Later writers have added the year on the basis of their calculations. It appears from *Qiwam-u'l-'Aqa'id* that his mother was alive at this time and he had undertaken this journey to Ajodhan with her permission (MS p. 16). She died soon after his return from Ajodhan (ibid. p. 18).

and famed across the whole of India, Nizam-u'd-din became nervous. The Shaikh welcomed him by reciting the following couplet:

اے آتش فراقت دلها کباب کرده

سیلاب اشتیاقت جانها خراب کرده

(The fire of your separation has burnt many hearts.
The storm of desire to meet you has ravaged many lives.)

With much effort Nizam-u'd-din mustered the courage to say that he wished to kiss the feet of the Shaikh. The old saint, noticing his nervousness, said, 'Every newcomer is nervous,'[15] and calmed him. He instructed his senior disciples, who looked after the management of the *Jama'at Khanah*, to provide a cot for the newcomer. Nizam-u'd-din hesitated to sleep on the cot while many *huffaz* (those who had committed the Qur'an to memory), devotees, and saints much senior to him in age and experience slept on the ground. When Maulana Badr-u'd-din Ishaq came to know of this hesitation, he sent a message: 'Will you do as you wish or will you obey the orders of the Shaikh?' Nizam-u'd-din quietly submitted and slept on the cot provided for him.[16]

Nizam-u'd-din was then initiated into the discipline. Contrary to his normal practice, Shaikh Farid did not ask the initiate to have his head shaved. Nizam-u'd-din had long curly hair and may have retained some attachment to it. However, when he saw others with shaven heads, he felt something attractive in them, and approached his master for permission to become *mahluq*. The permission was readily granted and Nizam-u'd-din was now like any other inmate of the *Jama'at Khanah*.[17]

In later life Shaikh Nizam-u'd-din told his audience that he visited his master three times in three years,[18] staying for several months each time. During these three visits the ageing saint completed his spiritual training.

---

[15] *Fawa'id-u'l-Fu'ad*, p. 30; *Siyar-u'l-Auliya*, p. 107.
[16] Ibid.
[17] Ibid.
[18] *Fawa'id-u'l-Fu'ad*, p. 42.

Though many significant incidents of Nizam-u'd-din's relationship with the great Baba Farid are mentioned in *Fawa'id-u'l-Fu'ad* and *Siyar-u'l-Auliya*, it is difficult to fix their sequence. Nevertheless, the psychological and moral significance of these incidents needs clear appraisal.

The first conflict in Nizam-u'd-din's mind was whether to complete his education or to give it up and turn singlemindedly to the cultivation of his soul. 'I never ask anybody,' Baba Farid told him, 'to give up studies. Knowledge also is necessary for a dervish. So do this [spiritual work] and that [studies] also till such time as one of them gets an upper hand over the other.'[19]

Baba Farid instructed Nizam-u'd-din in some basic texts; propounded the basic and fundamental principles of the order; illustrated through his own conduct the type of life a mystic was expected to lead; eliminated all traces of that intellectual arrogance which had quietly entered his mind when he won laurels in the highest academic circles of Delhi; and embellished his inner life with all the qualities necessary for a mystic entrusted with the stupendous task of looking after the spiritual well-being of others. He then appointed the young man, who had hardly attained the age of twenty-three years, as his chief successor.

(i) Nizam-u'd-din learnt six *paras* of the Qur'an, five chapters of *'Awarif-u'l-Ma'arif*, and Abu Shakur Salimi's *Tamhidat al-Muhtadi* from Shaikh Farid.[20] On his completion of the third book the Shaikh granted him a certificate.[21]

These three books were selected by Baba Farid for the instruction of his chief disciple. He considered a dedicated study of the Qur'an essential for awakening spiritual sensibilities in a human heart. His *Jama'at Khanah* was always humming with the voices of reciters of the Qur'an. It was at the instance of Baba Farid that Nizam-u'd-din committed the Qur'an to memory some time later and displayed keen personal interest in developing Qur'anic studies in his own *khanqah*.[22]

---

[19] *Siyar-u'l-Auliya*, p. 107.

[20] *Fawa'id-u'l-Fu'ad*, p. 75; *Siyar-u'l-Auliya*, p. 106. Teaching a few chapters of a book carefully and then leaving the rest for the independent study of the student was a common practice in medieval Muslim scholarship. Shah Waliullah of Delhi also followed it.

[21] See Appendix V for the document.

[22] See Nizami, *Tarikh-i-Masha'ikh-i Chisht*, I, pp. 406–7.

The *'Awarif-u'l-Ma'arif* was a book of practical importance. It was a manual of guidance for those who were entrusted with the task of organizing *khanqahs*. Baba Farid had great respect for Shaikh Shihab-u'd-din Suhrawardi, the author of the book, and had also, according to a later report, prepared a summary of it.[23] The day *'Awarif* was brought to the Shaikh, his wife gave birth to a child. The Shaikh named him Shihab-u'd-din.[24] The *Tamhidat* is a book on religious law (*fiqh*) and deals with the basic problems of faith with such clarity and depth that whoever mastered it developed an insight into the most subtle problems of Islamic law.

(ii) How Shaikh Farid's intuitive intelligence (*nafs-i-gira*) penetrated his disciples' characters may be gauged from the following incident. The Shaikh was teaching the *'Awarif-u'l-Ma'arif* from a manuscript that contained a number of scribal errors, and so he had to proceed slowly in order to correct the mistakes. Nizam-u'd-din interrupted the Shaikh and said that Shaikh Najib-u'd-din Mutawakkil had a good manuscript of the book. Shaikh Farid was annoyed and irritated. 'Has this dervish no capacity to correct a defective manuscript?' he exclaimed. When Nizam-u'd-din realized that his master had disapproved of his remark, he fell at his feet and humbly begged him to forgive his insolence. But Shaikh Farid's anger did not subside. Nizam-u'd-din was over-taken by deep grief. In a mood of extreme mental depression he even thought of committing suicide. He went into the wilderness, weeping and crying. Shaikh Farid's son, Shihab-u'd-din, who was a friend of Nizam-u'd-din, was touched by his condition. He interceded on his behalf and secured the Shaikh's pardon. Shaikh Farid called him to his presence and remarked: 'All this I have done for your perfection . . . A *pir* is a dresser of brides.'[25] He then bestowed his special dress on him.[26] On the face of it Shaikh Nizam-u'd-din Auliya's remark seems quite innocent, but the Shaikh perceived a trace of some intellectual snobbishness which distinctions and laurels in the academic circles

---

[23] *Gulzar-i-Abrar*, MS.

[24] *Fawa'id-u'l-Fu'ad*, p. 75.

[25] Ibid. pp. 26–7.

[26] *Siyar-u'l-Auliya*, p. 239.

of Delhi might have produced in him. He resorted to severe admonition in order to eradicate every trace of hidden conceit in him.

(iii) One day a classmate, with whom Nizam-u'd-din used to have academic discussions in Delhi, happened to meet him in Ajodhan. He was staying in an inn and had a servant to attend to his needs. Seeing Nizam-u'd-din in grimy and tattered clothes, he exclaimed: 'Maulana Nizam-u'd-din! What misfortune has befallen you? Had you taken up teaching work at Delhi, you would have become a leading scholar of the time in affluent circumstances.' Nizam-u'd-din said nothing in reply but reported the matter to Shaikh Farid. 'What would be your answer to such a question?', asked the saint. 'As the Shaikh directs,' replied Nizam-u'd-din. 'When you meet him next,' remarked Baba Farid, 'recite the following couplet':

نه همرهی تو مرا راه خویش گیر وبرو
ترا سعادت بادا مرا نگونساری

(You are not my travelling companion. Seek your own path. Move along. May prosperity be your portion in life and misfortune mine.)

The Shaikh further asked him to get a tray of food from the kitchen and carry it on his head to his friend. The friend came to see Shaikh Farid and was so charmed by his mystic ways that he decided to join his discipline.[27] There were a number of subtle hints and suggestions of psychological import involved in the way Shaikh Farid dealt with the matter. These were well taken by Nizam-u'd-din.

(iv) One day an old man came to Shaikh Farid and, while introducing himself, reminded him that he had met him in the *khanqah* of Shaikh Qutb-u'd-din Bakhtiyar Kaki. The old man was accompanied by his son, who was uncouth and insolent. He entered into an acrimonious discussion with the Shaikh and began to shout loudly. Shaikh Nizam-u'd-din and his son Maulana Shihab-u'd-din were at the door.

---

[27] Ibid. p. 239.

When they heard the youth talking rudely to the saint, Maulana Shihab-u'd-din entered the room and slapped his face. The youth was about to strike at Maulana Shihab-u'd-din when Shaikh Nizam-u'd-din caught hold of his hands. The Shaikh ordered his son to please the visitors. The Maulana gave some cloth and money to both the father and the son and they left the *Jama'at Khanah* happy and satisfied.[28]

Each one of these incidents at the *Jama'at Khanah* of Shaikh Farid had a lesson for Shaikh Nizam-u'd-din Auliya. No one could lead others on the path of spiritual discipline unless he was adequately educated in religious sciences and had developed an insight in *Shari'ah*. Arrogance and conceit had no place in mystic life. Nobody was to leave the portals of the *khanqah* displeased or hurt.

JAMA'AT KHANAH OF SHAIKH FARID

The *Jama'at Khanah* of Shaikh Farid was a large room where all the inmates slept, prayed, and studied on the ground. It was managed by the inmates themselves. They scattered to perform different duties: some went to the jungle to collect wood for the joint household, some plucked *delah* from the *kareel* trees, some fetched water from the well, some washed utensils in the kitchen, while others cooked the food.[29] They gathered again when their efforts succeeded in providing sufficient food for the inmates of the *Jama'at Khanah*. According to Shaikh Nizam-u'd-din Auliya it was like the day of 'Eid when the inmates got a full meal at dinner.'[30]

How Shaikh Nizam-u'd-din Auliya spent his time when he came to see his spiritual mentor may be gauged from the following incidents:

(i) He was assigned the duty of boiling *delah* brought from the jungle by his comrades. One day when boiling the *delah* he found that there was no salt available in the kitchen. He went

---

[28] *Fawa'id-u'l-Fu'ad*, p. 160.

[29] Ibid. p. 74; *Khair-u'l-Majalis*, p. 108; *Siyar-u'l-Auliya*, pp. 86–209. *Kareel* is capparis aphylla. See H. M. Elliot, *Memoirs on the History and Folklore and Distribution of the Races of the North Western Provinces of India*, ed. John Beames, London, II p. 373.

[30] *Khair-u'l-Majalis*, p. 150.

to a grocer in the neighbourhood and purchased some salt on credit. When the dish was ready, he placed it before Shaikh Farid. As soon as the saint put his hand into the dish, he said: 'My hand has become heavier. It may be that I am not permitted to take the morsel to my mouth. Perhaps there is something doubtful in it.' So saying the Shaikh put the morsel back into the dish. Shaikh Nizam-u'd-din trembled as he heard these words. He stood up, placed his head on the ground and submitted: 'My master! Shaikh Jalal, Maulana Badr-u'd-din Ishaq and Maulana Husam-u'd-din bring wood, *delah* and water for the kitchen. This humble fellow boils the *delah* and takes full care in its preparation, and brings it before the master. There seems to me nothing to doubt about. But what the position really is, is known to the master.' The Shaikh asked about the salt. Shaikh Nizam-u'd-din again placed his head on the ground and explained the position. Baba Farid then remarked: 'The dervishes prefer to die of starvation rather than incur any debt for the satisfaction of their desires. Debt and resignation are poles apart and cannot subsist together.' The Shaikh then ordered the dish to be removed from the *Jama'at Khanah*.[31]

(ii)   Many people came to the *Jama'at Khanah* of Shaikh Farid to get *ta'wiz* (amulets). It was difficult for the Shaikh to write all these *ta'wiz* in his own hand. He had, therefore, assigned this work to Maulana Badr-u'd-din Ishaq. On one occasion when Maulana Badr-u'd-din was not available, Shaikh Farid asked Nizam-u'd-din to prepare the amulets on his behalf. The number of supplicants was very large and Shaikh Nizam-u'd-din got tired of writing the amulets. Thereafter the Shaikh said: 'I give you permission to write amulets [in your own right] and give them to the supplicants.'[32]

(iii)   Once when Shaikh Nizam-u'd-din started for Ajodhan from Delhi, a neighbour, Muhammad, who had some serious ailment, requested him to bring an amulet for him from Shaikh Farid. When Shaikh Nizam-u'd-din placed his neighbour's

---

[31] *Siyar-u'l-Auliya*, p. 66.
[32] *Fawa'id-u'l-Fu'ad*, p. 200.

request before his master, the latter asked him to write a *ta'wiz* on his behalf. Shaikh Nizam-u'd-din wrote on a piece of paper—*Allah-u-Shafi*, *Allah-u-Kafi*, *Allah-u-ma'afi* (God is the Healer; God is Sufficient; God relieves from pain), and presented it to the Shaikh who touched it, read it and gave it back to him to be handed over to Muhammad.[33]

(iv) One day a hair fell from the beard of the Shaikh. Shaikh Nizam-u'd-din Auliya picked it up and obtained the Shaikh's permission to use it as *ta'wiz*.[34]

(v) A flourishing businessman of Kirman, Syed Mahmud, had settled at the *Jama'at Khanah* and adopted the life of a mystic. He lived there with his wife Bibi Rani, the daughter of a mint officer of Multan. Both of them lived in the *Jama'at Khanah* like other inmates and bore the hardships of penury and hunger. Bibi Rani was a kind and compassionate lady. She looked after the comforts of the inmates of the *Jama'at Khanah* like a sister looking after her brothers. One day she found that the clothes of Shaikh Nizam-u'd-din Auliya were extremely grimy and tattered. She requested him to give his clothes to her for washing. She gave him a *chadar* to cover his body and then washed his clothes and patched them.[35] All the time Shaikh Nizam-u'd-din sat in a corner, reading a book.

It was in the *Jama'at Khanah* of Shaikh Farid that Shaikh Nizam-u'd-din developed close personal contact with Syed Muhammad Kirmani and the Kirmanis became the life-companions of the Shaikh.[36]

(vi) Baba Farid fully realized the penury in which Shaikh Nizam-u'd-din's family lived in Delhi. Once when Nizam-u'd-din sought the Shaikh's permission to leave for Delhi, the latter gave him a gold coin (*ghiyasi*) for his expenses. Later Shaikh Nizam-u'd-din came to know that this was the last coin in Shaikh Farid's house. At *iftar* time Baba Farid had

---

[33] Ibid. pp. 62–3.
[34] Ibid. p. 63.
[35] *Siyar-u'l-Auliya*, p. 115.
[36] Ibid. pp. 115, 209.

nothing to break his fast with. Nizam-u'd-din placed his master's gift at his feet. It was accepted with the remark: 'I have prayed to God to grant you a portion of earthly goods.' Nizam-u'd-din was worried lest worldly comforts should destroy his spiritual personality. The Shaikh removed his anxiety by observing: 'Don't be afraid. This will not entangle you in any trouble or calamity.'[37]

(vii)   Once Baba Farid was indisposed. He sent Shaikh Nizam-u'd-din Auliya and a few other disciples to a graveyard of the martyrs to pray for his recovery from illness.[38] This was also the practice of Shaikh Nizam-u'd-din Auliya's mother. Whenever she fell ill, she asked her son to go to the graves of saints and martyrs and pray for her recovery.[39]

(viii) Whoever Shaikh Farid asked to commit the Qur'an to memory, he advised them to begin with *Surah Yusuf.* God blessed the person who started memorizing the Qur'an in this way.[40]

 (ix)   Shaikh Farid's practice was that whenever he referred to any incident of his life, he would say that such and such a thing happened to a dervish. He would never disclose his identity.[41] Shaikh Nizam-u'd-din Auliya also adopted this method.

  (x)   One day, six or seven young dervishes who belonged to the Chishti *silsilah* came to the *khanqah* of Shaikh Farid. They had some dispute and wanted the Shaikh's arbitration in the matter. Shaikh Farid entrusted the matter to Shaikh Nizam-u'd-din Auliya and Shaikh Badr-u'd-din Ishaq. The softness and humility with which these visitors presented the matter brought tears to the eyes of both arbitrators.[42]

 (xi)   Once on the eve of *Shab-i-Barat* Shaikh Farid offered some supererogatory prayers and asked Shaikh Nizam-u'd-din Auliya to lead the prayers.[43]

---

[37] *Siyar-u'l-Auliya,* pp. 131–2.
[38] *Fawa'id-u'l-Fu'ad,* p. 59; *Siyar-u'l-Auliya,* p. 123.
[39] *Fawa'id-u'l-Fu'ad,* p. 50.
[40] Ibid. p. 65.
[41] Ibid. p. 82.
[42] Ibid. p. 86.
[43] Ibid. p. 88.

SHAIKH FARID'S MORAL AND SPIRITUAL INSTRUCTIONS

Shaikh Farid naturally took a keen interest in the moral and spiritual education of his disciples. However, he was particularly interested in building up a morally autonomous and spiritually integrated personality in Shaikh Nizam-u'd-din Auliya, whom he wanted to appoint as his chief successor. Living in the *Jama'at Khanah* was in itself an education and the inmates learnt here the most difficult of human lessons—the subordination of human desires to moral and spiritual ideals. Example worked better than precept in moulding the personalities of the disciples in consonance with the ideals of the *silsilah*. Shaikh Nizam-u'd-din used to record in writing whatever he heard from his spiritual mentor.[44] This collection of *malfuzat* has not survived, as the Shaikh intended it as a personal memorandum only.

1. Shaikh Farid kept his doors open to all and sundry—whether mystics or the common people.[45] Shaikh Nizam-u'd-din followed his master's example and welcomed all sorts of people in his *khanqah*. Shaikh Farid liked to grant individual interviews and Shaikh Nizam-u'd-din Auliya also followed this practice.[46]
2. Shaikh Farid advised him to pacify his enemies and clear away any debts. Shaikh Nizam-u'd-din used to borrow money when in dire need, but now he decided to stop borrowing completely.[47]
3. Shaikh Farid told him that consistency and steadfastness in faith was an essential requirement for pursuing the mystic goal. He praised him on this account and expressed dissatisfaction at the behaviour of two other disciples whose faith diminished after they had left him.[48]
4. Shaikh Nizam-u'd-din Auliya had an aversion to worldliness from his very early years, but, as he himself once remarked, after he

---

[44] Ibid. p. 30.
[45] Ibid. p. 5.
[46] Ibid. p. 68.
[47] Ibid. p. 140.
[48] Ibid. pp. 171–2; *Siyar-u'l-Auliya*, p. 124.

joined the discipline of Shaikh Farid his attitude of *tark* (rejection of material means) was deepened because the Shaikh had completely forsaken all material attractions as things of no value.

5. Shaikh Farid used to advise his visitors to recite *Surat al-Jum'a* every Friday night if they desired increase in their means of livelihood. Shaikh Nizam-u'd-din Auliya advised others to read it every night but did not read it himself as he did not want to pray for that purpose.[49]

BLESSED BY THE SHAIKH

During his three visits to Ajodhan, Shaikh Farid blessed Nizam-u'd-din on different occasions and in different ways. Some of the incidents may be noted here:

(a) Once Nizam-u'd-din went with his master in a boat. It was midday of a summer month. All the companions went to sleep but he remained awake, driving the flies from his master. Baba Farid turned to him and said: 'When you get back to Delhi, busy yourself in religious exercises. It is not good to waste time. Half of the faith lies in observing fasts; the other half is prayers, Hajj etc.' Nizam-u'd-din heard the Shaikh with rapt attention but forgot to ask him what type of prayers he was referring to.[50]

(b) One day the saint asked Nizam-u'd-din if he remembered a particular prayer. 'Commit it to memory so that I may appoint you my successor,' remarked Shaikh Farid.[51]

(c) Perhaps it was the last visit of Shaikh Nizam-u'd-din to his master—in 664/1265 on 25 Jumada-u'l-Awwal—after the Friday prayers, Shaikh Farid put his saliva into the mouth of Shaikh Nizam-u'd-din and advised him to commit the Qur'an to memory. He added: 'I have given you both the worlds. Go and take the empire of Hindustan.'[52]

---

[49] *Fawa'id-u'l-Fu'ad*, p. 57.
[50] *Siyar-u'l-Auliya*, p. 112.
[51] Ibid. p. 116.
[52] Ibid. p. 123; *Qiwam-u'l-'Aqa'id*, MS p. 18.

(d) One day Shaikh Farid prayed to God that Shaikh Nizam-u'd-din's supplications be granted. The Shaikh then gave him his staff (*'asa*).[53]

(e) One day Shaikh Nizam-u'd-din entered the room of his master when he was alone. He placed his head on his feet and requested him to pray for the steadfastness of his faith. Shaikh Farid acceded to his request.[54]

(f) On 13 Ramadan 664/1265, Shaikh Farid granted him an *Ijazat Namah*,[55] a certificate permitting him to enrol disciples. He asked him to show this certificate to Maulana Jamal-u'd-din at Hansi and to Qazi Muntajib at Delhi. Shaikh Nizam-u'd-din was surprised that he did not mention the name of Shaikh Najib-u'd-din Mutawakkil in this connection. But on his return to Delhi he found that Shaikh Najib had already departed for the world beyond. While conferring the *Khilafat Namah* on him, Shaikh Farid prayed to God for his bright future and good fortune and remarked:

تو درختے شوی که در سایہء تو خلقے بیاساید

('You will be a tree under whose soothing shadow the people will find comfort.')[56]

Then Shaikh Farid observed with regret that Nizam-u'd-din would not be there at the time of his death.

Shaikh Nizam-u'd-din was overwhelmed by the kindness of his spiritual master. He submitted: 'You have bestowed great honour on me and have nominated me your successor. This is a great treasure for me. But I am a student and dislike worldly connection and have looked at it with disdain. This position is very high and beyond my capacity to shoulder . . . . For me your kindness and favour is enough.' When the Shaikh found him hesitant to accept this responsibility, he prophesied: 'This task will be efficiently performed by you.' When Shaikh Nizam-u'd-din still persisted in his request, Shaikh Farid remarked

---

[53] *Fawa'id-u'l-Fu'ad*, p. 52.

[54] *Khair-u'l-Majalis*, p. 225.

[55] For the *Khilafat Namah*, see Appendix IV

[56] *Siyar-u'l-Auliya*, pp. 116–17.

in great excitement, 'Nizam! Take it from me, though I do not know if I will be honoured before the Almighty or not, I promise not to enter paradise without your disciples in my company.'[57] Thereafter Shaikh Nizam-u'd-din left Ajodhan for Delhi. In Hansi he showed the certificate to Maulana Jamal-u'd-din, who recited the verse:

خدائے جهاں را هزاراں سپاس

که گوهر سپرده به گوهر شناس

(A thousand blessings and thanks to the Lord for having assigned the jewel to one who understands its value.)[58]

After Shaikh Nizam-u'd-din Auliya's return to Delhi, the saint, whose health had completely broken down as a result of continuous fasts and penitences, fell seriously ill. A few days before his death Syed Muhammad Kirmani reached Ajodhan from Delhi. The saint lay on a cot inside the *hujra*, while his sons and disciples were busy discussing at the door the problem of his succession. Syed Muhammad Kirmani expressed his desire to see the Shaikh but was not allowed in. However, he pushed open the door of the *hujra* and fell at the feet of the Shaikh. The Shaikh opened his eyes and asked: 'How are you Syed? How and when did you come here?' 'This very moment,' replied Syed Muhammad. In the course of his conversation he referred to Shaikh Nizam-u'd-din Auliya and conveyed his respects. On hearing Shaikh Nizam-u'd-din's name, the Shaikh enquired: 'How is he? Is he happy?' The Shaikh then entrusted all the articles of mystic regalia—prayer carpet, cloak, and staff—to him with instructions to convey them to Shaikh Nizam-u'd-din. It was a great disappointment for the sons of the Shaikh and they started quarrelling with Syed Muhammad Kirmani for having deprived them of the most precious things in their father's possession.[59]

---

[57] Ibid. p. 348.

[58] Ibid. p. 117.

[59] Ibid. pp. 121–2.

Shaikh Nasir-u'd-din Chiragh-i-Dehli has referred to a report which he had found circulating in this regard. Once Shaikh Farid was sailing in a boat with his sons and disciples. Everyone except the Shaikh and Shaikh Nizam-u'd-din Auliya had fallen asleep. All of a sudden the Shaikh called out: 'Nizam!' Shaikh Nizam-u'd-din Auliya immediately responded: 'I am present.' 'I mean my son Nizam-u'd-din,' remarked Shaikh Farid. After some time the Shaikh called out: 'Shaikh Nizam-u'd-din!' 'I am present,' replied Shaikh Nizam-u'd-din Auliya. 'Come! Mas`ud wanted to bless his son Nizam, [but] God wants to bless you.'[60] Whatever the basis of this report, the 'blessing' could have been some sort of spiritual favour in that particular moment, but not chief successorship, which was a very well thought-out decision taken very early by Shaikh Farid. Besides, the Shaikh's son was employed in the army[61] and was not much inclined towards mysticism. One day both Shaikh Nizam-u'd-din Auliya and the Shaikh's son, Nizam-u'd-din, were in the presence of Shaikh Farid. The saint said: 'Both of you are my sons,' and then, pointing towards his son, said, 'You are *nani* [of the bread],' and referring to Shaikh Nizam-u'd-din Auliya, said, 'you are *jani* [of the soul].'[62] A reference in *Fawa'id-u'l-Fu'ad* is significant in this context. Shaikh Nizam-u'd-din Auliya once told his audience: 'The youngest son of Shaikh-u'l-Islam Farid-u'd-din went to Delhi and got his head shaved [*mahluq shud*] at the grave of Shaikh-u'l-Islam Qutb-u'd-din Bakhtiyar Kaki. When Shaikh Farid-u'd-din heard about this he said: 'Shaikh Qutb-u'd-din is our spiritual mentor and master but this type of initiation has no meaning.'

No spiritual mentor could have exercised greater influence on the thought and character of his disciple than Shaikh Farid Ganj-i-Shakar on the personality of Shaikh Nizam-u'd-din Auliya. He found the young man receptive, conscientious, and dedicated, and passed on to him the essence of the mystic ideals and aspirations to be vigorously pursued in life. Shaikh Nizam-u'd-din Auliya lived up to the expectations of his spiritual master and made the Chishti *silsilah* a factor of immense significance in the lives of the people.

---

[60] *Khair-u'l-Majalis*, p. 224.
[61] *Siyar-u'l-Auliya*, pp. 189–90.
[62] Ibid. p. 124.

5

AT THE HEAD OF THE CHISHTI ORDER
IN INDIA

————·•◦•·————

At the age of twenty-three Shaikh Nizam-u'd-din Auliya was appointed
to succeed Shaikh Farid, directed to settle in Delhi and from there work
for the expansion of the *silsilah*. It was an enormous challenge and
responsibility—to work in the imperial capital without being tempted
by *shughl* (government service) and the company of princes and rulers;
to provide guidance to the disciples of Shaikh Farid who were dispersed
far and wide; to push forward the work of the *silsilah* in regions still
beyond the reach of the Delhi Sultans; and to evolve an effective mechan-
ism to deal with those associated with the order. Shaikh Nizam-u'd-din
Auliya not only rose to the occasion, he infused a new spirit into the
organization of the Chishti order. Amir Khusrau said of him:

شد سلک فرید از تو منظوم

زانست که شد لقب نظامت

(You gathered the beads of Shaikh Farid into a rosary. For this reason
your title has become Nizam [stringer of pearls].)

Through his ceaseless efforts, the entire country came to be stud-
ded with *khanqah*s of the Chishti *silsilah*. According to Muhammad
Ghauthi Shattari, he sent seven hundred senior disciples (*khalifah*s)

to different parts of the country, and 'in a short time the fame of his spiritual qualities and his concern for his disciples and his interest in their spiritual well-being and training reached every corner of the land and every ear, and his *khalifa*s reached every province of the country to train the novice and perfect the initiated.'[1]

Shaikh Nizam-u'd-din Auliya's decision to settle at Ghiyaspur marks the beginning of his career as a mystic teacher. The nucleus of his organization was laid there, and from there were initiated programmes of spiritual enlightenment and culture which transformed the Chishti order into a mass movement. The following account of the Shaikh's activities as given by Zia-u'd-din Barani in his *Hasrat Namah*, as quoted by Mir Khurd, throws considerable light on the aims and ideals of the Shaikh:

One day I was present in the assembly of Sultan-u'l-Masha'ikh and was busy listening to his life-infusing discourse from sunrise to midday. That day a large number of people got initiated into the discipline of Sultan-u'l-Masha'ikh and received his spiritual blessings. During this time it occurred to my mind that Sultan-u'l-Masha'ikh used to be restrictive in admitting people to his spiritual discipline but was now admitting all and sundry—special and ordinary—into that order. I wanted to ask the Shaikh about this change [in his practice]. The Shaikh's spiritual intuition got an inkling of what was passing in my mind. He [turned to me and] said: 'You put questions to me about everything. Why don't you ask me why I am admitting all visitors to my discipline without any enquiry [about their antecedents]?' I trembled and placed my head at the feet of Sultan-u'l-Masha'ikh and submitted: 'For some time this query was in my mind and it occurred to me today also and the Shaikh has come to know about it. The Shaikh then observed: 'God Almighty has, in His Wisdom, given a special characteristic to every age and the people of that age develop their customs, habits, and traditions accordingly in a distinct way. So much so that the temperament of the people [of one generation] and their nature does not agree with that of the preceding generation. This has been proved

---

[1] *Gulzar-i-Abrar*, MS.

by experience. The real purpose of initiation and disciplehood is severance of [all ties] from *ghair-i-Haqq* [what is not-Him] and involving [people] in Him as has been explained in books on spiritual discipline. The elders did not admit anybody to their discipline unless they saw total severance of [material ties] in a man. But from the time of Shaikh Abu Sa'id Abu'l-Khair . . . to the days of Shaikh Saif-u'd-din Bakharzi, and from the time of Shaikh-i-Shuyukh-u'l-'Alam Shihab-u'd-din Suhrawardi to the days of Shaikh-i-Shuyukh-u'l-'Alam Farid-u'd-din . . . all saints, whose exalted spiritual rank and blessings are beyond explanation—there were huge crowds surrounding them. All sorts of people gathered round them—kings, nobles, celebrities, the elite, and others who, out of fear of the Day of Judgement, sought shelter under the pro-tection of those lovers of God. These great saints admitted all people—special and ordinary—into their discipline and granted the Cloak of Repentance [*khirqah-i-taubah*] to them. Everyone cannot suppose his own affairs to be the same as those of Shaikh Abu Sa'id, Shaikh Saif-u'd-din Bakharzi, Shaikh Shihab-u'd-din Suhrawardi, Shaikh-i-Shuyukh u'l-'Alam Farid-u'l-Haqq wa'd-Din and say that since they have admitted disciples in this way I also do likewise . . . Regarding your question about my admitting disciples [without the conditions practised before], one reason is that I frequently hear that many people who join my discipline abstain from sinful acts, offer prayers in congregation, and keep themselves busy in litanies and supererogatory prayers. If I tell the conditions of initiation in the beginning and do not grant them the Cloak of Repentance and blessing, which is equivalent to *khirqah-i-iradah* [Cloak of Initiation], they will be deprived of whatever good thus comes to them. Secondly, I am permitted by a perfect Shaikh to initiate people without any recommendation, any intermediary, any hindrance. When I find a Muslim approaching me with humility, eagerness, and submissiveness and he says: 'I repent from all sins,' I take him at his word and initiate him in [my] discipline. I have also heard from truthful people that after getting initiated people abstain from sins. Another [and the] strongest of all considerations is that one day Shaikh-i-Shuyukh-u'l-'Alam Farid-u'l-Haqq wa'd-Din gave his pen and inkpot to me and ordered me to write amulets. 'I give you this permission to write amulets and give them to the supplicants.' When I started writing amulets the Shaikh-i-Shuyukh-u'l-'Alam found that I was out of spirits while writing prayer-words. He said: 'You feel depressed while writing these prayer-words. What will you do when large number of visitors will come to your door soliciting amulets?' As the Shaikh was alone at that time, I fell at his feet and submitted: 'My master! You have made me a spiritual guide and have conferred your *khilafah* on me . . . which is a treasure—but I am a student and have always shunned association with the world. This is a very responsible assignment. It is beyond my capacity to perform. Your affection is enough for me . . .' On hearing this submission of mine, the Shaikh said: 'You will perform this job well.' I made many excuses. The Shaikh was moved by ecstatic feelings. He sat erect, called me closer and bade me sit and said: 'Nizam! Know that tomorrow [on the Day of Judgement] Mas'ud does not know whether he will be admitted to His favour, but I promise you that I will not put my foot in Paradise without your disciples . . .'

Sultan-u'l-Masha'ikh smiled at this and said: 'I have been granted *khilafah* in this way. I perform this job well at times but not so well at others. Those who spend their lives in aspiring for it and obtain it through stratagems, lies, and fraud, how can they perform this delicate work well? Besides, when a saint about whom I know for certain and whom I have seen with my own eyes [that is, my Shaikh] to have been one of those blessed with *gnosis*, and who had on his body the same garment that Shaikh Bayazid, Junaid, and others who loved God had on their bodies, [when he] has promised the like of that to me, I do not refuse admission to my discipline.'[2]

In adopting this practice of universal admission to spiritual discipline Shaikh Nizam-u'd-din Auliya not only carried out the instructions of his spiritual mentor, but also converted the mystic movement, which earlier aimed at mere individual salvation, into a mass movement for the spiritual culture of man. It marks the beginning of a new phase in the history of Islamic mysticism in South Asia. No saint of any *silsilah*

---

[2] *Siyar-u'l-Auliya*, pp. 346–9.

before him had launched such an extensive movement for peoples' moral and spiritual regeneration.

When Shaikh Nizam-u'd-din Auliya settled at Ghiyaspur and made up his mind to carry the Chishti teachings to people of all walks of life, his *khanqah* emerged as the main centre of Chishti mystic activity in northern India. Many of the descendants and disciples of Shaikh Farid turned to him for spiritual training and blessing. He consolidated the principles of the *silsilah* as propounded by Shaikh Farid and gave a unity and cohesion to the discipline of the order. The following two incidents reflect the firmness with which he enforced his principles:

1. Maulana Burhan-u'd-din Gharib, who played an important role in propagating the Chishti order in the Deccan, was a senior disciple of Shaikh Nizam-u'd-din Auliya. He supervised the preparation of food in the kitchen. As he was an old man of seventy years, he sat leaning on a folded blanket. 'Ali Zambeli and Malik Nusrat—who were attendants of Sultan 'Ala-u'd-din Khalji and disciples of the Shaikh—reported to the Shaikh that Maulana Burhan-u'd-din sat like a shaikh on his carpet. The Shaikh was distressed at this report and when Maulana Burhan-u'd-din came to pay his respects to him, he did not speak to him. When he came down, Iqbal, an attendant of the Shaikh, came to him and conveyed the Shaikh's order to leave the place without delay. He was shocked and went to the house of Ibrahim Tashtdar. He had hardly been there for a couple of days when Ibrahim requested him to leave. No one who was not in the good books of the Shaikh could be a welcome guest at any house. Maulana Burhan-u'd-din returned to his own house overwhelmed with grief. Friends and colleagues came to console him. No one had the courage to plead for him before the Shaikh. Amir Khusrau took courage in both hands and broached the matter once but there was no response from the Shaikh. Then Amir Khusrau thought of making a dramatic appeal to the mercy of the Shaikh. With his turban wrapped round his neck as the criminals do when they surrender to justice, he appeared before the Shaikh. The Shaikh was moved to see him in that posture and asked the reason. He requested the Shaikh to pardon Maulana Burhan-u'd-din. Amir Khusrau

brought him to the Shaikh in the same posture of criminals. The Shaikh pardoned him. [3]

This was a warning to all disciples—to be humble and unassuming in their dealings with people.

2. Qazi Muhi-u'd-din Kashani was one of the most senior *khalifah*s of Shaikh Nizam-u'd-din Auliya. But when the Shaikh found that he had some inclination towards government service, he withdrew the *Khilafat Namah* from him and for one whole year he kept his *khilafah* under suspension. [4] It was a firm and clear warning to all disciples who were appointed *khalifah*s that the slightest leaning in them towards government service would incur the displeasure of the Shaikh. These admonitions administered to senior disciples made clear the basic principles on which the Shaikh wanted the *silsilah* to be organized in Delhi and elsewhere.

The following two principles determined the Shaikh's socio-religious approach and demonstrated in unmistakable terms his commitment to higher human values:

(a) The *murids* were expected to seek the blessings of God through service of His creatures. Service of mankind was considered by the Shaikh as of greater spiritual significance than mere formal prayers and penitences. [5]

(b) Baba Farid's ideals of love and amity in society were to inspire the lives of all those associated with the *silsilah*. Attempts were to be made to unite people rather than to divide them. [6] There was to be no discrimination between one human being and another. [7] All were to be treated as children of God.

It was on the basis of these organizational and ideological principles that Shaikh Nizam-u'd-din Auliya started his programme of spiritual enlightenment in Delhi after receiving *khilafah* from Shaikh Farid.

---

[3] Ibid. pp. 279–81.
[4] For details see below.
[5] *Fawa'id-u'l-Fu'ad*, pp. 13–14.
[6] Ibid. p. 226.
[7] Ibid. p. 207.

6

KHANQAH LIFE

———•◦•———

The *khanqah* of Shaikh Nizam-u'd-din Auliya was situated by the river Jumna,[1] the refreshing breeze from which added to the serenity of the place. Initially the building was a thatched structure of mud, but later a disciple, Zia-u'd-din, a clerk (*nawisinda*) of Malik 'Imad-u'l-Mulk, succeeded in obtaining the Shaikh's permission to make it of brick and mortar.[2] The remnants of this building may be seen near the tomb of Humayun.[3] The *khanqah* comprised a big hall (*Jama'at Khanah*) in the centre, with a series of pillars[4] on its two sides. An old banyan tree stood in the courtyard, somewhat away from the centre, its branches providing some shade to a part of the roof also.[5] A veranda surrounded the courtyard, but in order to provide separate rooms for some senior inmates, the parts of the veranda adjoining the hall were walled up. Opposite to the main gate was the gate-room (*dihliz*) with a door on either side. This was a large room and a few men could sit there comfortably without obstructing the passage of others. Adjoining the *dihliz* was a kitchen.

---

[1] *Siyar-u'l-Auliya*, p. 147; *Jawami'-u'l-Kalim*, p. 234.
[2] Ibid. p. 160. It appears from *Siyar-u'l-Auliya* (p. 318) that another disciple, Khwaja Shams-u'd-din Vihari, had also asked permission to construct a house for the visitors, but the Shaikh did not grant it. Reference is also found to a building constructed by Khwaja Jahan Ahmad Ayaz, but its nature is not clear. *Siyar-u'l-Auliya*, p. 137.
[3] Bayazid Bayat, *Tazkirah-i-Humayum-wa-Akbar*, p. 234.
[4] Referred to as *Suffah Sutun*.
[5] *Siyar-u'l-Auliya*, p. 362.

Later, the Shaikh lived in a small wooden-walled room on the roof of the hall.[6] During the day he took his rest in one of the small rooms in the main building. A low wall ran round the roof, but on the side of the courtyard the wall was raised higher to provide shade for the Shaikh and his visitors when they sat talking in the morning hours. Sometimes he had to appeal to them to sit closer so that all might find place in the shade provided by the branches of the banyan tree.[7] The Shaikh was the hub round which *khanqah* life revolved. Everything derived its hue and colour, its spirit and direction, from him. Even the minutest detail of its operation and administration had his direct or tacit approval. Though he himself followed a meticulously regulated programme, which kept him busy throughout the day, he did not neglect any detail of the *khanqah*'s functioning. Indeed, from the roof he could overlook what was going on in the *Jama' at Khanah* below. His word was law and deviation from it inconceivable. He dealt severely with any breach of the rule or the spirit of his *khanqah* organization.[8]

It appears that, though the Shaikh was available to visitors at all times, he had set aside certain hours for special categories of disciples. We find him asking Hasan Sijzi the reason for his coming at an inopportune hour.[9] In the *Jama'Masjid* of Kilugarhi, where he was thronged by large numbers of people, he told the regular visitors to the *khanqah* not to assemble there and add to the crowd.[10] His advice to visitors was to sit wherever they found an empty space and not bother about precedence.[11] He followed the tradition of Shaikh Farid in receiving new and regular visitors with equal warmth.[12] According to Jamal Qiwam-u'd-din, a beggar and a king had an equal status in the eyes of the Shaikh.[13] His clear instructions to his disciples, particularly those resident in the *khanqah* who managed its affairs, were to be

---

[6] Ibid. p. 281.

[7] *Fawa'id-u'l-Fu'ad*, p. 91.

[8] See e.g. how he dealt with Maulana Burhan-u'd-din Gharib when he came to know that he sat in the kitchen reclining on a folded blanket. *Siyar-u'l-Auliya*, pp. 279–81.

[9] *Fawa'id-u'l-Fu'ad*, pp. 6, 11.

[10] Ibid. p. 158.

[11] Ibid. p. 36.

[12] Ibid. p. 74.

[13] *Qiwam-u'l-'Aqa'id*, MS p. 165.

soft-spoken and treat people with affection.[14] During the *ayyam-i-Tashriq* (three days following the *'Eid-i-Azha*), the number of visitors swelled immensely. Food was served to parties of visitors continually for hours together. On one such occasion, the Shaikh commented in a lighthearted way: 'A dervish was asked what verse of the Qur'an he liked most? He replied: 'Eat always' (13: 35).'[15]

Shaikh Nizam-u'd-din Auliya cited Shaikh Farid's remark that whoever came to see him brought something for him, but if some poor fellow did not bring anything, it was his duty to give something to him.[16] Shaikh Nizam-u'd-din followed the same practice.

While sitting with the people, the Shaikh did not ignore even trivial rules of decorum. If he saw people sitting in the sun, he cried out: 'They are sitting in the sun, but I am burning from heat.'[17] Once he was sitting on a cot as he had pain in his legs. He apologized to his audience for this.[18] Once Shaikh Rukn-u'd-din Abu'l-Fath visited the *khanqah*. He came in a *dolah*. As he had some pain in his leg, he had difficulty in getting down. He asked people to help him but Shaikh Nizam-u'd-din insisted on his sitting in the *dolah* and himself sat down on the ground in the community hall (*Suffah Sutun*) and talked to the eminent visitor.[19]

OPEN FOR ALL

The *khanqah* of Shaikh Nizam-u'd-din Auliya was open for all types of visitors—the rich and the poor, the learned and the illiterate, the villagers and the townsfolk. Sometimes it became so overcrowded that the Shaikh asked his disciples to shorten their stay there. We find the Shaikh apologizing to Shaikh Nasir-u'd-din Chiragh, who had come all the way from Awadh in winter to see the Shaikh, about his inability to accommodate him in the *Jama'at Khanah*.[20] A few people did not

---

[14] *Fawa'id-u'l-Fu'ad*, p. 146.
[15] Ibid. p. 175.
[16] Ibid. p. 200.
[17] Ibid. p. 91.
[18] Ibid. p. 251.
[19] *Siyar-u'l-Auliya*, pp. 137–8.
[20] *Khair-u'l-Majalis*, p. 259.

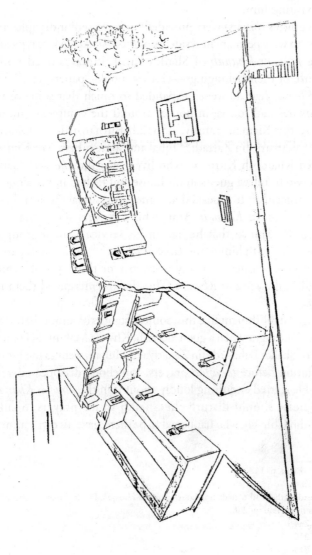

Conjectural reconstruction of Shaikh Nizam-ud-din Auliya's *khanqah* on the basis of its archaeological remains. (In July 1980 I undertook an archaeological survey of the area—near Humayun's tomb—with the agreement of B. K. Thapar, Director-General of the Archaeological Survey of India.)

appreciate the difficulties of the Shaikh in providing overnight accommodation to the visitors. A physician, son of Muslah Baqqal, who was not permitted to stay the night, became unhappy with the Shaikh and stopped visiting him.[21]

Small cubicles (*hujras*) were provided for some senior disciples and teachers who were permanent residents of the *khanqah*. More typically, as in the *Jama'at Khanah* of Shaikh Farid, inmates lived under pillars with all their belongings—clothes, books, papers, etc.[22] The *Jama'at Khanah* had, however, expanded so much that some of the senior inmates had to live in houses around the complex—among these were the Kirmani family,[23] Shaikh Burhan-u'd-din Gharib, Maulana Fakhr-u'd-din Zarradi,[24] Iqbal and some others. Mir Khurd's uncle Syed Khamosh Kirmani, who lived near the *khanqah*, could entertain two hundred guests in his house and he had in his service a party of musicians.[25] It appears that some professional musicians also lived in the *Jama'at Khanah*. Amir Khurd reports about Maulana Nizam-u'd-din Shirazi that he had in his service a small group of musicians living with him in the *Jama'at Khanah*.[26] Sometimes parties of wandering dervishes, as many as twenty or thirty people, came and stayed in the *Jama'at Khanah*. The Shaikh entertained them for three days.[27]

In a huge establishment like this, some instances of minor theft were inevitable. One night when a guest-dervish, Khwaja Mahmud Gazruni, a disciple of Shaikh Baha-u'd-din Zakariya of Multan, went to the Jumna to do ablution before *tahajjud* prayers, somebody disappeared with his robe. He started enquiring loudly about it in the *Jama'at Khanah*. Lest the noise should disturb the Shaikh in his prayers, Shaikh Nasir-u'd-din Chiragh, who happened to be there, gave his own garment

---

[21] *Siyar-u'l-Auliya*, p. 148.

[22] Ibid. p. 288.

[23] Mir Khurd's father had rented a big house near the *khanqah*. He used to give instruction to his pupils there. Ibid. p. 268.

[24] Ibid. p. 264.

[25] Ibid. p. 219.

[26] Ibid. p. 315.

[27] *Khair-u'l-Majalis*, p. 185.

to him. In the morning when the Shaikh came to know about this, he was pleased with Shaikh Nasir-u'd-din and bestowed upon him his personal garment.[28] Similarly, when somebody took away the shoes of Maulana Wajih-u'd-din Pa'ili, the Shaikh gave his own shoes to Wajih-u'd-din. He placed them on his head and went home barefoot, declaring, 'This is my crown.'[29]

Some provision of blankets was made for casual visitors. The Shaikh had a big Kashmiri blanket[30] which could be used by several persons.

The *Jama'at Khanah* was, in fact, the centre of a building complex that had grown up around the dwelling of the Shaikh. The whole area had a quiet spiritual atmosphere where visitors came in search of contentment and benediction.

TRAINING OF DISCIPLES

Instruction and training in spiritual discipline of large numbers of people cannot have been an easy affair. The Shaikh had resolved it in a simple but effective way—the senior disciples were to instruct the juniors.[31] When one group completed their initial training, they were assigned the duty of training new entrants. Thus the programme of instruction was carried on continually and covered all levels of disciples. The Shaikh himself concentrated on the most senior disciples. Every such disciple became, in the course of time, the centre of a small group of new entrants to the *khanqah*. This training inspired all disciples with a uniform mystic ideology and qualified them to carry on the work of the *silsilah* in their respective areas of residence. Their stay in the *Jama'at Khanah* had a profound impact on their thought and personality. They learnt there how to lead a communal life, to share the problems of others, and to develop an integrated personality imbued with the highest ideals of religion and mysticism.

---

[28] *Siyar-u'l-Auliya*, p. 236.
[29] Ibid. p. 297.
[30] *Sarur-u's-Sudur*, MS personal copy, p. 82.
[31] Barani, *Tarikh-i-Firuz Shahi*, p. 344.

INSTRUCTION THROUGH ANECDOTES

The Shaikh did not believe in giving direct advice to the visitors[32] who brought their problems to him, or to whom he wanted to explain some principle. His practice was kr.own to everybody, including the Sultan, 'Ala-u'd-din Khalji.[33] The Shaikh believed that example was more persuasive than precept. A mystic was expected to be a living embodiment of the virtues that he propounded.[34] The didactic import of the anecdotes recorded in the conversations of Shaikh Nizam-u'd-din Auliya is considerable. Every story that he narrated had a moral for the audience. *Fawa'id-u'l-Fu'ad* is filled with stories and anecdotes, behind each of which there is an individual problem that the Shaikh dealt with. Only a couple of instances can be given here to illustrate the point.

To bring home to his audience the value of living a life free of expectation from others, the Shaikh related an anecdote about Shaikh 'Ali. He was stitching his garment with his legs stretched out in front of him. An unexpected visit from the Khalifah was announced, the Wazir coming ahead and asking Shaikh 'Ali to fold his legs as a mark of respect. Shaikh 'Ali ignored him, and when the Khalifah arrived, he took hold of the hand of the Wazir and remarked to him: 'Look! I do not stretch out my hands to ask for favours and therefore I can stretch out my legs.'[35]

Admonishing his disciples against prayers offered with a distracted mind, the Shaikh related the following story: 'Shaikh Hasan Afghan was a disciple of Shaikh Baha-u'd-din Zakariya. He heard the call to prayer in the bazaar and stopped there to offer prayers. On finishing his prayers he came to the leader of the congregational prayer [*imam*] and said to him in a low voice: "When you began your prayer, I was with you. You went to Delhi from here. There you bought some slaves. Then you returned to Multan. Then you went to Khurasan with

---

[32] *Siyar-u'l-Auliya*, p. 349.

[33] Barani, *Tarikh-i-Firuz Shahi*, p. 331.

[34] He used to say that the *'Ulama* invited people to rectitude through their speech, the *masha'ikh* through their example. *Siyar-u'l-Auliya*, p. 321.

[35] *Fawa'id-u'l-Fu'ad*, p. 8.

those slaves. I too have been wandering like this from place to place. Where in the end have you left me?"[36]

ACADEMIC STATURE OF SENIOR DISCIPLES

The senior group of Shaikh Nizam-u'd-din Auliya's disciples connected with the *Jama'at Khanah* were learned scholars specialized in one or other branch of the Islamic sciences and of established academic reputation. Maulana Shams-u'd-din Yahya was known for his knowledge of *usul* (juristic principles), *fiqh* (law), and syntax.[37] He had written a commentary on *Mashariq-u'l-Anwar*,[38] and used to give lectures on *Kashshaf.*[39] Maulana Fakhr-u'd-din Zarradi, also learned in Islamic law, used to deliver lectures on *Hidaya*,[40] and had written some books on *sama'* from the legal point of view.[41] He was also an expert in adult education and had written a book called *Usmani* for the instruction of Akhi Siraj.[42] Qazi Muhi-u'd-din Kashani had extensive knowledge of Hadith.[43] Maulana 'Ala-u'd-din Nili was a powerful speaker with profound knowledge of *Kashshaf* and other exegetical literature.[44] Ibn Battuta witnessed a man so overcome by emotion during a lecture of 'Ala-u'd-din Nili that he died.[45] Maulana Wajih-u'd-din Pa'ili's insight in *fiqh* was unrivalled.[46] Khwaja Karim-u'd-din had extensive knowledge of mystic writing and a comprehensive collection of books written on the subject.[47] Students in the city gathered round Shaikh Nasir-u'd-din Chiragh to receive instruction from him in external

---

[36] Ibid. p. 10.
[37] *Siyar-u'l-Auliya*, p. 226.
[38] *Jawami'-u'l-Kalim*, p. 30; *Akhbar-u'l-Akhyar*, p. 96.
[39] *Siyar-u'l-Auliya*, p. 318.
[40] Ibid. p. 268.
[41] Ibid. p. 268–70.
[42] Ibid. p. 289.
[43] See below.
[44] *Siyar-u'l-Auliya*, p. 275.
[45] *Rihla* II, pp. 9–20.
[46] *Siyar-u'l-Auliya*, p. 296.
[47] *Qiwam-u'l-'Aqa'id*, MS pp. 173–4.

sciences.[48] There were others who were equally eminent in their special areas of study. Their presence added intellectual lustre to the *khanqah*.

DRESS

No special dress was prescribed for the residents of the *khanqah*. The Shaikh did cite the tradition of the Prophet, which indicates the preferability of wearing white.[49] However, the inmates of the *khanqah* were seen in different forms of dress. Maulana Wajih-u'd-din Pa'ili used to wear coarse garments of greyish-white colour.[50] Qazi Sharaf-u'd-din wrapped himself in two halves of a sheet—one half on the upper and the other on the lower part of his body.[51]

FUTUH

Strict rules about the acceptance of *futuh* (unsolicited gifts) were laid down by the Shaikh: (*a*) No guaranteed payment could be accepted.[52] Once a man named Kafur brought two *tanka*s to the Shaikh in his early life and said, 'I have orders to give something in charity every Friday for the sake of the soul of Sultan Ghiyas-u'd-din Balban. If you permit, I will send something to you every Friday.' The Shaikh agreed and the money came to him as promised. One day when in a *sama'* gathering he raised his hands in ecstasy, he felt an inner admonition that one who accepted guaranteed payment had no right to raise his hands in this way.[53] He decided to refuse the gift and never again accepted any guaranteed payment. (*b*) If the gift was conditional, with strings attached to it, its acceptance was forbidden. (*c*) No immovable property—lands, villages, buildings—could be accepted as *futuh*. (*d*) Everything received as *futuh* was to be distributed and nothing was to be retained for the morrow. (*e*) It appears that in the matter of *futuh* the Shaikh

---

[48] *Siyar-u'l-Auliya*, p. 279.
[49] Ibid. p. 298.
[50] Ibid.
[51] Ibid. p. 309.
[52] *Qiwam-u'l-'Aqa'id*, MS pp. 239–40.
[53] *Siyar-u'l-Auliya*, p. 506. Amir Khurd quotes a verse of Sa'di meaning: 'Raising the hands in ecstatic dance is permitted to you only if you have drawn away your skirts from both the worlds.'

used to advise his disciples according to their needs and capacities. According to Jamal Qiwam-u'd-din, he instructed some to use only one-tenth of what came to them and distribute the rest; to others the instruction was to use only one-fifth; others could use one-fourth or one-third of what came to them. It is said that Shaikh Burhan-u'd-din Gharib and Maulana Fakhr-u'd-din Zarradi distributed everything received by them as *futuh*. They retained no part of the *futuh* for themselves.[54]

The Shaikh told his disciples that one should follow the advice that the Prophet gave to Caliph 'Umar: 'Whatever comes to you unsolicited, eat it and distribute it.'[55] He quoted Caliph 'Ali to show that the Prophet never kept any presents with him even for one night.[56]

It was within these limits that gifts were accepted in the *khanqah* of Shaikh Nizam-u'd-din Auliya. The quantity of *futuh* that came to the *khanqah* was staggering. Shaikh Nasir-u'd-din Chiragh is reported to have observed that gifts flowed into the *khanqah* like a tributary of the Jumna that flowed in front of the *khanqah*.[57] Money, food, cloth, and a large number of miscellaneous articles poured in continually. The Shaikh was deeply appreciative of the gifts from people themselves in need and gave them rich rewards in return. He quoted with approval Shaikh Shihab-u'd-din Suhrawardi's appreciation of an old woman's gift of a *dirham*.[58] With such quantities of *futuh* coming to the *khanqah*, the Shaikh felt overburdened with responsibility. He considered himself merely a disbursing agency and was always anxious to clear away the stock. According to Mir Khurd the Shaikh felt at ease only when all *futuh* had been distributed among the needy and the poor.[59]

SERVING OF FOOD

Food was served to all visitors without discrimination. The Shaikh's urbanity and humanity did not allow the distribution of food to turn

---

[54] *Qiwam-u'l-'Aqa'id*, MS pp. 230–1.

[55] *Fawa'id-u'l-Fu'ad*, p. 125.

[56] Ibid. pp. 200–1.

[57] *Khair-u'l-Majalis*, p. 257.

[58] *Fawa'id-u'l-Fu'ad*, p. 180.

[59] *Siyar-u'l-Auliya*, p. 131.

into an act of ostentatious charity. His *khanqah* rules and discipline ensured the dignity of those who took food there. It was difficult to discover who did so out of need and who as a token of blessing. No visitor could be asked if he was fasting or not,[60] or, in other words, whether or not he needed food. The Shaikh was so considerate of visitors that he used to advise his disciples that eating twice was justified if it was done for the sake of guests.[61] 'First greet, then eat, then talk', was the rule of the *khanqah*.[62]

Since the Shaikh himself fasted, he could join others only at dinner. People were expected to wash their hands before they came to the table-spread. Those who served food had to wash their hands before others.[63] The Shaikh cited a Tradition of the Prophet advising hosts personally to assist guests in washing their hands.[64] The prayer of food (from *Surah* Ma'ida, Qur'an 5: 5) was recited before eating. The Shaikh used to say that complete silence at the time of eating was the habit of the Jews.[65] He, therefore, carried on light talk while taking food. On one occasion he said that if one began and ended his meal with salt, it protected one from leprosy. 'But,' he continued, 'salt should not be taken after dipping the finger in water.' Hasan Sijzi, with his quick wit, remarked: 'God be blessed that the right of salt (*haqq-i-namak*) has been refreshed.' Qazi Muhi-u'd-din Kashani said, 'You have uttered a 'salty' [spicy] sentence.' At this the Shaikh remarked: 'Yes, because he himself possesses salt [i.e. he is charming].'[66] The Shaikh enjoyed such light talk at the table. Once he said that when a ewer or a basin is brought for washing hands, the Arabs call it *Abu'l-Yas* (Lord of Despair) as it amounts to announcing the end of the feast. In India, he said, *Abu'l-Yas* is betel leaf which is served at the end of the meal.[67] Once

---

[60] *Fawa'id-u'l-Fu'ad*, pp. 12, 77; *Qiwam-u'l-'Aqa'id*, MS p. 177. The Shaikh quoted Shaikh Badr-u'd-din Ghaznavi who offered water to visitors if he had nothing else to offer. *Fawa'id-u'l-Fu'ad*, pp. 136–7.

[61] Ibid. p. 29.

[62] Ibid. p. 77.

[63] Ibid. p. 117.

[64] *Siyar-u'l-Auliya*, p. 413.

[65] *Siyar-u'l-Auliya*, p. 415.

[66] Ibid. p. 414.

[67] Ibid. p. 413.

while taking food in the *khanqah*, Shaikh Rukn-u'd-din Abu'l-Fath of Multan desired the vinegar cup to be brought nearer. 'It is good,' said Shaikh Nizam-u'd-din. 'Because it is sour,' added Shaikh Rukn-u'd-din. 'That is why it is liked,' remarked the Shaikh.[68]

Siyar-u'l-Auliya has three chapters which explain the principles and practices of the Shaikh pertaining to the entertainment of guests, table manners, and discouragement of gluttony.[69] The disciples were instructed to remember God while taking food. Maulana Fakhr-u'd-din Zarradi said 'In the name of God, Most Gracious, Most Merciful', with every morsel that he took.[70]

The table manners of the Shaikh's *khanqah* were carried by his disciples to different regions. We find Maulana Burhan-u'd-din Gharib exhorting his disciples in the Deccan to follow the rules laid down by the Shaikh.[71] Usually bread and gravy were served to all visitors and inmates. However, when 'Ala-u'd-din Khalji's spies came to find out what was served, the Shaikh instructed Mubashshir to add *tahiri* (a delicious dish of rice) to it.[72] Later on he ordered the supply of round cake, pudding, and savoury pastry (*qurs*, *halwa*, and *samosa*) at the time of the *sahri*.[73] Those who fasted continuously got their *sahri* from the Shaikh's *sahri* during the month of Ramadan. It consisted of *khichri* with purified butter.[74] It appears that sometimes vinegar was also served in small earthen pots.[75]

KITCHEN MANAGEMENT

Maulana Burhan-u'd-din Gharib looked after the preparation and distribution of food in the kitchen.[76] Iqbal managed the entire establishment. Mubashshir was present at the *ma'ida* (*sar-i-ma'ida buday*).[77]

---

[68] Ibid. p. 139.

[69] Ibid. pp. 407–20.

[70] Ibid. p. 414.

[71] See *Ahsan-u'l-Aqwal*, MS pp. 30–41.

[72] *Qiwam-u'l-'Aqa'id*, MS p. 178. When the Shaikh asked Iqbal to bring the left-over food of lunch for Maulana 'Ala-u'd-din, he brought *khichri* (rice boiled with lentil), *roghan* (purified butter) and *ahri* (perhaps *tahiri*). *Siyar-u'l-Auliya*, p. 277.

[73] *Qiwam-u'l-'Aqa'id*, MS p. 179.

[74] *Khair-u'l-Majalis*, pp. 186–7.

[75] *Siyar-u'l-Auliya*, p. 139.

[76] Ibid. pp. 279 *et seq.*

[77] *Qiwam-u'l-'Aqa'id*, MS p. 178.

We find the Shaikh instructing Mubashshir about the menu.[78] There must have been many persons serving in the kitchen. One name mentioned in that connection is that of Khwaja Abbu.[79]

The inmates considered it an honour to render any services in the kitchen. Shaikh Kamal-u'd-din, (later sent to Malwa by the Shaikh), used to clean the cooking utensils in the *khanqah*.[80] One day Amir Khusrau started licking the plates after food had been served. The Shaikh asked him what he was doing. He said that he wanted to be known as *kasa lais* (licker of the plates) of the Khwaja.[81]

STORES AND ESTABLISHMENT

A *khanqah* providing food and shelter on such a large scale had to have a large and efficient establishment to ensure its smooth and regular functioning. Articles of food were kept in the stores of the *Jama'at Khanah*. However, to maintain an atmosphere of *tawakkul* (trust in God) and resignation to His Will, the stores were swept and cleaned every Friday, before the Shaikh went to his Kilugarhi house to prepare for the Friday prayers.[82]

Apart from food articles, cloth, caps, *dastar*s, etc. were also kept in the stores of the *khanqah*. There is record of the Shaikh sending to his disciples in distant areas special robes, prayer-carpets, and a large number of caps (*kulah*).[83]

The stores were under the custody of Iqbal, who was a sort of major-domo for the *khanqah*. He kept and managed the *futuh*, made purchases,[84] controlled the stores, and supervised the kitchen. He enjoyed the confidence and trust of the Shaikh, who affectionately called him *Lalla* in his Purbi dialect. However, he sometimes did things which displeased the Shaikh. One such case has been reported by Syed Muhammad Gisu Daraz of Gulbarga. A Khurasani owed 700 *tankas*

---

[78] Ibid.
[79] *Jawami'-u'l-Kalim*, p. 123.
[80] *Siyar-u'l-Auliya*, p. 198.
[81] Ibid. p. 415.
[82] Ibid. p. 131.
[83] *Qiwam-u'l-'Aqa'id*, MS p. 102.
[84] *Durar-i-Nizami*, MS.

to the *khanqah* but was reluctant to pay. Iqbal chained him and locked him up in a room. People were so afraid of Iqbal that they dared not report the matter to the Shaikh. When Iqbal went home for his midday rest, the Khurasani made loud noises and struggled to come out of the room. The gate-keeper prevented him from getting out but the din of chains somehow reached the ears of the Shaikh, who anxiously enquired: 'Who is at the door?' The Khurasani showed his face. The Shaikh trembled at the sight and asked him: 'Who has put these chains on your legs?' 'Khwaja Iqbal,' he said, 'because I owe 700 *tanka*s to the *khanqah*.' The Shaikh immediately sent for Iqbal. 'Come Lalla! What are these things that you do? The money belongs to God; something out of it you eat; something this poor man has taken. What right have you to put this poor fellow in confinement?' He called a blacksmith, had the chains removed, and set him free.[85]

Surprisingly enough, another story about Iqbal mentioned by Syed Muhammad Gisu Daraz before his audience also does not give a good account of him. He said:

One day a man brought one hundred gold *tanka*s for the Shaikh. It was prayer time. The Shaikh [said to Iqbal]: 'Lalla! Keep it. We will distribute it tomorrow. The time is inappropriate now.' The Shaikh forgot it. . . . in his last years the Shaikh's memory had become weak. Iqbal thought that he had forgotten it completely. He took it to his house . . . [Then one day] the Shaikh abruptly remembered it [and asked Iqbal to bring it]. Iqbal ran here and there, searching for it in this corner and that. The Shaikh realized that Iqbal himself must have taken it. 'Lalla! We wanted to distribute it among several persons at *chasht* time. God has, however, given it to one man. Why run here and there looking for it?[86]

FAITH IN THE BREAD OF THE *KHANQAH*

People had great faith in the talismanic effect of the bread prepared in the kitchen of the *Jama'at Khanah*. Whenever anybody asked for

[85] *Jawami'u'l-Kalim*, p. 59.
[86] *Jawami'-u'l-Kalim*, p. 59.

any token of blessing, the Shaikh gave some pieces of bread to him. He gave a piece of bread to Hasan Gangu, and predicted that he would enjoy royal power.[87] When the Malika Jahan, wife of 'Ala-u'd-din Khalji, sent her sons, Khizr Khan and Shadi Khan, to the Shaikh and requested some token of blessing, the Shaikh sent two pieces of bread for her.[88] Qazi Muhi-u'd-din Kashani was once thrown into prison by 'Ala-u'd-din Khalji. He sent a message to the Shaikh requesting him to pray for his release. The Shaikh sent three loaves of bread to him with instruction to eat one every day. On the third day he was released from the prison.[89] Maulana Burhan-u'd-din Gharib used to keep left-over pieces of bread served on 'urs days and gave them to ailing people.[90] Once the Shaikh gave to Shaikh Nasir-u'din Chiragh a loaf of bread that was twenty or more days old.[91]

Besides bread, the Shaikh sometimes gave people some betel leaves chewed by him[92] or water from the vessel that he had drunk from.[93]

DISCUSSIONS BUT NO DEBATES

The Shaikh never allowed debates in the *Jama'at Khanah*. It was against Chishti principles of spiritual training. He rejected Maulana Jalal-u'd-din Awadhi's request to hold periodic debates[94] among the scholars of the *khanqah*. The Shaikh, however, did not discourage good-tempered academic discussions in the *khanqah*, which (as noted above) had within its confines many erudite scholars well able to task eminent scholars to the limit through learned explication of the subject in hand. Maulana Jamal-u'd-din Awadhi defeated a distinguished scholar of Khurasan, known as Maulana Bahas, in a discussion.[95] This foreign scholar had established his forensic eloquence in debates held in Delhi and people had been most impressed by his scholarship. Iqbal reported his defeat

---

[87] *Burhan-u'l-Ma'asir*, p. 12.
[88] *Qiwam-u'l-'Aqa'id*, MS p. 164.
[89] *Siyar-u'l-Auliya*, p. 143.
[90] *Ahsan-u'l-Aqwal*, MS p. 75.
[91] *Khair-u'l-Majalis*, p. 187.
[92] *Siyar-u'l-Auliya*, p. 142.
[93] Ibid. p. 144.
[94] Ibid. p. 305–6.
[95] Ibid. p. 319.

at the hands of Maulana Jamal-u'd-din to the Shaikh. 'Lalla!' the Shaikh
said, 'Bring him and his friends here.' When they arrived the Shaikh
said: 'Blessed be your coming. You did not barter away your learning.'[96]

It appears that discourse on different themes was listened to approvingly by the Shaikh. We find Maulana Fakhr-u'd-din Zarradi
discussing principles of *Tibb* (Unani medicine) before the Shaikh,[97]
and Qazi Muhi-u'd-din Kashani taking part in elucidation of the
Traditions of the Prophet.[98]

VISIT OF SUFI DIGNITARIES

Though many persons associated with other *silsilah*s visited the *khanqah*
and sometimes even joined the discipleship of the Shaikh,[99] the most
outstanding *sajjadah-nashin* saint of India who visited the *khanqah* of
Shaikh Nizam-u'd-din Auliya was Shaikh Rukn-u'd-din Abu'l-Fath
of Multan. He was grandson of the famous Suhrawardi saint Shaikh
Baha-u'd-din Zakariya and was held in high esteem both in Multan
and in Delhi. The Sultans of Delhi had deep respect for him and when
he proceeded to the royal palace in his *dolah*, people filled it with their
petitions to be forwarded and recommended to the Sultan.[100] Relations
between the Chishti saints of Delhi and the Suhrawardi saints of Multan
were extremely cordial. Shaikh Rukn-u'd-din had refused to oblige
Sultan Mubarak Khalji by setting up a rival *khanqah* in Delhi. Shaikh
Rukn-u'd-din's meetings with Shaikh Nizam-u'd-din were always
pleasant. They met at Hauz-i-'Alai, in the Kilugarhi mosque, and in
the *khanqah*. The two saints exchanged pleasantries and gifts, and talked
about different matters.

Once Shaikh Nizam-u'd-din Auliya directed Iqbal to present to Shaikh
Rukn-u'd-din a purse of gold coins, some pieces of cloth, and a beautiful
comb. He declined to accept the present. The Shaikh then gave these
things to Ruknuddin's brother Maulana 'Imad-u'd-din Isma'il.[101]

---

[96] Ibid.
[97] Ibid. p. 358.
[98] See *Durar-i-Nizami*, MS.
[99] See Chapter III of *Qiwam-u'l-'Aqa'id*, MS pp. 54 *et seq.*
[100] *Siyar-u'l-Auliya*, p. 139.
[101] Ibid. p. 139.

According to the author of *Qiwam-u'l-'Aqa'id* the present included some musk pods also. The Suhrawardi saint declined saying: 'Accepting these is beyond my limit [power].'[102] It is reported that Shaikh Rukn-u'd-din Multani used to send presents to the Shaikh through travellers setting out from Multan.[103]

There were subtle but significant ways of expressing respect for a distinguished visitor. Maulana 'Imad-u'd-din, brother of the saint, put a question: 'What was the intention of the Prophet in migrating to Madina from Makka?' Shaikh Rukn-u'd-din wanted Shaikh Nizam-u'd-din to speak on it, but the Shaikh requested him to express his views. The perfection and honours of apostlehood, Shaikh Rukn-u'd-din said, which had been reserved for the Prophet from the Day of the Creation, could reach their perfection after the Prophet's migration to Madina. Then Shaikh Nizam-u'd-din spoke and expressed the view that the migration of the Prophet was intended for the perfection of the people of Madina, who had not benefited as long from his presence.[104] Each showed his respect to the other in an oblique but courteous way.

Another very significant incident shows how deep the Shaikh's respect was for Shaikh Rukn-u'd-din Multani. One day a visitor asked Shaikh Nizam-u'd-din Auliya the reason for bestowing gifts on everyone who came to see him. The Shaikh referred to a Tradition of the Prophet in which it is said that if one did not present anything to one's visitor, it was as if the latter had visited a dead person. On hearing this, the visitor immediately commented on Shaikh Rukn-u'd-in Multani, who did not give anything to his visitors. The Shaikh said that while his own gifts were physical, Shaikh Rukn-u'd-din bestowed spiritual gifts on every visitor. On another occasion he told a visitor that Shaikh Rukn-u'd-din managed both the material world and the (world of) religion (*din-o-dunya*).[105]

It is reported by Jamal Qiwam-u'd-din that when Shaikh Rukn-u'd-din came from the court and turned to the *khanqah* of Shaikh Nizam-u'd-din, he renewed his ablution. 'I cannot meet the Shaikh

[102] *Qiwam-u'l-'Aqa'id*, MS p. 77.
[103] Ibid. MS p. 81.
[104] *Siyar-u'l-Auliya*, p. 138.
[105] *Qiwam-u'l-'Aqa'id*, MS p. 131; *al-Durar al-Manzum*, pp. 28–32.

with the same ablution with which I have seen the Sultan,' he is reported to have remarked.[106]

PRINCES AND NOBLES AS VISITORS

Large numbers of nobles, *maliks*, princes, and government officers came to the *khanqah* to pay their respects to the Shaikh. We find Khizr Khan, Shadi Khan, and Juna Khan in the *Jama'at Khanah* of the Shaikh. Whenever the commotion or fanfare of their arrival reached the ears of the Shaikh, he was distressed and sighed: 'Ah! Where do they come from to waste the time of the dervish.'[107]

VISITORS AND THEIR PROBLEMS

The visitors to the *khanqah* of Shaikh Nizam-u'd-din Auliya came with different motives—some spiritual, some material. The expectations of these two categories of visitors were different. The Shaikh's intuitive mind penetrated to the anxiety and anguish of every heart and he offered appropriate healing and comfort. Where immediate solution of a problem was not possible, he gave to his visitor that inner strength, courage of conviction, and trust in God which mitigated his worries and reduced the stress they provoked.

The Shaikh possessed *nafs-i-gira* (intuitive intelligence) of a very high order. He could read a man's motives on his face. We give in the following a few examples from the records of personal contact with the Shaikh:

1. An externalist scholar (*danishmand*) from Nagaur requested the Shaikh to enrol him as his disciple. The Shaikh did not accede to his request but asked him to say honestly what his real intention was in joining his discipline. The man was not prepared to disclose his mind, but when the Shaikh pressed, he confessed that he had been granted some land in Nagaur which the *muqta'i* of that place did not allow him to occupy. The Shaikh asked: 'If I write

[106] Ibid. MS p. 77.
[107] *Siyar-u'l-Auliya*, p. 131.

a recommendatory letter and give it to you, will you give up the idea of joining my discipline?' The visitor agreed. The Shaikh gave him the letter and he left.[108]

2. A *danishmand* from Meerut complained, 'I have a daughter but do not possess means to arrange her marriage.' The Shaikh gave him a *tanka* as a token of blessing. Then, somehow, the man's need was brought to the notice of the ladies of 'Ala-u'd-din Khalji's *harem*, whereupon the need was met.[109]

3. Whenever Khwaja Mubarak Gopamawi came to Delhi and visited the court of 'Ala-u'd-din Khalji he would get a *khil'at* (robe of honour). But one time the Sultan gave him a white sheet and not the usual *khil'at*. He was depressed on that account. When the Shaikh came to know about this, he recited a couplet meaning:

> A gift from the king is valuable
> Whether it be a gold coin or a shell (*pishez*)

It had an extremely soothing affect on Mubarak and he felt relieved of great pressure on his heart.[110]

4. Amir Khusrau requested the Shaikh to pray to God to grant charm to his lyrics and melodies. The Shaikh asked him to get a plate of sugar and put it under his cot. He then directed him to circulate it over his head and eat something from it.[111]

5. Qazi Muhi-u'd-din Kashani's relations with his wife had become so unpleasant that he wanted to divorce her. He sought the advice of the Shaikh, who did not approve the divorce. The Qazi's relations with his wife become pleasant again.[112]

6. Maulana Wajih-u'd-din Pa'ili had been diagnosed with tuberculosis. On a winter evening he reached the *khanqah*. The Shaikh had just broken his fast. A man brought fresh *mundi* (*sphaeranthus indicus*) to the Shaikh. He asked Pa'ili to eat it with him.

---

[108] Ibid. p. 148.
[109] *Qiwam-u'l-'Aqa'id*, MS pp. 133–4.
[110] *Siyar-u'l-Auliya*, p. 148.
[111] Ibid. pp. 301–2.
[112] *Qiwam-u'l-'Aqa'id*, MS p. 118.

He hesitated at first as *mundi* is heat-producing and could have been detrimental to his condition, but he took it and felt better.[113]

7. Muhammad Haji had just returned from Hajj. Instead of enjoying inner peace and tranquillity, he was distracted and disturbed at heart. He sought the Shaikh's blessings through Qazi Muhi-u'd-din Kashani. The Shaikh prescribed a few verses from *Surat al-Fath* (48: 4) meaning—

> It is He Who sent down tranquillity into the hearts of the believers, that they may add faith to their faith: for to God belong the forces of the heavens and the earth; and God is full of Knowledge and Wisdom

—and directed him to recite them seven times a day with his right hand over his chest.[114]

8. Qazi Muhi-u'd-din Kashani's son 'Abdullah was seriously ill. He reported his condition to the Shaikh, who listened to it attentively. Then he narrated the story of a man whose only son died of some serious illness, and who bore this bereavement with patience and was blessed by God on that account.[115]

9. A disciple apologized on behalf of someone who had delayed in accepting a recommendation of the Shaikh. 'I should take it ill,' remarked the Shaikh, 'still I don't and forgive him.'[116]

10. A grandson of Shaikh Najib-u'd-din was a man of unsound character. He came and placed ink-pot, pen, and paper before the Shaikh and asked him to write a letter of recommendation to a particular *malik* so that he could get something from him. 'How can I write to him?' the Shaikh apologized, 'He does not come to me. But tell me what you expect from him and I will give it to you.' 'Give me what you like but write the letter also,'

---

[113] *Siyar-u'l-Auliya*, p. 143.
[114] Ibid. p. 426.
[115] *Qiwam-u'l-'Aqa'id*, MS pp. 116–17.
[116] *Fawa'id-u'l-Fu'ad*, p. 146.

said the visitor. 'No', replied the Shaikh, 'it is not the custom of dervishes to write letters, particularly when I have never met him and he has never come to me.' The man started abusing the Shaikh: 'Nizam-u'd-din! You [are] the disciple of my grandfather and his slave (*banda*). I am the descendant of your Khwaja. I say write this letter and you do not.' So saying he raised the ink-pot, threw it on the ground, and rose to depart. The Shaikh stretched his hand, caught hold of his robe and said: 'You are going away displeased. Cast aside your anger and then you can go.'[117]

SAMA'

The Shaikh was extremely fond of music (*sama'*) as a form of spiritual nourishment. The *khanqah* often resounded to the mystic songs recited by the disciples as well as the professional musicians. But the Shaikh had strict rules regarding the participation of like-minded people, a ban on musical instruments, and the timings of audition parties. He did not agree with the view of the *'Ulama* that music as such was forbidden and tried to argue his position in the light of the Traditions of the Prophet. The *'Ulama*, however, insisted on his producing a verdict of Imam Abu Hanifa in favour of his practice. It appears that during the time of Ghiyas-u'd-din Tughluq some restrictions were placed on *sama'* meetings at public places. However, the Shaikh continued with his audition parties in the *Jama'at Khanah*, preferably in his room on the upper storey. When the Shaikh heard mystic songs he went into ecstasy and tears flowed from his eyes. Iqbal tore strips of fine cloth and gave them to him one by one. He would put the strip on his eyes to wipe the tears and throw it before the *qawwal*. An account of some mystic songs recited by Hasan Bhaddi, Amir Haji (son of Amir Khusrau), and others is given by Amir Khurd. Sometimes, when overwhelmed by emotion, the Shaikh motioned to Khwaja Musa (a grandson of Shaikh Farid) to stand up and dance in ecstasy. Sometimes the Shaikh

---

[117] *Khair-u'l-Majalis*, p. 106.

was so moved by some verse of Sa'di that he remained in a state of emotional excitement throughout the day.[118] The Shaikh enjoyed Hindi verses also and went into ecstasy on hearing them.[119]

'URS CELEBRATIONS

One day a visitor asked the Shaikh what the word '*urs* stood for. He said: 'It means to arrange a wedding feast and also the alighting of a caravan.'[120] Death anniversary celebrations of his spiritual master, Shaikh Farid Ganj-i-Shakar, were a grand affair in the *khanqah* of Shaikh Nizam-u'd-din Auliya. Huge crowds gathered there on 5 Muharram every year. Special arrangements were made for the preparation and distribution of food. The Shaikh called all *langardars* (cooks and those who ran *langars* in the city) to help in the preparation of food.[121] The Shaikh enquired about his friends and disciples if they had attended the celebrations. Food was sent to the houses of those who could not participate for some reason. Perhaps to deter the attendance of pimps and prostitutes, the Shaikh sent food and money to them—either two dishes of food and two *tankas* or one dish and one *tanka* to each.[122] Once on an '*urs* day Iqbal sent a tray of food and one *tanka* to a woman through Abbu. The woman was used to getting two trays and two *tankas*. She thought that Abbu had embezzled the rest. She came to the *khanqah* and started creating a fuss about it. The Shaikh overheard all this from his room above. 'Lalla! What does Abbu say?', he enquired from there, and instructed Iqbal to send the full sum and the tray to the woman as usual.[123]

JAMA'AT KHANAH AT NIGHT

The *Jama'at Khanah* at night was the scene of quiet but brisk spiritual activity. Disciples kept vigil for different durations—busy in prayers

---

[118] *Siyar-u'l-Auliya*, pp. 511–15.
[119] Ibid. p. 512.
[120] *Fawa'id-u'l-Fu'ad*, p. 121.
[121] *Khair-u'l-Majalis*, p. 185.
[122] *Jawami'-u'l-Kalim*, pp. 122–3.
[123] Ibid. p. 123.

and meditation. Many of them offered *tahajjud* prayers for several hours. An hour before dawn those who fasted had their food (*sahri*); thereafter, they resumed prayers. Before the morning prayers many inmates went to the river, performed *wuzu* (ablution), and returned to the prayer carpet.

VISITORS—INQUISITIVE CRITICS

Among the visitors were some inquisitive critics also who came to test the Shaikh's scholarship or gauge his spiritual stature. Often their arrogance melted before the dignified and scholarly bearing of the Shaikh, and they would plead with him to admit them to his discipline. One such instance may be cited here. Shams-u'd-din and Sadr-u'd-din Nawli, two bright but indigent students, were washing their clothes on the banks of the Jumna, near the *khanqah*. Shams-u'd-din turned to his cousin and said: 'Shah Nizam-u'd-din lives here in the vicinity. Many people of the city have faith in him but we do not know what the depth of his learning is. Come, let us go to him and assess his scholarship. But we will not show much respect to him and will not put our head on the ground. We will simply greet him and take our place.' But both, on entering the *khanqah* and seeing the face of the Shaikh, instinctively kissed the ground. The Shaikh asked them to be comfortably seated, and then conversed with them. They told him that they lived in the city and were studying *Bazudi* with Maulana Zahir-u'd-din Bukhari. The Shaikh then asked them to explain a passage that happened to be the one their teacher had not been able to explain and deferred for later reflection. They mentioned this to the Shaikh. He explained it with such insight and understanding that both visitors were taken by surprise. When they stood up to leave, the Shaikh gave a loincloth of his to Shams-u'd-din and a *dastar* to Zahir-u'd-din. Both returned and joined in the discipline of the Shaikh.[124] Shams-u'd-din attained such scholarship that Shaikh Nasir-u'd-din Chiragh, who later studied some books with him, paid eloquent tribute to it.

---

[124] *Siyar-u'l-Auliya*, pp. 223–4.

OPPONENTS OF THE SHAIKH

There were some people who were hostile towards the Shaikh and resented his popularity and prestige. They spoke ill of him, ridiculed his *khanqah*-life and criticized his audition parties. Shaikhzada Husam-u'd-din Farjam and Qazi Jalal-u'd-din Saqanji displayed great hostility towards the Shaikh in the *mahzar* meeting convened by Sultan Ghiyas-u'd-din Tughluq to consider the legality of *sama'*. What annoyed the Shaikh was not their insolence but their refusal to listen to the Traditions of the Prophet in support of *sama'*.

But the Shaikh was most distressed by the attitude and behaviour of the sons of Shaikh Nur-u'd-din Firdausi. Young, immature, and boisterous they often sailed past the *khanqah*, dancing and shouting insolently at the saint. One morning when Shaikh Nizam-u'd-din Auliya was sitting on his wooden staircase, lost in contemplation, these boys rowed their boat near the *khanqah* and started shouting and dancing. The Shaikh took his arms out from the sleeves and observed sadly: 'What a wonder! A man has sacrificed many years of his life in this [religious] work and there are people who still ask: Who are you that claim equality with us?' As luck would have it, the boat sank and the merrymaking group of insolent youths disappeared in the water.[125]

THE *JAWALIQS*, *QALANDARS*, AND *HAIDERIS*

Among the wandering dervishes of different backgrounds who came to the *khanqah* were *Jawaliqs*, *Qalandars*, and *Haideris*. Despite the arrogance and insolence of their behaviour, the Shaikh treated them with consideration and courtesy and fulfilled their demands.[126] He justified being patient with people who addressed him insolently in this way: 'This sort of behaviour should also be tolerated. Many people come, touch the feet [of the one they are visiting to show respect] and leave gifts. Such [insolent] people should also be allowed to come and speak what they like. Such action offsets [the behaviour of others who follow the other course].'[127]

---

[125] Ibid. p. 147.
[126] *Fawa'id-u'l-Fu'ad*, p. 48.
[127] Ibid.

IMPACT OF THE MONGOL INVASIONS

Shaikh Nizam-u'd-din Auliya's ancestors had been driven out from Bukhara by the Mongols. India was also threatened by Mongol invasions. Whenever reports of such threat reached Delhi, people would flock to the *khanqah* of the Shaikh for protection. It was a safer place, at some distance from the city, and it was under the spiritual umbrella of the saint. Once Maulana Shams-u'd-din Yahya, Maulana 'Ala-u'd-din Nili, and some other disciples came from Awadh to pay their respects to the Shaikh. At the time there was widespread panic in Delhi due to an impending Mongol invasion. Hardly four days had passed since the arrival of this group that the Shaikh told them that they had his permission to return. They left as instructed but were disappointed and depressed. They had only reached Tilpat when 'Ala-u'd-din Nili fell seriously ill with a high fever. They sent word to the Shaikh and sought his instructions. The roads to Awadh had also become unsafe. The Shaikh immediately sent some money and his carriage to bring 'Ala-u'd-din back to the *khanqah*. Out of respect, 'Ala-u'd-din Nili did not sit in the carriage of the Shaikh. He hired a *doli* and travelled in it behind the Shaikh's carriage. The Shaikh received them with great kindness, asked after the illness of 'Ala-u'd-din Nili and had Iqbal bring them some food from the kitchen. He brought some *khichri* with purified butter, which the Shaikh gave to Nili. It suited him immensely and he recovered from his illness. 'The Mongol invasion is causing great worry everywhere,' the Shaikh explained. 'Those living in the suburbs were forced back to the city and there was scarcity of water and food, and travellers in particular were subject to hardships. That is why I asked you to go back home. You felt depressed at this, though there was no reason to feel so.'[128]

JAMA'AT KHANAH—A WELFARE CENTRE

The *Jama'at Khanah* of Shaikh Nizam-u'd-din Auliya was, in fact, a centre of service and welfare for the entire locality, not just for its own residents. People living in the neighbourhood were also helped

---

[128] *Siyar-u'l-Auliya*, pp. 276–7.

and supported. The Shaikh distributed alms and gifts with a generosity that surprised people. His gifts reached the '*Ulama*, even the nobles and the elite.[129]

Jamal Qiwam-u'd-din writes:

When the Shaikh opened the door of granting awards to people it reached such a stage that '*Ulama* and *masha'ikh*, nobles and *maliks* and princes all became his stipend receivers (*wazifa khawar*). To everyone he gave something, 10, 5, or 4 silver *tanka*s. The people in general received stipends daily, or every week, or in a month or in four months or half-yearly or yearly. Those who lived in the vicinity got it daily; those living in the city got it on weekly basis. Those who came from neighbouring *qasbat* received monthly stipends. Six-monthly or yearly stipends were given to those who came from distant places like Uchch, Multan, Gujarat, or Deogir. Whoever came after the morning prayer, and before the Shaikh retired for midday rest, got *jital*s, gold and silver *tanka*s—10, 20, 50, or 100—according to his needs . . . Very good and costly clothes were also distributed. . . .Whoever came got something. The house of the Shaikh had two doors, both on the riverside. The crowd swelled immensely . . . If anybody (in the neighbourhood) had his earthen vessel (*subu'i*) broken, he had the broken one exchanged for a new one at the door . . . People were surprised where this large number of earthen pots came from. The Shaikh was so concerned about the welfare of the people that even [such items of need] were not ignored.[130]

One very hot summer day many houses in Ghiyaspur caught fire. The Shaikh was deeply perturbed. He rushed to the roof barefoot and stood there with only a cap (*taqiya*) on his head (and not the *dastar* he used to wear in summer) till the fire was completely extinguished. He then asked Iqbal to go and count the houses which had been burnt. He sent to every house two silver coins, two trays of food, and one pitcher of cold water. In those days two silver *tanka*s sufficed for buying all essential things for the household.[131]

---

[129] *Qiwam-u'l-'Aqa'id*, MS pp. 201 *et seq.*

[130] Ibid. MS pp. 204–6.

[131] *Jawami'-u'l-Kalim*, p. 123.

After the death of Shaikh Nizam-u'd-din Auliya his *khanqah* continued to perform this service of helping the poor through stipends and daily food. 'Ain-u'l-Mulk Mahru wrote to Shaikh-i-Shuyukh-u'l-Islam Sadr-u'd-din Muhammad about stipendary help from the *khanqah*— 150 silver *tankas* annually and two trays of food daily—to the descendants of Malik Qutb-u'd-din Dabir.[132]

---

[132] *Insha-i-Mahru*, pp. 39–41, 56.

7

ROUTINE AND SCHEDULE

———•◦•———

Shaikh Nizam-u'd-din Auliya had an extremely busy and highly
regulated schedule. It was a self-imposed discipline which he followed
meticulously, hardly ever deviating from it, even when ailing or
indisposed.[1] His routine was adjusted according to the time of the
obligatory prayers (*salat*). Since he fasted almost every day he woke up
at the time of *sahri* (the pre-fast meal) in the small hours of the morning.
When Khwaja 'Abd-u'r-Rahim brought *sahri* to him an hour before
the dawn, he found the Shaikh awake. In the morning, one could see
an inexplicable spiritual radiance on his face and his nocturnal devotions
beaming through his red sleep-laden eyes.[2] The Shaikh offered all his
obligatory prayers in the *Jama'at Khanah*. Even when he passed the
age of 80 he negotiated the dangerous wooden staircase and came down
to offer the obligatory prayers in congregation.[3]

After sunrise the Shaikh sat on his carpet facing towards the Ka'ba
and received the people on the roof of the *Jama'at Khanah*. People
put their problems to him at that time and he listened quietly. He
would offer consolation, and his promise to pray to God for the solution
of their problems infused hope and confidence in them. The presents
brought at this time were distributed among the audience. At about
noon he retired to a room on the ground floor for a brief rest. He offered his midday (*zuhr*) prayer in the community hall below and then

---

[1] *Nafa'is-u'l-Anfas*, MS Nadwat-u'l-'Ulama Library, p. 7.
[2] *Siyar-u'l-Auliya*, pp. 126–8.
[3] Ibid. p. 124.

went to his room on the upper-storey and received visitors there. After a break for the mid-afternoon (*'asr*) prayer, he resumed meeting his visitors until sunset.

At the time of breaking the fast (*iftar*) he came down to the community hall, and invited others to join him. He did the sunset (*maghrib*) prayer in the *Jama'at Khanah*. During the summer he then went to his room upstairs, but in winter to his room on the ground floor. Till the *'isha* prayers he granted interviews to the visitors who had collected there. After that, dinner was served upstairs. The Shaikh himself took very little but asked others to enjoy the dinner. He did the *'isha* prayer in the community hall, after which the visitors left and the Shaikh went to his room upstairs. There he busied himself in his devotions for some time. Then he sat down on his cot for rest and Iqbal put a rosary in his hand. Amir Khurd informs us that at that time none except Amir Khusrau remained in his presence.[4] The poet—who was always ready with reports, news, and reviews—talked about different matters and the Shaikh nodded his head to keep him going. Sometimes the Shaikh would ask: 'What more, O Turk?', and Khusrau would expatiate on different matters with the genius of a court poet. It was also at this time of the day that the Shaikh met some of his relations and children. When all had left, Iqbal would come and bring some water for ablution and retire. The Shaikh then bolted the door, and nobody tried to approach him thereafter. But the light could be seen in his room burning through the silent hours of the night.[5] He often recited the following Persian couplet:

بارے بتماشـــائے من وشمع بیا

کز من دمکے نماند وازوے دودے

(Come sometimes to have a glimpse of me and the candle
When breath leaves me and flame goes out of the candle.)[6]

---

[4] Ibid. p. 125.
[5] Ibid.
[6] Ibid.

Most of his time at night was spent in prayer, study, and meditation. He once told a disciple that in the early hours of the morning some ideas and verses flashed across his mind and gave immense spiritual pleasure to him.[7] Some of his time at night was spent in study. He read books and noted down his comments in them or on separate sheets of paper. His eyesight was good and he could easily read closely-written manuscripts in candlelight.[8]

The visitors flowed into his presence like a stream till about noon. Then the stream became thin and the saint retired for his midday rest in the room adjoining the *Jama'at Khanah*. But very often he was unable to have a proper rest from the strains of the day. He used to say that he was most happy on two occasions—when he was attending *sama'*, and when somebody came to him and talked about spiritual matters. He felt depressed when people talked of everyday worries (*anduh-i-ruzgar*).[9]

Though punctilious about his schedule, he was always available to visitors who called at odd hours. One day he told Amir Hasan Sijzi:

> The general custom of the Shaikhs is that no one goes to them except between sun-rise (*ishraq*) and midday (*zuhr*) prayers. This is, however, not my practice. Any one can come to me at any time: "In the lanes of taverns and in the inns of vagabonds There is no restriction— come, sit, and be at home."[10]

A man once called on the Shaikh while he was having his midday rest. Akhi Mubarak, an inmate of the *Jama'at Khanah*, sent him away. At that very moment the Shaikh saw Shaikh Farid in a dream, telling him: 'If you have nothing to give to a visitor, at least receive him cordially.' Thereafter the Shaikh gave instructions to the inmates to wake him up whenever a visitor came to see him. He always put two questions on getting up from his siesta: 'Has the shadow declined [towards evening]? Has any visitor come?'[11]

---

[7] Ibid. p. 127.
[8] Ibid. p. 383.
[9] *Nafa'is-u'l-Anfas*, MS Nadwat-u'l-'Ulama Library, pp. 10–11.
[10] *Fawa'id-u'l-Fu'ad*, p. 98.
[11] *Siyar-u'l-Auliya*, p. 129.

The Shaikh never enjoyed good health. According to Shaikh Nasir-u'd-din Chiragh he suffered from one complaint or the other—painful flatulence, fever, or piles—and when one ailment was cured, another appeared.[12] His illness always sent a wave of anxiety all over the *Jama'at Khanah*. Special prayers were held and alms distributed by the disciples after circumambulating his cot.[13] Once his legs became swollen and excruciating pain made him restless. Disciples from places like Badaon, Chanderi, and Awadh came in large numbers to ask after him. When he recovered and had a 'bath of recovery' (*ghusl-i-sayhat*) people sent propitiatory offerings according to their means for distribution as *sadaqah* and felicitated him warmly.[14] The Shaikh often suffered from stomach trouble.[15] Once his eyesight was temporarily affected by some illness. Maulana Burhan-u'd-din Gharib noticed it and arranged litanies and prayers for the Shaikh's health in the *Jama'at Khanah*. Burhan-u'd-din Gharib has reported that the Shaikh did not give up his litanies and supererogatory prayers even when seriously ill: 'He offered some *rak'as* and then put his head on the pillow [for rest]. Then he raised it again and offered more genuflexions.'[16]

On one occasion the Shaikh was so overpowered by ecstasy during *sama'* that he fell from the roof of the *Jama'at Khanah* and fractured his leg. Thereafter, he could not walk without limping. Some critics attributed this accident to lack of spiritual agility. Shaikh Rukn-u'd-din Abu'l-Fath of Multan was saddened on hearing this criticism and condemned the critics for their ignorance of what they considered to be the spiritual implications of the accident.[17]

Though the Shaikh's face and his demeanour always gave the impression of his being absorbed in contemplation,[18] he neither performed innumerable *rak'as* in prayer nor kept on reciting the Qur'an all the time. Once a visitor mustered courage to ask him how much

---

[12] *Khair-u'l-Majalis*, p. 257.

[13] *Nafa'is-u'l-Anfas*, MS Nadwat-u'l-'Ulama Library, p. 13; *Siyar-u'l-Auliya*, p. 285.

[14] Ibid.

[15] *Nafa'is-u'l-Anfas*, MS Nadwat-u'l-'Ulama Library, p. 10–11; *Siyar-u'l-Auliya*, p. 217.

[16] *Nafa'is-u'l-Anfas*, MS Nadwat-u'l-'Ulama Library, pp. 6–7.

[17] *Bahr-u'l-Ma'ani*, p. 193.

[18] *Siyar-u'l-Auliya*, p. 129.

Qur'an he recited every day. The Shaikh's reply was, 'One *para*.'[19] Amir Khurd informs us that the Shaikh recited *darud* and *Surat al-Fatiha* one thousand times after *'isha* prayers every day. In addition, he read something from *Jawahir-u'l-Qur'an* of Imam Ghazzali, *Hirz-i-Yamani* and *Hirz-i-Kafi* daily.[20]

Of the servants of the Shaikh, Iqbal was pre-eminent. Mubashshir[21] had been in the service of the Shaikh from his early youth. Among others who served the Shaikh, the names of Khwaja Nasir[22] and Khwaja 'Abd-u'r-Rahim[23] are mentioned in contemporary accounts. Khwaja Razi has been referred to as a special courier of the Shaikh (*paik-i-hazrat bad*),[24] and 'Abdullah Koli as his *Rakabdar*.[25] However every person in the *Jama'at Khanah* was not only ready to render any service to the Shaikh but felt elated if a task were assigned to him.

The disciples of the Shaikh had built a small, neat house for him in Kilugarhi, about two miles away from Ghiyaspur.[26] It was located opposite the door of the Kilugahri Jama' Masjid.[27] On Friday mornings the Shaikh went there, had his bath there, changed his clothes and busied himself in meditation. It appears from *Fawa'id-u'l-Fu'ad* that here also he addressed visitors before prayers.[28] In the mosque he used to sit at a fixed place near the southern gate.[29]

During the early years at Ghiyaspur he had no transport and walked to the mosque. Sometimes he felt so exhausted from fasting that he had to rest in some shop on the way. A disciple of Malik Yar Parran presented a horse to him but he did not accept it till his spiritual master told him in a dream to do so.[30] Thereafter the Shaikh was never without

---

[19] Ibid. p. 383.
[20] Ibid. p. 108.
[21] Ibid.
[22] Ibid. p. 238; *Khair-u'l-Majalis*, p. 187.
[23] *Siyar-u'l-Auliya*, p. 128.
[24] Ibid. p. 259.
[25] Ibid. p. 265.
[26] Ibid. pp. 144, 257.
[27] *Fawa'id-u'l-Fu'ad*, p. 80.
[28] Ibid. pp. 80, 82.
[29] *Siyar-u'l-Auliya*, p. 136.
[30] Ibid. p. 144.

a horse in the *khanqah*.[31] In later years, however, he used *singhasan, dolah*, etc. Iqbal and 'Abdullah Koli walked on the right and the left of the *dolah*, reciting verses in soft but moving tones. Tears flowed from the eyes of the Shaikh as he rode on the *dolah* in a state of ecstasy.[32]

The Shaikh did not go out often. But he visited some graves of saints in Delhi, and sometimes went for a stroll on the bank of the Jumna. In his early years he went to *Bagh-i-Jasrat* and other places for contemplation and prayer in seclusion. One day while walking by the Jumna he saw an old woman drawing water from a well. He stopped to ask her why she put herself to this trouble when the Jumna flowed nearby. The woman explained that she and her husband were poor people; since the water of the Jumna increased the appetite, she preferred the water of the well. The Shaikh was deeply moved. 'Lalla,' he said to Iqbal, 'in our Ghiyaspur there is a woman who does not take the water of Jumna for fear of hunger. Go and ask her how much she needs for her daily expenses and send her all she needs every month without fail.'[33]

The Shaikh often visited the graves of his mother, Shaikh Najib-u'd-din Mutawakkil, and Khwaja Qutb-u'd-din Bakhtiyar Kaki. Many prostitutes would come out on the street when they heard about the Shaikh's visit to some place. To avoid being surrounded by them, he sent some people ahead to distribute money to them and persuade them to leave the road and sit in the shade.[34]

The Shaikh used to sit and pray in the vacant space between the graves of Khwaja Qutb-u'd-din Bakhtiyar Kaki and Qazi Hamid-u'd-din Nagauri. He felt great spiritual exhilaration in praying there.[35] Sometimes he visited the grave of Maulana Rashid-u'd-din, known as Shaikh Rasan, in Sarai Jasrat and sat there meditating under an *imli* tree.[36] In his early career he had even performed *chillah* (forty days seclusion and meditation) at his tomb.[37]

[31] Ibid.
[32] Ibid. p. 510.
[33] *Jawami'-u'l-Kalim*, p. 123.
[34] Ibid.
[35] *Siyar-u'l-Auliya*, p. 57.
[36] *Durar-i-Nizami*, MS.
[37] *Siyar-u'l-Auliya*, p. 149.

The Shaikh did not go to Badaon after he settled in Delhi. He went to Ajodhan nine or ten times—three times when Shaikh Farid was alive, and six or seven times after his death.[38] He did not go out to any other place during his long stay in Delhi.

The Shaikh sometimes attended *sama'* meeting and feasts arranged in gardens, *khanqah*s, and private residences in Delhi. He used to attend sermon meetings (*tazkir*) at the home of Qazi Minhaj-u's-Siraj, the famous author of *Tabaqat-i-Nasiri*, every Monday. Verses recited there threw him into ecstasy.[39] During the time of 'Ala-u'd-din Khalji things were cheap and great feasts could be arranged for a few *tanka*s. There were *langardar*s in Delhi who managed such feasts.[40] The Shaikh was also invited to these feasts and audition parties.

The Shaikh attached great importance to the proper use of time. 'Time is the most precious thing with a mystic,' he used to say, 'it is lamentable if he wastes it.'[41] Every breath that a man draws had a value realized if the moment was spent in devotion to Him.[42] Life for him was only that period which was spent in contemplation of Him.[43] This was the guiding principle of his use of time.

---

[38] Ibid. p. 107.
[39] Ibid. pp. 501–2.
[40] *Khair-u'l-Majalis*, p. 240.
[41] *Siyar-u'l-Auliya*, p. 376.
[42] Ibid.
[43] *Fawa'id-u'l-Fu'ad*, p. 20.

8

LAST ILLNESS AND DEATH

Shaikh Nizam-u'd-din Auliya approached death at about eighty-two years of age. He had attended to his gigantic mission with remarkable devotion and sincerity. Years of penitence, vigils, and fasts, however, told on his health. During the closing years of his life his health had so declined that he always suffered from one ailment or the other—acute pain caused by wind in the bowels, fever, headache, or piles (*khala, tap, suda, bowasir*)[1]—but he never allowed these physical afflictions to disturb his daily routine.

The final warning about the breakdown of his health came when the Shaikh was offering his Friday prayers in the mosque. Ecstasy combined with loss of memory suddenly overcame him. He went on bowing and prostrating again and again. He came back home in this condition. He would recover consciousness for a short while but again lapse into coma.[2] On recovering consciousness he would ask about prayers and due to forgetfulness offer the same prayer several times over again. Time and again he asked: 'Today is Friday. Have I offered the prayers?', and repeated the words: 'We are going. We are going. We are going.'[3] His every moment was symbolic of his inner craving:

> I hope to see my Pilot face to face
> When I have crossed the bar.

---

[1] *Khair-u'l-Majalis*, p. 257.
[2] *Nafa'is-u'l-Anfas*, MS p. 7.
[3] *Siyar-u'l-Auliya*, pp. 152–3.

Tears constantly flowed from his eyes during this period. One day he summoned all his relations, friends, and servants and said: 'Be a witness if this man [turning to Iqbal] holds back a single thing from distribution to people, he will himself be responsible before God on the Day of Judgement.' So saying he ordered Iqbal to give away in charity everything that he had in the stores of his *Jama`at Khanah*. Iqbal doled out everything, holding back some corn for a few days' consumption in the *khanqah*. When the Shaikh came to know about it from Syed Husain Kirmani, he was displeased with Iqbal. 'Why have you kept this dead sand?' He then called poor people and mendicants and asked them to break open the doors of the granaries and take away everything.[4]

Two problems now exercised the minds of the inmates of the *khanqah*, the relatives, and the senior disciples of the Shaikh: what about their livelihood after the Shaikh?, and where to bury him when he was dead?

When the first problem was brought to the notice of the Shaikh, he said that those who would live at his tomb would get enough for their livelihood. On being asked further who would collect, control, and distribute this income, the Shaikh replied that the one who surrendered his own share would do this job.[5]

Maulana Shams-u'd-din Damghani, maternal grandfather of the author of *Siyar-u'l-Auliya*, was a friend and class-mate of the Shaikh. He was persuaded to ascertain the Shaikh's preference for his last resting place, as a number of people had constructed buildings in the hope that the Shaikh would be buried in their building. To Damghani's query, the Shaikh's reply was: 'Maulana! I am not worthy to sleep under any building. I would lie under the open sky.'[6]

For about forty days the Shaikh remained in a state of semi-consciousness. His diet, already very meagre, further decreased and he stopped eating anything. Akhi Mubarak brought some fish soup for him. The Shaikh declined to take it and said: 'Throw it in the running water.'[7]

---

[4] *Siyar-u'l-Auliya*, p. 153.
[5] Ibid.
[6] Ibid. pp. 153–4.
[7] Ibid. p. 154.

During this last illness Shaikh Rukn-u'd-din Abu'l-Fath of Multan came to enquire about his health. The Shaikh was too weak to rise and receive him. Shaikh Rukn-u'd-din insisted that the Shaikh should remain on his cot, but he would not, out of respect for him. A chair was then brought for him. Shaikh Rukn-u'd-din recited a Hadith to the effect that prophets are given an option by God to live in the world for some time longer if they so desired. And since *walis* (saints) were successors of the Prophet, they too might pray for an extension in their lifespan. Shaikh Nizam-u'd-din Auliya burst into tears on hearing this and said: 'I have seen the Prophet in a dream saying: "Nizam! We are anxiously waiting for you."'[8] As soon as he uttered this sentence, the entire audience, including the distinguished visitor, began to weep. Everybody present felt that it was the last glow of a setting sun.

The Shaikh died on 18 Rabi'-u'l-Akhir 725/3 April 1325, after sunrise. Shaikh Rukn-u'd-din led the funeral prayers and he was buried, as he had desired, in an open space.

Sultan Muhammad bin Tughluq[9] carried his bier on his shoulders. It is said that in his last days the Shaikh had directed that musicians should sing *sama'* for three days before his burial. He even obtained a promise to this effect from Maulana Shihab-u'd-din. Shaikh Rukn-u'd-din, however, advised against it and said, 'I will be responsible on the Day of Judgement for not carrying out this direction of the Shaikh.' Muhammad bin Tughluq heard about this and was sorry that the Shaikh's wish had not been fulfilled.[10] It was indeed a longstanding desire of the Shaikh. Once when asked by Shaikh Farid what he wished from God that he could pray for, he had asked him to pray for his steadfastness in mystic effort (*istiqamah*). Later on he lamented that he had not requested his spiritual master to pray that he should die listening to *sama'*.[11]

It is reported that Shaikh Rukn-u'd-din Multani enquired from Iqbal: 'Did the Shaikh fix any place [for his burial]?' 'Yes,' replied Iqbal, 'in

---

[8] Ibid. pp. 140–1; *Qiwam-u'l-'Aqa'id*, MS p. 83.

[9] *Masalik-u'l-Absar*, English translation. p. 37; *Jawami'-u'l-Kalim*, p. 132; Ibn Battuta, II p. 33. The confusion in Ibn Battuta's statement has been removed by the translator of *Masalik-u'l-Absar*, p. 37 n. 48.

[10] *Jawami'-u'l-Kalim*, p. 132; *Nafa'is-u'l-Anfas*, MS p. 87.

[11] *Khair-u'l-Majalis*, p. 225.

this garden.' 'If the Shaikh came to this place, where did he sit?' enquired Shaikh Rukn-u'd-din. Iqbal pointed to an orange tree under which, he said, the Shaikh used to sit. Shaikh Rukn-u'd-din offered two *rak'a*: of prayer there and exactly at that spot his grave was dug.[12] The mystic cloak (*khirqa*) which Shaikh Farid Ganj-i-Shakar had bestowed on him was spread over his body and his prayer-carpet was placed on his head.[13] As his body was lowered into the grave, a historic phase of the Muslim mystic movement in South Asia came to an end. When Amir Khusrau heard about his master's death, on his return from Awadh, he tore his garments, blackened his face and went to the grave of the Shaikh. He recited the following Hindivi verse and fell down in a swoon:

کوری سووے سیج پر مکھ پر ڈارے کھیس
چلو خسرو گھر اپنے رین بھئی سب دیس

(The fair one lies on the couch with her black tresses scattered on her face:
O Khusrau, come home now, for night has fallen all over the world.)

Sultan Muhammad bin Tughluq built a dome over his grave.[14] The building near the mausoleum of the Shaikh, generally known as *Jama'at Khanah*, was built by Firuz Shah Tughluq, as he himself says in his *Futuhat*:

'And I constructed a new *Jama'at Khanah* which was not there'[15]

---

[12] *Qiwam-u'l-'Aqa'id*, MS p. 84.

[13] *Siyar-u'l-Auliya*, p. 342.

[14] *Siyar-u'l-Auliya*, p. 155.

[15] *Futuhat-i-Firuz Shahi*, Aligarh, p. 17. Its attribution to Khizr Khan is wrong. Jamali's incorrect statement (*Siyar-u'l-Auliya*, p. 74) led to this confusion.

9

MORAL AND SPIRITUAL TEACHINGS

————•◦•————

Discussing the role of mystics in society, Bergson said: 'A great mystic feels the truth flow into him from its source like a force in action. His desire is with God's help to complete the creation of the human species. The mystic's direction is the very direction of the *élan* of life.'[1] Shaikh Nizam-u'd-din Auliya's life reflects the truth of this statement. His moral and spiritual teachings centred round three basic ideals:

(a) To teach man the moral and spiritual significance of obeisance to the Lord of the Universe;

(b) To bring happiness to the human heart amid the distress and struggle of life in the world; and

(c) To inculcate respect for moral values and reduce sin.

With these ideals in view, the Shaikh sought to build his disciples into morally autonomous persons.

The Shaikh realized that no spiritual exercise, penitence, prayer, or vigil had greater value in the eyes of God than bringing consolation to distressed hearts and helping the needy and the downtrodden.[2] All his efforts were, therefore, directed towards the alleviation of human misery. It was beyond the power of any human being to solve every problem brought to him, but what was more important was to create in the sufferer a sense of security, which reduced tensions and gave

---

[1] As cited by Toynbee, *A Study of History*, Abridgement, p. 212.
[2] *Siyar-u'l-Auliya*, p. 128.

inner peace and equanimity. This reorientation of the personality, by altering its motivations and impulses, was of greater significance than doling out a few coins in charity. With change in a man's outlook, his hopes and fears, his ambitions and aspirations, underwent a complete metamorphosis. Shaikh Nizam-u'd-din Auliya strove to achieve this objective throughout his life.

SERVICE OF MANKIND HIGHER THAN FORMAL PRAYERS

The roots of Shaikh Nizam-u'd-din Auliya's moral and spiritual teachings lay in his concept of devotion to God. He said:

> Devotion to God is of two kinds, *lazmi* [intransitive] and *muta'addi* [transitive]. In *lazmi* devotion the benefit which accrues is confined to the devotee alone. This type of devotion includes prayers, fasting, pilgrimage to Makka, recitation of religious formulae, turning the beads of the rosary, etc. The *muta'addi* devotion, on the contrary, brings advantage and comfort to others; it is performed by spending money on others, showing affection to people, and by other means through which a man strives to help his fellow human beings. The reward of *muta'addi* devotion is endless and limitless.[3]

This radical attitude to religion provided motive power to the spiritual discipline of Shaikh Nizam-u'd-din Auliya, and made the mystic movement a humanitarian activity to remove sin and suffering from society. It emanated from the Shaikh's concept of God as an all-embracing Reality present in his ethical, intellectual, and aesthetic experience. He lived for the Lord alone. His cosmic emotion, rooted in his faith in God as the Supreme Nourisher, supplied motive power to his mystic mission. He believed in following the ways of the Lord of the Creation. (تخلقوا بـأخلاق اللّه)

---

[3] *Fawa'id-u'l-Fu'ad*, pp. 13–14; *Siyar-u'l-Auliya*, p. 411. The opposition between *lazmi* and *muta'addi* is adopted from grammatical terminology. The *muta'addi* verb being transitive, i.e. its action exercising an effect upon an object, and the *lazmi* being intransitive, i.e. its action being confined to the subject. Sir Hamilton Gibb once wrote to me: 'The transference of these terms to mystical devotion is, in fact, remarkably apt.'

Divine bounty does not discriminate between one individual and another. When the sun rises, it gives light and warmth to all people, whether living in palaces or in huts. When it rained, the poor and rich alike benefited from it. Once Shaikh Mu'in-u'd-din Chishti of Ajmer was asked to explain the highest form of religious devotion which endeared man to God. He said:

> Develop river-like generosity, sun-like
> Bounty, and earth-like hospitality.[4]

Shaikh Nizam-u'd-din Auliya demonstrated the significance of this advice as an inspiring motive in his own life.[5] A mystic was expected to transcend all barriers of cult, race, language, and geography in dealing with human beings, who were all God's creatures.

LIVE FOR THE LORD ALONE

Shaikh Nizam-u'd-din Auliya believed that if man learnt 'to live for the Lord alone' there would be love, peace, and amity in this world, and the very basis of human relationship would change. Human beings are 'like children of God on earth' and one who seeks His pleasure must strive for the welfare of all people, regardless of any consideration. 'Living for the Lord alone' meant a total transformation of human psychology through a fundamental change in approach to life and its problems. Inspired by this ideal, whatever a man did or applied his mind to, became devotion to God. It led to sublimation of motivations in life. The moral of the following anecdote, the miracle element apart, is to teach man to live for the Lord alone and subordinate sex and hunger to higher and nobler ideals of life:

A saint lived by the bank of a river. One day this saint asked his wife to take food to a dervish living on the other side of the river. His wife protested that crossing the water would be difficult. He said: 'When you go to the bank of the river tell the water to provide a way for you out of respect for your husband who never slept with

---

[4] *Siyar-u'l-Auliya*, p. 46.
[5] *Fawa'id-u'l-Fu'ad*, p. 207.

Chillah Khanah of the *Khanqah* of Shaikh Nizam-u'd-din Auliya, near the tomb of Humayun.

his wife.' His wife was perplexed at these words and said to herself: 'How many children have I borne by this man? Yet how can I challenge this directive from my husband?' She took the food to the bank of the river, spoke the message to the water, and the water gave way for her passage. Having crossed, she put food before the dervish, and the dervish took it in her presence. After he had eaten, the woman asked: 'How shall I recross the river?' 'How did you come?' asked the dervish. The woman repeated the words of her husband. On hearing this the dervish said, 'Go to the water and tell it to make way for you out of respect for the dervish who never ate for thirty years.' The woman, bewildered at these words, came to the river, repeated the message, and the water again gave way for her passage. On returning home, the woman fell at her husband's feet and implored him: 'Tell me the secret of those directives which you and the other dervish uttered.' 'Look!' said the saint, 'I never slept with you only to satisfy the passions of my lower self but to provide you what was your due. In reality I never slept with you, and similarly that other man never ate for thirty years to satisfy his appetite or to fill his stomach. He ate only to have the strength to do God's will.'[6]

Shaikh Nizam-u'd-din Auliya taught sublimation of desires through the development of cosmic emotion. This gave real spiritual peace and poise to those who practised it. The Shaikh never tried to curb or control an individual's natural aptitudes. He just sublimated them through development of counter-attractions. From his early life Amir Khusrau was interested in romantic and lyrical poetry. When he joined the Shaikh's discipline, he thought of changing the trend and tenor of his poetry. The Shaikh did not permit him to check the natural flow of his emotions.[7] However, in course of time he changed his amorous fancies into cosmic emotion. What was material and mundane became spiritual and cosmic. Similarly, the Shaikh's nephew Khwaja Rafi'-u'd-din was interested in archery and somatic arts. The Shaikh did not prevent him from pursuing his hobbies.[8] However, by making him commit the Qur'an to memory he gave a different orientation to his personality.

---

[6] *Fawa'id-u'l-Fu'ad*, pp. 60-1.

[7] *Siyar-u'l-Auliya*, p. 301.

[8] Ibid. p. 203.

RENUNCIATION OF THE MATERIAL WORLD

The Shaikh believed that one could not live a life of divine significance unless one firmly rejected all material attractions (*tark-i-dunya*).[9] This did not necessarily mean leading the life of a recluse or denying oneself the good things of life. It meant rejection of that attitude of mind which involved man in material struggles in such a way that he ceased to look at the divine significance of life and frittered away his energies in petty worldly pursuits. Like Wordsworth he felt:

Getting and spending we lay waste our powers
Little we see in nature that is ours.

He thus explain his views in this regard:

Rejection of the world does not mean that one should strip himself of his clothes or put on a loincloth and sit idle. Instead, rejection of the world means that one may put on clothes and take food. What comes to him [unasked], he should accept it, but not hoard it. He should not place his heart in anything. Only this is the rejection of the world.[10]

He made a distinction between 'appearance' and 'reality' of the world. What one did to provide for the needs of his wife and family was the world (*dunya*) in appearance, but not so in reality.[11]

The Shaikh thought that possession of private property deepened a man's links with the material world and cut him off from the energizing

---

[9] *Fawa'id-u'l-Fu'ad*, pp. 72–82.

[10] Ibid. p. 9; *Siyar-u'l-Auliya*, pp. 543–5. Very similar is the explanation of Rumi who says:

چیست دنیا از خدا غافل بودن

نی قماش ونقره وفرزند وزن

(What is the [material] world? [Nothing but] becoming neglectful of God: it is not wealth, sons, or wife [which one considers material wealth.])

[11] *Fawa'id-u'l-Fu'ad*, p. 130.

currents of spiritual life. One should hold only the bare minimum and distribute the rest among the needy and the poor. Real happiness, according to him, lay not in accumulating money but in spending it.[12] He thought that there were three types of persons so far as involvement in material pursuits were concerned. 'First, those who want worldly goods and spend their days in search of them . . . Secondly, those who consider the world to be their enemy and speak disdainfully about it. Thirdly, those who consider the world neither an enemy nor a friend and do not refer to it either with enmity or friendship. They are the best of all.'[13] The Shaikh believed in following the last course—free from all unnecessary inner struggles and tensions.

PACIFISM AND NON-VIOLENCE

Shaikh Nizam-u'd-din Auliya was a firm believer in pacifism and non-violence. Violence, he said, created more problems than it solved. In forgiveness and large-hearted tolerance lay the supreme talisman of human happiness. 'If a man places a thorn in your way', he said, 'and you place another thorn in his way, it will be thorns everywhere.'[14] He advised his disciples to be good to their enemies also, and often recited the following verses of Shaikh Abu Sa'id Abu'l-Khair:[15]

هر که مارا یار نبـــــــود ایزد اورا یار باد

وانکه مارا رنجـــه دارد راحتش بسیار باد

هر که او در راه ما خارے نهد از دشمنی

هر گلے کز باغ عمرش بشکفد بے خار باد

(He who is not my friend—may God be his friend,
And he who bears ill-will against me may his joys [in life] increase.

---

[12] Ibid. p. 190.
[13] Ibid. p. 189.
[14] Ibid. pp. 86–7.
[15] Ibid.; *Durar-i-Nizami*, MS.

He who puts thorns in my way on account of enmity,
May every flower that blossoms in the garden of his life be without
thorns.)

BASIS OF HUMAN RELATIONSHIP

The Shaikh thought that a man could relate to others in any one of
three ways: (*a*) He could be neither good nor bad to others. This is
what happens in the non-living world (*jamadat*). (*b*) He could do no
harm to others but only what is good. (*c*) He could do good to others,
and if others do harm to him, remain patient and not retaliate. This
was the course adopted by the people of Reality, and he advised his
disciples to follow it.[16]

This approach was based on Sufi interpretation of human nature:
there is *nafs* (the material ego) and *qalb* (the soul). *Nafs* is the abode
of mischief, animosity, and strife; *qalb* is the centre of peace, resignation,
and good will. If a man acting under the influence of his *nafs* is dealt
with by responding under the direction of *qalb*, strife would end. On
the other hand, if *nafs* is met by *nafs*, there will be no end to strife and
enmities.[17]

Every human action covers the stages of *knowing, feeling,* and *willing*.[18]
All programmes of reform should be initiated at the stage of knowing.
True knowledge would lead to right action.

Not only in action but in thought also, the Shaikh preached an
approach of large-hearted forgiveness. In patience and tolerance he
saw the secret of social well-being. He advised his disciples thus:

If one man vents his wrath on another and the second man is patient,
the virtuous attitude belongs to him who is patient and not to him
who gives vent to his wrath.[19]

---

[16] *Fawa'id-u'l-Fu'ad*, p. 237.
[17] Ibid. p. 124.
[18] The Shaikh calls them *khatra, azimat,* and *fay'l*. Ibid. p. 18; *Siyar-u'l-Auliya*, pp. 565–7.
[19] *Fawa'id-u'l-Fu'ad*, p. 138.

He told his disciples that suppression of anger was not the right course, as it directed the virus to other channels of thought and action. His advice was: 'Forgive the person who has committed a wrong and thus eliminate your anger.'[20] Forgiveness rather than retribution was the reliable route to peace and happiness in society. The Shaikh said:

If there is a strife between two persons—say, between me and some other person—its solution is this: I should on my part, cleanse my heart of all ideas of revenge. If I succeed in doing that, the enemy's desire to do some harm to me would also be lessened.[21]

One day a person said to him: 'People speak ill of you from the pulpits and elsewhere. We cannot bear hearing it any longer.' The Shaikh replied:

I have forgiven them all. You also should forgive them, and not bear ill-will against them.[22]

Round these ideals of tolerance, forbearance, patience, and sympathy was built the entire structure of the spiritual discipline of Shaikh Nizam-u'd-din Auliya. He influenced the behaviour of his disciples through his own example. His moral and spiritual teachings may be thus summarized:

1. A spiritual mentor should not instruct his disciple openly, but use hints and suggestions to bring about change in his thought and behaviour.[23]
2. One who repents sincerely after committing a sin and one who has committed no sin hold an equal position in mystic discipline (*Fawa'id-u'l-Fu'ad*, pp. 2–3).
3. Lordship and slavery are not known to mystic life. A slave may succeed his master to the spiritual *gaddi* (Ibid. p. 4).

---

[20] *Siyar-u'l-Auliya*, pp. 552–6.
[21] Ibid. p. 555.
[22] *Fawa'id-u'l-Fu'ad*, p. 94.
[23] *Siyar-u'l-Auliya*, p. 349.

4. Though God's bounty is always there, whatever one can achieve is through the dint of his own effort (Ibid. p. 7). Under no circumstances can one earn anything without struggle.

5. Whatever one does not like for himself, he should not under any circumstances, recommend to others (Ibid. p. 8).

6. One should pitch his ambitions high and should not involve himself in material allurements. He should rise above sex and appetites (Ibid. p. 11).

7. One should scrupulously abstain from the display of his spiritual achievements (Ibid. p. 12).

8. Spiritual control and sobriety (*sahw*) is superior to (spiritual) intoxication (*sukr*) (Ibid. p. 13).

9. Food should be distributed to all and sundry, without discrimination (Ibid. p. 18).

10. Women are equally endowed with spiritual power and talent (Ibid. p. 22). They are equal to men in spiritual discipline.

11. Books of *masha'ikh* (spiritual mentors) should be regularly studied for enlightenment and culture (Ibid. p. 24).

12. Intention (motive) alone counts. One's intention should be good (Ibid).

13. Every work, spiritual or otherwise, appears difficult in the beginning but perseverance makes it easy.

14. Spiritual guidance and training should be received from one spiritual source (Ibid. p. 29). 'Hold one door and hold it fast', should be the guiding principle.

15. A miracle is like a screen (Ibid. p. 33) which obscures the reality from view.

16. Bread earned through permitted means provides greater spiritual enlightenment than livelihood obtained through doubtful means (Ibid. p. 40).

17. On the Day of Judgement one would be asked to give account of his earnings through permitted means and will be punished for earnings secured through dubious methods (Ibid).

18. Real pleasure lies not in the accumulation but in the distribution of wealth (Ibid. p. 49).

19. When one prays he should think of His mercy alone. He should neither brood over his penitences nor over his past sins (Ibid. p. 62).
20. Food should not be taken alone (Ibid. p. 67).
21. Fasting is half the prayer, the other half is patience (Ibid. p. 75).
22. Love of God and love of money cannot subsist in one heart (Ibid. p. 85).
23. Seclusion from human society is not desirable. One should mix with people and face their blows and buffeting (Ibid).
24. There should be no expression of anger when points of difference are discussed (Ibid. p. 86).
25. Malice and ill-will should be rooted out from the hearts (Ibid. p. 95).
26. One who serves becomes the master (Ibid. p. 98).
27. Resignation to the will of God is the real key to peace and satisfaction in life (Ibid. p. 101–2).
28. The purpose of prayer is to get rid of self-conceit. One who is egocentric and selfish cannot achieve anything spiritually (Ibid. p. 121).
29. Every wealth has its *zakah* (alms tax on surplus or stored wealth). The *zakah* of knowledge and learning is to act upon it (Ibid. p. 103).
30. God's relation with man is of '*adl* (justice) and *fazl* (bounty). Man's relationship with man is all '*adl, fazl,* and *zulm* (tyranny) (Ibid. p. 110).
31. Dishonest dealings lead to destruction of cities (Ibid. p. 116).
32. Self-criticism and disputing with one's self is better than seventy years of prayer (Ibid. p. 121).
33. Every visitor should be served something; if there is nothing to offer, a cup of water may be offered (Ibid. pp. 136–7).
34. One should be kind-hearted and should deal with people with clemency (Ibid. p. 146).
35. Prayers should be inspired neither by fear of hell nor by love of heaven. Love of God should be the only inspiring motive (Ibid. p. 152).

36. One should pray for the salvation of all. There should be no discrimination in it (Ibid. p. 162).
37. Honest dealings alone lead to lasting fame (Ibid. p. 164).
38. Poetry and scholarship are vain and valueless if used for praise and cajolery of others (Ibid. p. 182).
39. One who does not love children cannot treat grown-ups well (Ibid. p. 185).
40. One should hide, rather than disclose, the evil deeds of others (Ibid. p. 196).
41. Emancipation of slaves is an act of spiritual reward (Ibid. p. 202).
42. A man is in his worst state when he considers himself good and pious (Ibid. p. 216).

10

ATTITUDE TOWARDS THE SULTANS
AND THE STATE

The Chishti attitude towards the rulers and the State was firmly stated by Shaikh Farid Ganj-i-Shakar in these words: 'If you aim to achieve the [spiritual] position attained by [our] elders, keep away from the princes of the blood.'[1] The early saints of the Chishti order always kept this admonition in view. They not only gave a wide berth to the government of the day, but eschewed politics and *shughl* (government service) also. Stipends and grants (*idrar*) too were refused by them.[2]

This isolationist attitude of the early Sufis was based on a variety of considerations—pragmatic, legal, and historical. First, it was believed that government service created serious obstacles in the development of one's spiritual personality. It rendered attainment of gnosis (*ma'rifat*) impossible. Acceptance of government service thus virtually amounted to signing one's own spiritual death warrant. Secondly, the days when government service was a service of religion were long dead. It had become the service of dynastic and class interests. Thirdly, as Imam Ghazzali pointed out, almost the entire income of the Sultans was from prohibited sources—sources that had no sanction in *Shari'ah*.[3]

---

[1] *Siyar-u'l-Auliya*, p. 75.

[2] I have discussed the attitude of the early Indo-Muslim mystics towards the State in a series of articles published in *Islamic Culture*, Oct. 1948 to Jan. 1950.

[3] See *Ihya al-'Ulum* for a detailed analysis of the problem (Beirut: Dar al-Fikr, 1991), 2: 148–9.

Consequently, services paid from these sources were illegal. Fourthly, all Muslim political organizations, from the fall of the *Khilafat-i-Rashidah* to the rise of the Sultanate, were essentially secular organizations and had nothing to do with religious ideals. The government organization as well as the court life breathed an atmosphere absolutely alien to the true spirit of Islam. Face to face with this situation, argued Imam Ghazzali, the only course open was to keep away from kings. Fifthly, if a mystic associated himself with the governing class and the bureaucracy, he cut himself off completely from the main sphere of his activity—the masses. He ceased to be one of them and became part of a bureaucratic machinery. Sixthly, one could not help being infected by materialistic allurements and ambitions if he lived in the court and witnessed the grandeur and glory of the rulers. He was bound to be attracted towards a life of ease, pleasure, and plenty. Under the circumstances one who served a king could not consider his soul as his own. Shaikh Nizam-u'd-din Auliya brought home to his senior disciples the basic considerations involved in this approach through stories and anecdotes of the elder saints.[4]

This approach was not born of inertia, ignorance, or indifference to social problems. The mystics found government service a serious impediment to the realization of their objective to mitigate human misery and reduce sin. The rule to abjure government service was, however, confined to those senior disciples who had dedicated themselves to the spiritual work of the *silsilah*. There was no such restriction for those who were not granted *khilafat namah*s to carry further the work of spreading the *silsilah* and its teachings. Amir Khusrau and Amir Hasan Sijzi were associated with the court and so the Shaikh did not appoint them as his *khalifah*s. Considered purely from the social point of view, this isolationistic attitude of the Sufis towards the rulers provided them with time and energy to look to the social and spiritual needs of the people. A morally starved society, they believed,

---

[4] e.g., the Shaikh reported to his audience that Shaikh Abu Sa'id had earth dug out from those parts of his *khanqah* where the couriers from the ruler had placed their feet, *Fawa'id-u'l-Fu'ad*, p. 181.

could not survive for long. It was therefore incumbent upon some groups of people to concentrate on the moral and spiritual welfare of the people.

Shaikh Nizam-u'd-din Auliya followed the instructions of his elders in this regard and throughout his life kept away from the courts of kings and refused to accept *jagirs* and stipends from them. The *khilafat namah* which he granted to his senior disciples contained a clear instruction: 'You will not go to the doors of kings and will not seek their rewards.'[5] If anybody was suspected of the slightest disregard of this principle, he was sternly dealt with by the Shaikh. Qazi Muhi-u'd-din Kashani, a native of Awadh, was granted *khilafat* by the Shaikh. The *khilafat namah* contained the instruction:

> Reject the world and its transient glories and turn to God. Do not turn your attention to the world and worldly people. Do not accept grants of villages or the gifts of kings. If travellers come to you and you have nothing [to offer them] consider it one of the blessings of God . . .
> If you will act like this you are my *khalifah* (deputy) . . .[6]

Muhi-u'd-din's family had been a family of *qazis*. Sultan 'Ala-u'd-din Khalji sent a *farman* to him offering to make him the qazi of Awadh along with some *jagir* land and gifts. He came to Delhi with the *farman* to seek the Shaikh's advice. The Shaikh was distressed to learn this and said: 'There must have been some desire in your heart [for this post]. That is why this *farman* has come to you.'[7] He then took back the *khilafat namah* from him as a punishment and kept his *khilafat* in abeyance for a year. His view was that a person entrusted with the task of showing people the way to God could not involve himself in any government assignment without seriously jeopardizing his spiritual responsibilities.

Shaikh Nizam-u'd-din Auliya always remembered a few incidents in which his spiritual mentor had adopted a clear and firm attitude

---

[5] *Siyar-u'l-Auliya*, pp. 204, 295 *et seq.*
[6] Ibid. p. 295.
[7] Ibid.

towards contact with worldly authorities. Sayyidi Maula, a saint from Jurjan, came to India during the time of Balban and stayed at Ajodhan for some time with Shaikh Farid Ganj-i-Shakar. When he sought the Shaikh's permission to leave for Delhi, he said:

> Sayyidi! You are going to Delhi and wish to keep an open door and earn fame and honour. You know well what is good for you. But keep in mind one counsel of mine. Do not mix with the *amir*s and the *malik*s. Consider their visits to your house as calamitous. A saint who opens the door of association with *malik*s and *amir*s is doomed.[8]

Sayyidi Maula ignored Shaikh Farid's advice and got himself in trouble: Jalal-u'd-din Khalji had him crushed under the feet of an elephant as punishment for his involvement in baronial conspiracies. Another incident relates to Shaikh Badr-u'd-din Ghaznavi, a disciple of Shaikh Qutb-u'd-din Bakhtiyar Kaki. He had attached himself to Malik Nizam-u'd-din Kharitadar, who constructed a *khanqah* for him and undertook to bear all its expenses. Not long afterwards, the Kharitadar was thrown into prison on an embezzlement charge. This created a financial crisis in the *khanqah* of Shaikh Badr-u'd-din and in great distress he wrote to Shaikh Farid Ganj-i-Shakar soliciting his spiritual help in the matter. The Shaikh expressed his strong disapproval of the ways of Shaikh Badr-u'd-din and said that all this was due to his deviation from the tradition of his elder saints.[9]

ATTITUDE OF SULTAN JALAL-U'D-DIN KHALJI

Shaikh Nizam-u'd-din Auliya resolved early in life to follow the path shown by his spiritual master. During the reign of Balban he had already gained some fame, but by the time Jalal-u'd-din Khalji came to power he was a prominent figure in Delhi. The Sultan offered some villages for the expenses of his *khanqah*. The Shaikh declined, saying that it did not behove a dervish to have orchards and villages to look after. He put the matter before his disciples in order to test their determination

---

[8] Barani, *Tarikh-i-Firuz Shahi*, p. 209.
[9] *Fawa'id-u'l-Fu'ad*, p. 79; *Khair-u'l-Majalis*, p. 188.

to lead a life of penury and hunger. He appreciated the spirit of those, particularly the Kirmanis, who were firmly opposed to the offer. This decision set the tone of his *khanqah* in the years that followed. Sultan Jalal-u'd-din sought an interview with the Shaikh but it was politely refused. The Sultan then thought of visiting the *khanqah* without informing the Shaikh. 'My house has two doors,' remarked the Shaikh, 'if the Sultan enters by one, I will make my exit by the other.' The Sultan planned a surprise visit to the Shaikh. Amir Khusrau, who was the Sultan's *mushafdar* (keeper of the royal copy of the Qur'an), reported this to the Shaikh, who avoided meeting the Sultan by undertaking a journey to the tomb of his spiritual mentor at Ajodhan. When the Sultan came to know about the divulgence of this secret by Amir Khusrau, he took him to task for it. 'In disobeying the Sultan I stood in danger of losing my life, but in playing false to my master, I stood in danger of losing my faith,' replied Amir Khusrau.[10] Jalal-u'd-din was dumbfounded.

SURROUNDED BY NOBLES

While Shaikh Nizam-u'd-din Auliya had closed his doors to the Sultan, he could not restrain the nobles, *malik*s, government officers, military men and others from visiting him in order to seek his blessings.[11] The Shaikh was in good spirits when he was with the poor and the destitute, but when thronged by nobles and officers he would sadly remark: 'These people waste the time of this *faqir*.'[12] However, it appears that many princes, *malik*s, and others had joined his spiritual discipline.

THE SHAIKH AND SULTAN 'ALA-U'D-DIN KHALJI

When 'Ala-u'd-din Khalji came to power, Shaikh Nizam-u'd-din Auliya's fame and popularity were at their highest level. In addition to the common people—who came to him in large numbers—princes,

---

[10] *Siyar-u'l-Auliya*, p. 135.

[11] Barani, *Tarikh-i-Firuz Shahi*, p. 345. See also *Qiwam-u'l-'Aqa'id*, MS pp. 25, 176 *et seq.*, particularly chapters VI and VII, which deal with the devotion of nobles, *malik*s, and Sultans to the Shaikh.

[12] *Siyar-u'l-Auliya*, p. 131.

courtiers, soldiers, government officers, merchants, and scholars also visited his hospice and sought his blessings. Some government officers gave up their jobs on joining his discipline and concentrated on the culture of their soul.[13] Some hostile courtiers mischievously suggested to the Sultan that the Shaikh's popularity had grave political dangers. In order to pry into the saint's intentions, 'Ala-u'd-din wrote a letter to him offering to be guided by his advice in all matters. The Shaikh did not even care to open this letter, which was delivered to him by Khizr Khan. 'We dervishes have nothing to do with the affairs of the state,' he replied, 'I have settled in a corner away from the men of the city and spend my time praying for the Sultan and other Muslims. If the Sultan does not like this, let him tell me so. I will go and live elsewhere. God's earth is spacious enough.'[14] This reply convinced the Sultan that the Shaikh had no political ambitions. That suspicion once set aside, the Khalji Sultan showed great respect for the saint and developed faith in his spiritual excellence.

SPIES IN THE *KHANQAH*

It appears from the *Qiwam-u'l-'Aqa'id* that at one stage Sultan 'Ala-u'd-din Khalji had sent spies to the *khanqah* to report about its functioning, particularly the nature and extent of free food (*langar*) distributed to the people. The Sultan, who did not permit even two persons to sit at a place for a feast, was disturbed at the mass feasts of the *khanqah*. One day the Shaikh was informed that a person sitting near Khwaja Muhammad Imam was an informer (*mukhbir*).[15] The Shaikh said nothing to him, but ordered the addition of a dish of rice (*tahiri*)[16] to the menu normally served. The Sultan was displeased at the functioning of the *langar*. His displeasure was reported to the Shaikh who did not utter a word on hearing it but called Mubashshir and ordered that for those who fasted, the *sahri* (food taken before dawn)

---

[13] e.g., Khwaja Mubarak Gopamavi (*Siyar-u'l-Auliya*, p. 310), and Khwaja Mu'in-u'd-din (*Siyar-u'l-Auliya*, p. 311).

[14] Ibid. pp. 133–4.

[15] *Qiwam-u'l-'Aqa'id*, MS p. 177.

[16] *Tahiri*: a dish of rice cooked with *bari* (pulse). See *Farhang-i-Asafiya*, III p. 239.

should further include cake (*qurs*), pudding (*halwa*), and savoury pastries (*samosa*).[17] The Sultan, however, did not react to it. The otherworldly atmosphere of the *khanqah* was so obvious that he did not press matters further. His suspicion gradually faded away. It is very significant that, despite all his regulations of rationing and control he did not interfere in the functioning of the *langar* in the *khanqah* of Shaikh Nizam-u'd-din Auliya.[18]

Zia-u'd-din Barani informs us:

Although the Sultan never met the Shaikh, he never uttered throughout his reign a single word about the Shaikh that could have annoyed him in any way. The enemies of the Shaikh and those jealous of him reported with considerable exaggeration to such a jealous king [as 'Ala-u'd-din] about the great gifts of the Shaikh, the crowd of people frequenting his place and the Shaikh's feeding of the people and his generosity towards them. But 'Ala-u'd-din paid no attention to what they said about him. In the last days of his reign he became a sincere and firm believer in the Shaikh. Nevertheless the two never met.[19]

KHIZR KHAN AND SHADI KHAN JOIN THE DISCIPLINE

Once Sultan 'Ala-u'd-din Khalji was satisfied about the intent and scope of the Shaikh's humanitarian activities and his concern for the moral and spiritual welfare of society, he developed a respectful attitude towards him.[20] He sent Khizr Khan and Shadi Khan to become his disciples.[21] The princes came again and again to the *khanqah* and pleaded with the saint to admit them to his discipline, but the Shaikh was adamant. He told the princes:

You are sons of the king and are privileged to use the royal *chatr* (parasol). Governance and military campaigns and conquest of realms

---

[17] *Qiwam-u'l-'Aqa'id*, MS pp. 179–80.
[18] For 'Ala-u'd-din's restrictions on assembly and feasts among nobles, see *Tarikh-i-Firuz Shahi*, p. 286.
[19] Ibid. p. 332.
[20] *Qiwam-u'l-'Aqa'id*, MS pp. 179–80.
[21] Ibid. MS pp. 163–4, 180.

suits your position. On the other hand this is the house of poverty, humility, abstinence, and self-abasement. You cannot stand [the strain of] it.[22]

When they persisted in their request, the Shaikh told them to consult their father again and obtain his permission. When 'Ala-u'd-din Khalji joined the princes in their request, the Shaikh admitted them to his discipline.[23]

Thereafter the princes obtained the Shaikh's permission to arrange a feast at an open space in Ghiyaspur. It was a big feast for which preparations were made for seven nights and days, and distinguished nobles and *maliks* were deputed by the Sultan to make arrangements and to serve food. The princes were directed by the Sultan to circulate the ewer (*tasht*) and the washbasins (*aftaba*) themselves and serve personally sherbet and betel leaves.[24] Purses containing gold and silver coins were put before the guests by the princes. It appears that in addition to Khizr Khan and Shadi Khan, other princes also—four or five in number—were present there. The Shaikh came to the feast. The feast being over, *sama'* was arranged. The Shaikh left the function at the time of the midday prayer.[25]

Khizr Khan once presented to the Shaikh a rosary of precious jewels, every bead of which, according to Muhammad Jamal, was such as one could buy a whole city for it. The Shaikh accepted it but when he came to know that these were all gems, he threw it away in the courtyard.[26]

THE QUEEN'S FAITH IN THE SHAIKH

It appears that the Malika Jahan, mother of these princes, had also developed faith in the Shaikh. She told the princes to request from the Shaikh some token of blessing for her. The Shaikh asked Iqbal to bring some pieces of bread, which he gave for the Malika Jahan.[27]

---

[22] Ibid. p. 180.
[23] Ibid. p. 181.
[24] Ibid. p. 185.
[25] Ibid.
[26] Ibid. p. 206.
[27] Ibid. p. 164.

Another wife of the Sultan, a daughter of Sultan Mu'izz-u'd-din, gave a huge amount in charity to a person who was worried about the marriage of his daughters, when she came to know that he was associated with the Shaikh.[28]

'ALA-U'D-DIN'S FAITH IN THE SHAIKH

It is sometimes suggested that Sultan 'Ala-u'd-din Khalji had no special regard for or faith in Shaikh Nizam-u'd-din Auliya. Barani's remark— that while travellers and pilgrims from thousands of miles came to meet Shaikh Nizam-u'd-din Auliya, and the young and the old of the city, both scholars and illiterates paid visits of respect to him, 'it never crossed 'Ala-u'd-din's mind to call on the Shaikh or to request him to come to him and meet him'[29]—is cited in support of this view. But the conclusion drawn is not justified. Barani himself states in two places that (a) In the last days of his reign 'Ala-u'd-din became a sincere and firm believer in the Shaikh, though the two did not have an opportunity to meet;[30] and that (b) Sultan 'Ala-u'd-din, along with his family, became a firm believer in the Shaikh.[31]

His earlier statement is just an expression of his amazement that 'Ala-u'd-din Khalji made no special effort to visit the Shaikh or adopt some device to have an interview with him. In fact 'Ala-u'd-din knew the Shaikh's attitude in this respect and he did not ask for something that went against the convictions of the Shaikh. That the Sultan and his nobles held the Shaikh in deep respect is clear from the following incidents recorded in *Tarikh-i-Firuz Shahi*, *Fawa'id-u'l-Fu'ad*, *Siyar-u'l-Auliya*, and *Qiwam-u'l-'Aqa'id*:

1. Malik Naib was sent on the southern campaign by the Sultan. For forty days he received no information about the welfare of the army. The Sultan was very anxious and the *amirs* and *maliks* in Delhi began to suspect that the army had either revolted or

---

[28] Ibid. pp. 133–4.
[29] *Tarikh-i-Firuz Shahi*, p. 366.
[30] Ibid. p. 332.
[31] Ibid. p. 345.

been defeated. The Sultan sent Malik Qara Beg and Qazi Mughis-u'd-din of Bayana[32] to the Shaikh and told them: 'Convey my respects to Shaikh Nizam-u'd-din and tell him that my mind is anxious owing to lack of any news of the army of Islam.[33] You have more concern for Islam than I have. If owing to the inner light of your mind anything has been revealed to you about the condition of the army, send me the good news.' The Sultan also told the messengers that after conveying his message they were to report to him exactly every story or incident that the Shaikh narrated.[34] The Shaikh, after hearing the message, narrated a story about the victories and conquests of a king. And after a time he said to the messengers: 'What is this victory? I am waiting for further victories.' The messengers reported this to 'Ala-u'd-din who was immensely pleased on hearing these words of the Shaikh. He tied a corner of his handkerchief into a knot and said : 'I have taken the words of the Shaikh for a good omen. I know that no vain words would come from the tongue of the Shaikh. Warangal has been conquered and I should expect further victories.' Soon afterwards reports of victory came and 'the Sultan's faith in the spiritual greatness of the Shaikh increased.'[35]

Amir Khusrau has described in *Khaza'in-u'l-Futuh* how the enormous booty brought from the south by Malik Naib was displayed on *Chabutrah-i-Nasiri*.[36] The next day the Shaikh spoke about wealth in his assembly and said that it should be used for the good of the people.[37]

2. Amir Hasan records on 19 Jumada-u'l-Awwal, 713/11 September 1313 that grants of orchards, land, and other enormous gifts came to the Shaikh. The Shaikh refused to accept them and said that none of the elder saints of his *silsilah* had accepted such

---

[32] According to *Qiwam-u'l-'Aqa'id* (p. 186), it was Maulana Hamid-u'd-din Sadr-i-Jahan who was sent by the Sultan.

[33] The number of the army is given as 50,000 in *Qiwam-u'l-'Aqa'id* (p. 186).

[34] According to *Qiwam-u'l-'Aqa'id* (p. 188), the Sultan enquired later about the stories mentioned by the Shaikh.

[35] *Tarikh-i-Firuz Shahi*, pp. 331–2; *Qiwam-u'l-'Aqa'id*, MS pp. 185–9.

[36] *Khaza'in-u'l-Futuh* (Calcutta, 1953), p. 112.

[37] *Fawa'id-u'l-Fu'ad*, p. 49.

things.[38] Significantly enough Sultan 'Ala-u'd-din, who had resumed all grants[39] of land and was not in favour of such grants, made an exception in the case of the Shaikh.[40]

3. Khwaja Muiyyid-u'd-din of Kara was in the service of Prince 'Ala-u'd-din who liked him very much. On ascending the throne he called him to the court, but by now he had become a disciple of the Shaikh and lived the life of a dervish. 'Ala-u'd-din sent his messenger to the Shaikh to request him to send Khwaja Muiyyid-u'd-din to the court. The Shaikh declined. The messenger was peeved. He told the Shaikh: 'Revered Sir! You want to make others also like you.' 'No, better than myself,' replied the Shaikh. The Sultan did not press his request further.[41]

4. Malik Qiran, the Amir-i-Shikar, was one of the trusted nobles of 'Ala-u'd-din Khalji. He joined the discipline of Shaikh Nizam-u'd-din Auliya and offered to pay off the debt of any disciple of the Shaikh who stood in need of financial help. All through his life he stood by his pledge and cleared debts without any hesitation. Khwaja Taj-u'd-din had to pay 500 *tankas* to his creditors, but did not want to approach him. Somebody informed Malik Qiran about it and he sent the amount to him. Throughout his life he disbursed his earnings in charity,[42] inspired by the teachings of the Shaikh.

5. Malik Husam-u'd-din Qalagh was a sister's son of 'Ala-u'd-din Khalji.[43] He became a disciple of Shaikh Nizam-u'd-din Auliya and beseeched the Shaikh to visit his house. The Shaikh agreed. Malik Husam-u'd-din collected all his belongings—property, horses, gold, silver, precious stones, etc.—and divided them into two parts: one he gave to his mother; the other half he doled out in charity in the name of his spiritual master. He set free all

---

[38] Ibid. pp. 98–9.

[39] *Tarikh-i-Firuz Shahi*, p. 283.

[40] The Sultan made a similar exemption in the case of Rashid-u'd-din Fazlullah to whom he gave some villages in *inam*: the revenues of these villages were remitted to the Ilkhanid *wazir* in Hamadan, *Mukatabat-i-Rashidi*, pp. 166–7.

[41] *Siyar-u'l-Auliya*, p. 311.

[42] *Qiwam-u'l-'Aqa'id*, MS p. 232.

[43] Ibid.

his slaves to commemorate the visit of his Shaikh. The Shaikh came there seated in a palanquin (*dolah*) and had to cross two or three courtyards before he reached the meeting hall. Costly carpets (of *nasich* and *deba*) were spread out on which the carriers of the palanquin were to place their feet. These carpets were given to the bearers of the *dolah*. The Shaikh blessed him.[44]

6. Mali Qir Bak was another eminent noble of 'Ala-u'd-din Khalji. One day a visitor sought the Shaikh's help in connection with the marriage of his two daughters. The Shaikh wrote a prayer on a piece of paper and gave it to him with instructions to take it to Qir Bak. Qir Bak had made arrangements for the marriage of his own daughter, and transferred everything to the person sent by the Shaikh. When Qir Bak attended the court the next day, 'Ala-u'd-din Khalji enquired about it. Though puzzled about how the Sultan came to know about it at all, Qir Bak narrated the whole incident. 'Ala-u'd-din appreciated his gesture and bestowed on him wealth ten times more than he had given.[45]

7. Maulana Sharaf-u'd-din Jamakal [*sic*] was the teacher of a nephew of 'Ala-u'd-din Khalji. He repeatedly requested the Shaikh to enrol him among his disciples, but the saint refused. In order to draw attention, he thought of a plan: he had some food cooked, put the pot on his head and, with a rope tied round his neck, passed through the streets covering a distance of more than a mile, and then reached the *khanqah*. The Shaikh called him in and admitted him into his discipline.[46]

8. Maulana 'Ala-u'd-din, a pious and erudite scholar, was appointed Qazi of Jhain by Sultan 'Ala-u'd-din Khalji. He was associated with the Suhrawardi order. A noble was brought before him charged with offences that could be punished by death. The Qazi had him executed. When the Sultan heard about his execution, he was furious. He ordered that the Qazi be brought to him in chains and fetters. On his way to the court, he somehow

---

[44] Ibid. pp. 233–4.
[45] Ibid. pp. 234–5.
[46] Ibid. pp. 50–1.

persuaded his custodians to take him to the Shaikh, who prayed for his exoneration as he had acted according to the *Shari'ah*. The next day he was produced before the Sultan who unexpectedly set him free and indeed conferred a robe of honour on him.[47]

9. Shaikh Nizam-u'd-din's spiritual help was extended to Sultan 'Ala-u'd-din when Qutlugh Khwaja invaded Delhi with a huge army[48] and the battle of Kili took place. It appears from *Fawa'id-u'l-Fu'ad* that the Shaikh remained in the city during the days of the battle.[49] Jamal Qiwam-u'd-din would have us believe that even Qutlugh Khwaja had developed faith in the Shaikh. Qutlugh's orders were that nobody should take horses into India, and 'Ala-u'd-din's orders were that no slaves should be taken to the Mongol lands. An Indian purchased horses in Mongol territories intending to smuggle them into India. He was caught and presented before Qutlugh Khwaja who, according to Qiwam-u'd-din, excused him when he mentioned the name of Shaikh Nizam-u'd-din Auliya as his spiritual mentor. 'On returning home,' he resolved, 'I will repent before the Shaikh for my lapse.'[50]

EXECUTIONS OF KHIZR KHAN AND SHADI KHAN

The closing years of 'Ala-u'd-din Khalji's reign were marked by rapid decline of his royal authority and the rise of Malik Kafur as a power behind the throne. Anxious to consolidate his position, Malik Kafur removed important nobles from the scene, and imprisoned Khizr Khan and Shadi Khan in the Gwalior fort. 'Ala-u'd-din died on 7 Shawwal 715/4 January 1316. His body had not yet been lowered in his grave when Malik Kafur dispatched Malik Sumbul to Gwalior to remove the eyes of the princes. Mubarak Khalji ascended the throne on 20 Muharram 716/14 April 1316. During the interregnum of about

---

[47] Ibid. pp. 60–1.
[48] Ibid. pp. 110–11.
[49] *Fawa'id-u'l-Fu'ad*, p. 145.
[50] *Qiwam-u'l-'Aqa'id*, MS p. 109.

three months Kafur raised a child, Shihab-u'd-din 'Umar, to the throne and ruthlessly applied himself to the liquidation of the family of 'Ala-u'd-din Khalji.

The execution of the blinded princes[51] was carried out on the orders of Mubarak in 1318. The details of their ghastly end are appalling. When evil days fell on Khizr Khan and Shadi Khan and their eyes were taken out of their sockets, somebody asked them: 'Of what use has been your faith in the Shaikh?' The reply of the princes, as quoted by Muhammad Jamal Qiwam-u'd-din, was:

O misguided prosecutor! This [association with the Shaikh] has caused [us] neither any loss nor ill fortune. On the contrary, due to the blessings accruing from the discipleship to the Shaikh, we have been saved from the evil effect of involvement in this sordid world and from shedding innocent blood and illegally usurping the property of others. He [the Shaikh] thus relieved us from the Qur'anic threat (4: 93): 'If a man kills a believer intentionally, his recompense is hell, to abide therein.' He also saved us from the punishment laid down in the Qur'an (4: 10): 'Those who unjustly eat up the property of orphans, eat up a fire into their own bodies: they will soon be enduring a blazing Fire.' If eyesight has been taken away from us and the inner light has been opened [in our hearts], it is all due to the blessings of the Shaikh and because we held his hand as his disciples and entrusted all our affairs to him. We hope that tomorrow on the Day of Judgement we shall be under the banner of the Shaikh.'[52]

During the years 715–19/1315–19, a period of alarming political developments, Hasan Sijzi recorded sixty-two conversations of the Shaikh. It is difficult to find in them any reaction from the Shaikh to these developments, particularly the fate of Khizr Khan and Shadi Khan. The Shaikh never discussed political events in his assemblies. Rulers came to the throne and disappeared; princes struggled for succession; nobles won and lost the confidence of rulers, but the Shaikh never turned his attention to the drama of their rise and fall.

---

[51] *Tarikh-i-Firuz Shahi*, p. 393.
[52] *Qiwam-u'l-'Aqa'id*, MS p. 190.

RELATIONS WITH SULTAN MUBARAK KHALJI

Mubarak Khalji, vain fulsome mediocrity that he was, departed from the tradition of his father in all spheres. He assumed the title of *Khalifah*, something no previous Sultan had done, and declared Delhi as *Dar-u'l-Khilafah*.[53] He developed ill-will towards Shaikh Nizam-u'd-din Auliya because he had been the spiritual mentor of Khizr Khan.[54] He adopted an independent, aggressive attitude towards the Shaikh and started using foul language about him in the court. Arrogant and impudent, he offered a reward of one thousand *tanka*s to whomever brought him the head of the Shaikh.[55]

THE ATTITUDE OF THE NOBLES

Mubarak issued orders banning the visit of *amir*s and *malik*s to the *khanqah* of the Shaikh. He was under the impression that this would dry up the sources of his income and lead to the collapse of his *langar* establishment. But this did not happen. According to Shaikh Nasir-u'd-din Chiragh, the Sultan enquired about the kitchen of the Shaikh and, on being informed that its expenditure had doubled, regretted his move.[56]

The story of Talbagh Yaghda, a noble with Mubarak, is significant in this context and reveals the attitude of the Shaikh during this period. He presented one hundred gold *tanka*s to the Shaikh, who declined to accept them. He felt depressed, whereupon the Shaikh agreed to take just one coin. He insisted on more but the Shaikh would not yield,[57] perhaps because he did not want the Sultan or his nobles to think that their gifts kept the *langar* going. Tablagh Yaghda had great respect for the Shaikh and was influenced by his traditions of generosity and large-heartedness in helping the poor. He used to get 70,000 *tanka*s as his emoluments during the time of Mubarak and spent the whole amount in charity on the needy and the poor.[58]

---

[53] *Nuh Sipihr*, p. 77.
[54] *Tarikh-i-Firuz Shahi*, p. 395.
[55] Ibid. p. 396.
[56] *Khair-u'l-Majalis*, p. 258.
[57] Ibid. p. 257. See also *Qiwam-u'l-'Aqa'id*, MS p. 200.
[58] Ibid. p. 231.

Muhammad Jamal says that one day in a state of intoxication Mubarak asked Tablagh Yaghda to take off the cap that symbolizes of his association with Shaikh Nizam-u'd-din Auliya. The Sultan asked him thrice and even took out his sword but the *malik* would not dishonour the cap bestowed upon him by his spiritual mentor. It is said that the Sultan was pleased with his steadfastness and said: 'Bravo Tablagh Yaghda! A *murid* should be like this.'[59] He then increased his emoluments and conferred a robe of honour on him. Tablagh reported the matter to Shaikh Nizam-u'd-din Auliya and offered the entire money he had received from the Sultan for the expenses of the kitchen. The Shaikh asked Iqbal to bring something for Tablagh Yaghda. Iqbal brought a handful of gold *tanka*s and threw them in Yaghda's lap. The Shaikh then returned the money Yaghda had presented with the remark: 'This is not needed.'[60]

The attitude of Amir Khusrau also deserves to be mentioned in this context. Notwithstanding all the ill-will that the Sultan had for the Shaikh, he paid eloquent tribute to his spiritual master in *Nuh Sipihr*[61] — a *masnawi* written for the Sultan and presented to him. How the Sultan reacted to this is not known, but it is certain that he had realized the limits to which he could expect the nobility to cooperate with him in this matter.

THE SULTAN'S MEASURES TO HUMILIATE THE SAINT

Bent upon humiliating the Shaikh, the Sultan sent a message to him saying : 'Shaikh Rukn-u'd-din comes to see me all the way from Multan. How is it that you, though living in Delhi, do not come to the court?' The Shaikh apologized and said that it was not the practice of his elder saints to attend the court.[62] The Sultan's repeated efforts to meddle in the Shaikh's peaceful life eventually annoyed him and he sent Hasan 'Ali Sijzi to the Sultan's *pir*, Shaikh Zia-u'd-din Rumi,[63] with the message: 'You should advise the Sultan against annoying the dervishes, as his

---

[59] Ibid. p. 199.
[60] Ibid. p. 200.
[61] *Nuh Sipihr*, pp. 23–8.
[62] *Siyar-u'l-'Arifin*, p. 75.
[63] For Shaikh Zia-u'd-din Rumi, see *Akhbar-u'l-Akhyar*, p. 62.

safety in both the worlds depends on his not doing so.'[64] But as Shaikh
Rumi was ill, the message could not be delivered. A few days later,
Shaikh Rumi died and the Sultan and the Shaikh came face to face at
the *siyyum*[65] of Shaikh Zia-u'd-din Rumi. Mubarak Khalji assumed an
attitude of arrogance and did not even acknowledge the Shaikh's
greetings.[66]

MUBARAK'S DISSOLUTE LIFE AND THE SHAIKH'S ADVICE

Mubarak lapsed into licentiousness and debauchery soon after his accession. All sorts of undesirable characters—eunuchs, ribald and dissolute
women, courtesans and boys—surrounded him, and he himself put
on female attire and indulged in revelries.[67] Shaikh Nizam-u'd-din Auliya,
despite the strained relations between them, could not help advising
him when he saw him at the *siyyum* of Shaikh Zia-u'd-din. He recited
before him the following tradition of the Prophet:

Whoever sits in the company even for a short while will be inter-
rogated by God as to whether he fulfilled the obligation to God in
that company.[68]

It is not known how the Sultan reacted to it, but the Tradition quoted
contained much relevant counsel, had he been minded to heed it.

THE SULTAN'S MEASURES TO DIMINISH
THE SHAIKH'S POPULARITY

What most exasperated the Sultan was the Shaikh's popularity, and
he resorted to various devices to pull the Shaikh down in public estima-
tion. He summoned Shaikh Rukn-u'd-din Abu'l-Fath from Multan

---

[64] *Siyar-u'l-'Arifin*, pp. 75–6.

[65] A gathering on the third day after a death to recite the Qur'an and pray for blessings on
the soul of the departed.

[66] The accounts of this meeting differ. Barani says that the Sultan did not return the Shaikh's
greetings (p. 396). Jamali (p. 76), Ferishta (p. 35), and others say that the Shaikh himself
refrained from greeting the Sultan and explained his action by saying 'as he is reciting the
Qur'an, there is no need of offering compliments to him.' Barani's account deserves greater
credence.

[67] *Tarikh-i-Firuz Shahi*, p. 396.

[68] *Siyar-u'l-Auliya*, p. 558; *Durar-i-Nizami*, MS.

in order to turn the public away from him.[69] But Shaikh Rukn-u'd-din was an old friend of Shaikh Nizam-u'd-din Auliya and considered him 'the best man in Delhi'. The Sultan's scheme failed.[70] He then set up one Shaikhzada Jam, an opponent of Shaikh Nizam-u'd-din Auliya,[71] as an officially sponsored saint to whom people were expected to pay homage, ignoring Shaikh Nizam-u'd-din Auliya. This ruse did not work either as people continued to visit Shaikh Nizam-u'd-din's *khanqah* as before.

REFUSAL TO OFFER PRAYERS AT MASJID-I-MIRI

The Sultan built a mosque, called Masjid-i-Miri, in Delhi and invited the leading men of the capital to join at the first congregational prayer there. The Shaikh was also invited but he apologized, saying: 'The mosque nearest my house has greater claims upon me.'[72] The Sultan was vexed by this reply, but the Shaikh remained determined not to budge from his position.

REFUSAL TO VISIT THE COURT TO GREET THE KING

There was a custom in Delhi that on the first day of the month, *'Ulama*, saints, and nobles assembled in the court to offer their greetings and good wishes to the Sultan. The Shaikh, however, never went to felicitate 'Ala-u'd-din Khalji and the Sultan for his part never expected it from him. Mubarak Khalji, however, insisted on the Shaikh's presence at the court. The Shaikh sent his servant, Iqbal, to represent him.[73] The Sultan took this as an affront and threatened to punish the Shaikh if he did not come to the palace in person the following month. The Sultan sent Syed Qutb-u'd-din Ghaznavi, Shaikh 'Imad-u'd-din Tusi, Shaikh Wahid-u'd-din Qanzi, Maulana Burhan-u'd-din, and others to

---

[69] *Tarikh-i-Firuz Shahi*, p. 396; *Qiwam-u'l-'Aqa'id*, II MS p. 75; *A'in-i-Akbari*, II p. 209; *Akhbar-u'l-Akhyar*, p. 64.

[70] *Siyar-u'l-'Arifin*, p. 136. He had such regard for Shaikh Nizam-u'd-din that he renewed his ablution *(wuzu)* when he went to see the saint. See *Qiwam-u'l-'Aqa'id*, MS p. 77.

[71] *Tarikh-i-Firuz Shahi*, p. 396.

[72] *Siyar-u'l-'Auliya*, p. 150.

[73] *Siyar-u'l-'Arifin*, p. 151.

warn the Shaikh about the consequences of non-compliance with his orders.[74] When people heard about the Sultan's intention to punish him on that count, there was a civic commotion in Delhi. The Shaikh, however, did not give way to worry and behaved with patience. But one day he went to his mother's grave, shed tears there, and said: 'If the Sultan's life does not end by the first of the next lunar month, I won't come to you again.'[75] Thoughtful people sensed great disaster in the tussle between the saint and the Sultan. When the day approached, men who had the courage to make a point before the Shaikh on such a delicate issue requested him to proceed to the court as the Sultan was a reckless youth and could take any rash action, regardless of consequences. Compliance with the order could avert the crisis. The Shaikh did not heed their advice and kept quiet. When they persisted, the Shaikh told them: 'Last night I saw in my dream a bull rushing towards me. I caught hold of its horns and pushed it back.'[76] The disciples interpreted this dream as an indication that no harm would come to the Shaikh and were for the moment satisfied. Iqbal twice sought permission to bring the palanquin (*palki*) but the Shaikh firmly told him: 'Do something else.' Some people suggested that the Shaikh turn to the soul of Shaikh Farid Ganj-i-Shakar and seek his help in the matter. 'I feel ashamed of turning to my Shaikh about a worldly affair,' he replied.[77] Residents of the *khanqah* and the people of Delhi spent several hours of anxious suspense and feared summons from the court at any moment, but things moved in a different direction. Hardly a few hours had passed when Mubarak Shah met his end at the hands of the Parwaris.

The murder of the Sultan, the pious Amir Khurd would have us believe, was due to the prayers of the Shaikh, not to the crime of the Parwaris. 'The decision of such problems,' Professor Mohammed Habib has rightly observed, 'is fortunately beyond the province of the historian.'[78]

---

[74] Ibid. pp. 76–7.
[75] *Siyar-u'l-Auliya*, p. 151.
[76] Ibid. p. 80.
[77] *Siyar-u'l-'Arifin*, p. 77.
[78] *Hazrat Amir Khusrau of Delhi*, p. 40.

SHAIKH NIZAM-U'D-DIN AULIYA AND SULTAN GHIYAS-U'D-DIN TUGHLUQ

Shaikh Nizam-u'd-din Auliya's relations with Sultan Ghiyas-u'd-din Tughluq were far from cordial. The reasons for this estrangement are given as follows:

> First, when Khusrau Khan came to power after the assassination of Mubarak, he distributed huge sums of money among the saints and *'Ulama* of Delhi in his eagerness to win their confidence and goodwill. He sent 50,000 *tanka*s to Shaikh Nizam-u'd-din Auliya. He accepted the gift[79] and, as was the practice of his *khanqah*, disbursed the money among the needy and the poor. When Ghiyas-u'd-din Tughluq came to power, he asked all the recipients of Khusrau Khan's favours to refund the money. Some saints complied with the order but when Shaikh Nizam-u'd-din Auliya was approached, he told the royal emissaries that the money belonged to the public treasury (*bait-u'l-mal*) and he had, therefore, distributed it among the people. This reply is said to have offended the Sultan.

Secondly, the Shaikh, following the tradition of the earlier saints of the *silsilah*, used to hold audition parties (*sama'*). The *'Ulama* objected to this. Shaikhzada Husam-u'd-din Farjam and Qazi Jalal-u'd-din Soranji, *Naib Hakim-i-Mumlakat*, worked up the orthodox sentiments of the Sultan and persuaded him to take action against the Shaikh. The Sultan convened a meeting (*mahzar*) of the *'Ulama* to discuss issue. The Shaikh attended this meeting[80] and, despite all the unpleasant discussion that took place between him and the *'Ulama*, the *'Ulama* did not succeed in persuading the Sultan to promulgate any order against the mystic

---

[79] Perhaps it was the acceptance of this money by the Shaikh which led Dr R. P. Tripathi to observe: 'There is also reason to think that he [Khusrau] had the moral support of Shaikh Nizamuddin who exercised considerable influence over the people' (*Some Aspects of Muslim Administration*, p. 54). But this conjecture is not warranted in view of the Shaikh's well-known aversion to rulers and politics.

[80] This was the first and last occasion that the great Shaikh attended the Delhi court. It should be remembered that he was summoned to the court to explain a matter involving interpretation of *Shari'ah*. In his mind he attended not a Sultan's court, but a *Shari'ah* court.

practice, though audition parties in public were discouraged. It is said that the incident led to estrangement between the saint and the Sultan.

Thirdly, it is said that when the Sultan was coming back from his Bengal expedition, he sent an order to the Shaikh to quit Delhi before he reached the capital. On receiving the imperial order, the Shaikh is reported to have remarked: 'Delhi is still far off' (*Hunuz Dilli dur ast*).[81] Elaborate arrangements were made by Prince Juna Khan, the future Muhammad bin Tughluq, for the reception of the Sultan at Afghanpur. The wooden pavilion which had been hastily constructed to receive the Sultan suddenly collapsed, and the Sultan was buried under the debris.[82]

These incidents have led some historians to emphasize the hostility between the Shaikh and the Sultan, though Barani and Amir Khurd do not say anything concerning unpleasantness between them. The following aspects of the problem may, however, be considered:

1. The Shaikh's acceptance of Khusrau Khan's gift, and his subsequent inability to reimburse the money to the state treasury, could not have led to the bitterness some writers have read into the incident. The Sultan must have known the Shaikh fairly well as he was deeply respected by the Delhi public and by the preceding Sultans. Ghiyas-u'd-din was an old servant of the state and could hardly have been ignorant of the practice of the Shaikh's *khanqah*. Whatever *futuh* reached there was immediately distributed among the poor and the needy who thronged there. The saint's failure to reimburse the money could not be a reason for displeasure. However, it remains a possibility that it was the acceptance of the gift in the first place that annoyed the Sultan.

2. The *sama'* episode, as narrated by Amir Khurd, shows no ostensible hostility between the Sultan and the saint. But the entire atmosphere in which the *mahzar* proceedings were conducted, and the behaviour of the externalist scholars towards the Shaikh in the royal presence—in particular their refusal to listen to the traditions

---

[81] *Tarikh-i-Mubarak Shahi*, p. 97.
[82] *Tarikh-i-Firuz Shahi*, p. 452.

of the Prophet that the latter wanted to cite—gives the impression that all this happened with the connivance of the Sultan. The Shaikh returned from the court disgusted and exasperated, but on account of the *'Ulama* rather more than the Sultan.

3. So far as the last incident is concerned, some writers have expressed the opinion that the Shaikh died before the Afghanpur tragedy took place. But this is not correct. Ghiyas-u'd-din Tughluq died some time in the month of Rabi'-u'l-Awwal 725 AH,[83] while the Shaikh died on 18th of the following month.[84] However, he was so ill during the last forty days of his life[85] as to be only semi-conscious. He ate nothing and hardly talked to anyone during this illness.

4. It appears from the *Qiwam-u'l-'Aqa'id* that Ulugh Khan, future Muhammad bin Tughluq, had great faith in the Shaikh and used to visit him. Perhaps this led some uncritical writers to build fantastic theories of conspiracy. Even after the Shaikh's death, Sultan Muhammad bin Tughluq continued to believe that the Shaikh's spiritual blessings were with him. Muhammad Jamal Qiwam-u'd-din records on the authority of Maulana Shihab-u'd-din Imam that one day Iqbal reported to the Shaikh: 'Ulugh Khan has come.' The Shaikh said: 'Say the Sultan has come.' Thrice Iqbal said 'Ulugh Khan has come,' and every time the Shaikh corrected him: 'Say the Sultan has come.' The Shaikh then turned to Iqbal and said: 'Lalla! Didn't I tell you to say Sultan?'[86] In the meantime Ulugh Khan appeared before the Shaikh. He heard and noted the Shaikh's remark. The Shaikh asked Iqbal to bring something for him. The Prince remained standing and left paying his respects.[87]

---

[83] *Tarikh-i-Mubarak Shahi*, p. 96.

[84] *Siyar-u'l-Auliya*, p. 155.

[85] Ibid. p. 154.

[86] Some reckless and uncritical writers, like Sleeman (*Rambles and Recollections* II, p. 54) and Cooper (*The Handbook of Delhi*, p. 97), have cast aspersions on the character of the Shaikh and expressed the view that he was involved in a conspiracy against the Sultan with the Prince. This is absurd. No one who has the slightest knowledge of the Shaikh's character can entertain such suspicions.

[87] *Qiwam-u'l-'Aqa'id*, MS pp. 191–3.

When the Sultan was in Lakhnauti, Prince Ulugh came to enquire about the health of the Shaikh, seriously ill at that time. The Shaikh asked him to sit on his cot; the Prince, being respectful, was reluctant to do so. 'We ask you to sit on the cot. Sit.' It was then not possible to refuse. He rested only a part of his body on the cot. Later, the Shaikh asked Iqbal to bring a chair on which he motioned Khwaja Jahan to sit. Ulugh Khan told Khwaja Jahan: 'The Shaikh has given the throne to me and the chair of *Wizarat* to you.'[88] It may be pointed out that the Shaikh had made a similar prophecy about 'Ala-u'd-din Bahman Shah, the founder of the Bahmanid kingdom.[89]

The sequence of these events—the Prince's visits to the Shaikh, the Shaikh's remarks, the fall of the pavilion—led many people to interpret the Sultan's death as divine retribution for displeasing the Shaikh. Others who were ignorant of the character of the Shaikh saw some conspiracy in the death of the Sultan. It was neither the one nor the other. The Shaikh never cursed the Sultan. In fact, he was so ill at this time that he hardly talked to people. The death of the Sultan was due to the accidental collapse of the pavilion[90] and no human mind had engineered it.

It appears that on some of the campaigns during his reign, Muhammad bin Tughluq turned to the soul of Shaikh Nizam-u'd-din Auliya for blessing and help. In his campaign against Kishlu Khan he asked Qutb Dabir, a disciple of Shaikh Nizam-u'd-din Auliya, for litanies prescribed by the Shaikh for critical situations. His success against Kishlu Khan is attributed by Jamal Qiwam-u'd-din to his faith in the Shaikh.[91]

It is therefore surprising that some of the senior disciples of Shaikh Nizam-u'd-din Auliya suffered great hardships at the hands of the Sultan Muhammad bin Tughluq. The reasons were ideological: the Sultan,

---

[88] Ibid. pp. 193–4.

[89] Tabataba'i, *Purhan al-Ma'asir*, ed. G. Yazdani, p. 12.

[90] Modern scholars (Wolseley Haig, *JRAS*, July 1922); Ishwari Prasad, *A History of the Qaraunah Turks in India*, pp. 46 *et seq.*, Mahdi Husain, *Rise and Fall of Muhammad. Tughluq*, pp. 66 *et seq.*, and Moinul Haq, 'Was Muhammad bin Tughluq a Patricide?' in *Muslim University Journal*, 1939) have discussed the incident in detail. Mahdi Husain and Moinul Haq have exonerated Muhammad bin Tughluq of complicity in any conspiracy against Ghiyas-u'd-din and have shown that the Sultan's death was an accident. Haig and Ishwari Prasad hold Muhammad bin Tughluq responsible for the tragedy.

[91] *Qiwam-u'l-'Aqa'id*, MS pp. 195–96.

under the impact of Ibn Taimiya's ideology,[92] considered state and religion as twins[93] and expected the Sufis to accept government services and work under the direction of the Sultan. The Chishti saints, taught to eschew politics and abstain from government service, resented this, with the result that conflict became inevitable.[94]

The titles, like *Sultan-u'l-Masha'ikh* and *Sultan-u'l-Auliya*, that were given to Shaikh Nizam-u'd-din Auliya, reflect deeper traits of the medieval psyche than have hitherto been appreciated. That psyche refused to accept greatness, grandeur, and glory as the exclusive monopoly of the rulers. In the spiritual domain the Sufi masters held a position in no way inferior to the rulers in the political sphere. Indeed, it was higher.[95] Amir Khusrau could tell Sultan Jalal-u'd-din Khalji that in disobeying him he stood in danger of losing his head, but showing disregard to his spiritual master meant loss of his faith, which he was not prepared to suffer. The concept of *walayat*[96] further buttressed the position of Sufi saints and their hierarchical status, like *Qutb*, *Abdal*, or *Autad*, made it functionally effective. When Baba Farid Ganj-i-Shakar conferred the realm of Hindustan[97] on Shaikh Nizam-u'd-din Auliya, he confirmed the working of this principle in the world of spiritual discipline. When Firuz Shah Tughluq once visited Shaikh Nasir-u'd-din Chiragh, the latter kept him waiting for some time before he came out. Firuz Shah turned to Tatar Khan and said: 'We are not the king.

---

[92] See Nizami, 'The Impact of Ibn Taimiyya on South Asia', in *Journal of Islamic Studies* (Oxford, 1990), i. 125–34.

[93] *Siyar-u'l-Auliya*, p. 196; Nizami, *Salatin-i-Dehli Kay Mazhabi Rujhanat*, pp. 334–8.

[94] See Introduction, *Khair-u'l-Majalis*, pp. 49–59.

[95] Khusrau says about the Shaikh:

در حجرهٔ فقر بادشاهے

در عالم دل جهاں پناهے

(He is a king living in a cell of poverty. He is the refugee in the realm of the heart). *Majnun Laila*, p. 13.

[96] See Nizami, *Some Aspects of Religion and Politics in India During the Thirteenth Century*, pp. 175–7.

[97] *Siyar-u'l-Auliya*, p. 123; *Qiwam-u'l-'Aqa'id*, MS p. 18.

He is the [real] king.'[98] There was a clear ring of displeasure at the position of the Shaikh. When Amir Khusrau wrote about his master—

شاهنشاه بے سریر وبے تاج

شاهانش بخاکپائی محتاج

(He is an Emperor without throne and without crown. But the rulers stand in need of the dust under his foot.)[99]

—he placed Shaikh Nizam-u'd-din Auliya above all temporal authorities. He declared this before a Sultan like 'Ala-u'd-din Khalji, who was both very conscious and jealous of his authority.[100]

---

[98] *Jawami'-u'l-Kalim*, p. 219.
[99] *Majnun Laila*, p. 13.
[100] Barani, *Tarikh-i-Firuz Shahi*, p. 332.

11

RELATIONS WITH NON-MUSLIMS

———————•◦•———————

Shaikh Nizam-u'd-din Auliya's relations with non-Muslims were determined by two basic principles—that all human beings are, figuratively, children of God on earth; and that one should adopt the ways of God in his dealings with human beings.[1] The bounties of God— sun, rain, earth—do not discriminate between one individual and another. So also, one should not treat human beings differently. Two incidents very neatly bring out the working of these principles in the Shaikh's social attitudes and relations. First, one morning, looking down from the roof of his *Jama'at Khanah*, he saw Hindus worshipping idols on the bank of the river Jumna. He remarked:

هر قوم راست راهے دینے وقبله گاهے

(Every people has a religion and a house of worship.)[2]

---

[1] *Khair-u'l-Majalis*, pp. 106–7.

[2] *Anwar-u'l-A'yun*, *malfuz* of Shaikh Ahmad 'Abd-u'l-Haqq, p. 1. Amir Khusrau is reported to have completed the verse instantly by saying:

من قبله راست کردم جانب کج کلاهے

(I have adjusted my *qibla* towards one wearing a slanting cap). The Shaikh used to wear his cap in a slanting way at that time. Amir Hasan Sijzi wrote a whole poem on this verse (*Diwan*, pp. 390–91). See also *Tuzuk-i-Jahangiri*, Sir Syed Ahmad Khan (ed.), p. 81; Rukn 'Imad, *Shama'il-u'l-Atqiya*, MS p. 127.

This remark, inspired by tolerance, reflects the true spirit of medieval Indian culture—coexistence of different religions and diverse patterns of life. It was rooted in the conviction that religions are different paths to the same goal. Second, to show that God did not approve discrimination between human beings, he narrated a story about the Prophet Abraham who, he said, never took his meals unless he had a guest to share the food. Sometimes he went out for miles in search of a guest. One day a polytheist was with him. He hesitated somewhat about inviting him to share his meal with him. Divine admonition came to the Prophet Abraham: 'O Abraham! We can give life to this man but you cannot give food to him.'[3]

True tolerance is not a concession but the overflowing of a spiritually vigorous character which, 'while jealous of the frontiers of its own faith, can tolerate and appreciate all forms of faith other than its own.' Iqbal[4] thought that this couplet of Amir Khusrau reflected that spirit in a remarkable way:

اے کہ ز بت طعنہ بہ ھندو بری

ھم زوے آمــــوز پرستش گری

(Oh you who sneer at the idolatry of the Hindu,
Learn also from him how worship is done.)

This verse is symbolic of Shaikh Nizam-u'd-din Auliya's cosmopolitan spirit, which inspired the remark quoted above. Love and amity in social relationship, tolerance in religious approach, and concern for the welfare of all men irrespective of caste or creed—these were the ideals that were dear to his heart, and his relations with the Hindus were based upon them.

The following incident should also be considered in the context of the Shaikh's appreciation of Hindu attachment to religion. Hasan Sijzi was employed in the army. He had not been paid his salary for some time and was greatly worried on that account. When the Shaikh came

---

[3] *Fawa'id-u'l-Fu'ad*, p. 207.
[4] *Islam and Ahmadism*, p. 7.

to know of this, he narrated the following story of a Brahman: 'There
was a Brahman in a city. He possessed huge wealth. The ruler of that
city confiscated all his property and reduced him to abject penury . . .
One day the Brahman was walking on the road. A friend stepped in
and asked: "How are you?" "Very well," replied the Brahman. "Everything has been taken away from you. What is then the source of this
happiness of yours?" "I still have my holy thread (*zunnar*)," replied
the Brahman.'[5]

Some other anecdotes recounted by the Shaikh before his audience—
and this was his preferred method of teaching—help us to determine
his socio-religious outlook, particularly with regard to the non-Muslims.

1. An Arab of the desert used to pray to God in this way: 'O Creator!
   Be merciful to me and to Muhammad. Don't include others in
   this mercy.' When the Prophet heard about this, he advised the
   Arab not to limit God's mercy like this. God's mercy is general
   (*'amm*).[6]

2. A dervish who had gone to Gujarat met a mystic overpowered
   by ecstasy. He stayed with him. One night he went to a water
   tank to get water for ablution. The guardians of that tank did
   not allow just anybody to do this, but as he had some acquaintance
   there, he was allowed. A number of women were standing there
   with their pitchers. An old woman asked him to fill her pitcher.
   Then, one after the other, several women gave their pitchers to
   him and he filled them all. When he returned to his cell, he found
   the mystic still in his trance. As soon as he started his prayers,
   the mystic awoke from his trance and shouted: 'Why all this
   fuss? The real work [for seeking spiritual bliss] was to fill the
   pitchers of women.'[7]

3. Khwaja Hamid-u'd-din Nagauri even addressed a Hindu as '*wali*'
   (saint). This was because of the belief that God alone knows what
   the end of a man will be.[8] So one should abstain from being
   judgemental.

[5] *Fawa'id-u'l-Fu'ad*, pp. 55–6.
[6] Ibid. p. 162.
[7] Ibid. p. 176.
[8] Ibid. p. 70.

4. Shaikh Farid had advised Shaikh Nizam-u'd-din Auliya to placate everyone and settle the accounts of all. On his return from Ajodhan he went to a cloth-dealer, who was perhaps a Hindu, to whom he owed twenty *jital*s. He gave ten *jital*s to him and promised to pay the balance. The cloth-dealer, who had come to know about his visit to Ajodhan, offered to remit the balance. 'You are coming from the [real] Muslim,' he said.[9]

Now these stories and incidents mentioned by the Shaikh in his mystic gatherings indicate his attitude towards the Hindus and his anxiety to inculcate the same approach among his disciples.

There are references to the visits of yogis to the *khanqah* of Shaikh Farid Ganj-i-Shakar at Ajodhan[10] and Shaikh Nizam-u'd-din Auliya's exchange of views with them. On one occasion he informed his audience:

Once I was in the presence of the Great Shaikh in Ajodhan. A yogi came. I asked him: 'Which way do you follow? What is the real thing in your discipline?' He replied: 'Our science says that there are two worlds (*'Alam*) in the human *nafs*. One is the *'Alam-i-'ulwi*, the other is *'Alam-i-sifli*. From head to navel it is *'Alam-i-'ulwi* and from navel to feet it is *'Alam-i-sifli*. The way to discipline is that there is all sincerity, purity, good manners, and good dealings in *'Alam-i-'ulwi*; in *'Alam-i-sifli* there is observation, purity, and chastity.[11]

Having narrated this, Shaikh Nizam-u'd-din Auliya commented that he liked what the yogi had said.

On another occasion a Hindu yogi explained to Shaikh Nizam-u'd-din his views about the birth and character of children, the appropriate time for conjugal relations, and other similar matters. As the conversation developed the Shaikh asked him about the effect of sexual relationship on particular days and remembered it. When he reported this conversation to Baba Farid, he remarked, 'You will have nothing to do with this in your life.'[12]

---

[9] Ibid. p. 140.
[10] See Nizami, *The Life and Times of Shaikh Farid-u'd-din Masud Ganj-i-Shakar*, pp. 105–6.
[11] *Fawa'id-u'l-Fu'ad*, pp. 84–5.
[12] Ibid. pp. 245–6.

With this background of early contact with Hindu yogis in mind, it becomes easier to analyse the nature and extent of Shaikh Nizam-u'd-din Auliya's contact with the Hindu religious men during his stay in Delhi.

Once six yogis came to the *khanqah* of the Shaikh and busied themselves in meditation at the gate (*dihliz*) of the *Jama'at Khanah*. They did not talk to anybody. Iqbal reported this to the Shaikh, who directed him to bring in the yogis. One of the yogis disclosed that his other companions had been maintaining silence for decades and living in mountain caves. On hearing about the Shaikh's spiritual eminence they had come to Delhi to receive his blessings. They had no other wish except this. The Shaikh received them cordially.[13] Jamal Qiwam-u'd-din says that wise men and ascetics of other faiths recognized the spiritual greatness of the Shaikh.[14] Once a Brahman happened to see the Shaikh, who was on his way to the city. He was so enamoured of him that he started visiting Ghiyaspur and sought an interview with him through Maulana Yusuf of Kilugarhi. Khwaja Muhammad Imam was then sitting with the Shaikh. He sent him to bring in the Brahman. Soon after appearing before the Shaikh, the Brahman fell into contemplation and remained in that state for quite some time. He then stood up and abruptly left. Later Maulana Yusuf asked him why he had not spoken to the Shaikh. He said that all the time he had been trying to assess the spiritual position of the Shaikh, but had not succeeded in his efforts.[15]

One day a person present in the assembly asked the Shaikh: 'If a Hindu recites the Muslim formula of faith (*kalima*), believes in the Unity of God and affirms the Prophethood of Muhammad, but remains silent when a Muslim comes, what will be his end?' The Shaikh replied, 'His affair is with God. He may punish him or forgive him, as He likes. There are some Hindus who know that Islam is the correct creed, but they will not adopt it.'[16]

One day a disciple of the Shaikh came with a Hindu, introduced the stranger and said: 'He is my brother.' The Shaikh asked if he had

---

[13] *Qiwam-u'l-'Aqa'id*, MS p. 106.
[14] Ibid.
[15] Ibid. p. 108–9.
[16] *Fawa'id-u'l-Fu'ad*, p. 135.

any inclination towards Islam. 'I have brought him to your feet,' the disciple replied, 'so that the blessings of the Shaikh's glance may turn him into a Muslim.' The Shaikh said with tears in his eyes: 'You may talk to people as much as you please, but nobody's heart is changed by mere talking. But if he lives in the company of a pious man, that company may make him a Muslim.' The Shaikh then narrated a long story about Caliph 'Umar and the ruler of Iraq, pointing out that lack of character among the Muslims had reduced the impact of their contact with non-Muslims. The Shaikh said that a Jew who lived in the neighbourhood of Shaikh Bayazid was asked: 'Why do you not become a Muslim?' The Jew replied: 'If Islam is what Bayazid possessed, it is beyond me. If it is what you possess, I would feel ashamed of such Islam.'[17]

No cases of conversion by the Shaikh are reported in any of his *malfuzat*. In fact the Shaikh believed in living a pious and dedicated life which attracted people to piety and good conduct, rather than striving for immediate formal change of faith. 'What the *'Ulama* seek to achieve through speech,' he used to say, 'we achieve by our behaviour.'[18] The Shaikh appreciated Maulana 'Ala-u'd-din Usuli's approach in a matter, which involved choice between losing a convert and winning a heart.[19] He was more concerned with bringing happiness to human hearts than making converts.

Amir Khurd's verses, indicating that after the Shaikh's death, Hindus and other non-Muslims visited his grave,[20] shows that Hindus had developed respect and love for him during his lifetime.

It is not known if the Shaikh could converse in Hindivi, but we find Hindivi sentences being uttered in Badaon in his presence.[21] His spiritual mentor's *Jama'at Khanah* at Ajodhan was one of the earliest cradles of the Urdu language,[22] and it is highly improbable that he

---

[17] Ibid. pp. 182–3.

[18] *Siyar-u'l-Auliya*, p. 321. The *Tarikh-i-Mubarak Shahi* (p. 95) refers to a single case of conversion, but in a different context.

[19] See above.

[20] *Siyar-u'l-Auliya*, p. 155.

[21] *Khair-u'l-Majalis*, p. 191.

[22] 'Abd-u'l-Haqq, *The Sufis' Work in the Early Development of the Urdu Language*, (Urdu), pp. 5–7.

did not pick up the Hindivi language. His musician Hasan Mahmandi recited Hindi verses [23] and Amir Khusrau was known for his Hindivi compositions of great appeal. The Shaikh once heard a cultivator driving his bull to draw water from a well with the Hindi words *bahar-i-hu-bahar*. He was overpowered by feelings of ecstasy at these words.[24] Shaikh Burhan-u'd-din Gharib once heard the following Hindivi *dohah* from the Shaikh:[25]

> *Des bhulaven handkar rati sakli soe!*
> *Bahut bura yeh jivana, yun bhi jeevana koe?*
> (Sleeping the night through, forgetting home [the destination] is vain and futile. Who lives like this?)

Mir 'Abd-u'l Wahid Bilgrami and Dara Shukoh have referred to a remark made by the Shaikh showing his preference for and love of Purbi songs. 'I took my oath on the day of [my] creation in the Purbi language,' the Shaikh is reported to have said.[26]

---

[23] *Jawami'-u'l-Kalim*, p. 150.
[24] Ibid.
[25] *Ahsan-u'l-Aqwal*, MS p. 88.
[26] *Saba ' Sanabil*, p. 63; *Hasanat-u'l-'Arifin*, MS Nadwat-u'l-'Ulama *Library* , p. 21.

12

THE MAN

————◆•◆•◆————

A profound humanity and constant moral idealism characterized the thought and activity of Shaikh Nizam-u'd-din Auliya throughout his life. Amir Khusrau calls him *sharaf-i-Adam* (the Glory of Man).[1] In the words of Shakespeare one could say about him:

> His life was gentle and the elements,
> So mixed in him that Nature might stand up
> And say to the world: 'This was a man.'

Generous, compassionate, and forgiving, his heart went out in sympathy to those in distress. He could hardly bear the sight of human suffering— be it physical, mental, spiritual, or financial. When Khwaja Rashid, who was flogged by the *Shuhna* of Delhi, reported his punishment to the Shaikh, he was deeply pained. He put his hand on his own back in agony and said: 'He did not whip you. He flogged my back.'[2] His

---

[1] *Hasht Bihisht*, p. 13.

[2] *Qiwam-u'l-'Aqa'id*, MS p. 127. In the Shaikh's assembly someone alluded to an incident in Shaikh Abu Sa'id Abu'l-Khair's life when a man inflicted two strokes of stirrup-leather on an animal in his presence. Shaikh Abu Sa'id groaned as if the strokes had hit him. An objection was raised against this. Shaikh Nizam-u'd-din Auliya explained it thus: 'When the soul becomes strong and attains perfection, it absorbs the body. In consonance with this law, it is possible that when a man's heart is affected, the effect of it should appear on the body.' (*Fawa'id-u'l-Fu'ad*, p. 77). Perhaps Maulana Kaithali had impressed this on his mind. In his early years Maulana Kaithali came to see Shaikh Nizam-u'd-din Auliya. Mubashshir, who was a young boy at that time, misbehaved with him. Shaikh Nizam-u'd-din struck him with a cane. Maulana Kaithali felt it as if he had himself been struck. *Fawa'id-u'l-Fu'ad*, p. 60.

spiritual mentor had prayed to God to make his life that of a shady tree[3] under which people find shelter from scorching heat and sun. His life was one long illustration of the way he lived up to the hopes and expectations of his master. One day Khwaja 'Aziz-u'd-din told the Shaikh about an after-meal conversation at a feast he had attended. The people present there were saying that Shaikh Nizam-u'd-din's life was free from all sorts of worries. On hearing this the Shaikh said with deep anguish: 'Nobody in this world has more worries and agonies than myself. So many people come to me and report their woes and misfortunes to me. All these [accounts] sear my heart and my soul.'[4]

In fact the man in Shaikh Nizam-u'd-din Auliya was as responsive and resplendent as the mystic in him. His greatness was the greatness of a loving heart. He identified himself with the problems of the people and sought Divine mercy through service of mankind. 'Ali Jandar informs us that the Shaikh used to say that Shaikh Junaid found God in the lanes of Madina. When they asked him how he replied, 'Because God is with the destitute and the broken-hearted.'[5] A life spent in alleviating the misery of people and in doing good to mankind fulfilled the divine purpose of creation, and Shaikh Nizam-u'd-din Auliya's whole life was spent in bringing happiness to the human heart.[6] Shaikh Farid-u'd-din Nagauri, son of Shaikh Hamid-u'd-din Nagauri, wrote in a letter to Najib-u'd-din that he did not find in the whole of Delhi a single man with more agonized concern (*dard*) for human beings than Shaikh Nizam-u'd-din Auliya.[7] In fact, whenever Shaikh Farid Ganj-i-Shakar was happy with somebody, he prayed to God to grant him *dard*.[8]

PERSONALITY

The Shaikh possessed an extremely attractive personality. A tall,[9] handsome figure, fair in complexion, with a fully grown beard,[10] red

---

[3] *Siyar-u'l-Auliya*, p. 117; *Qiwam-u'l-'Aqa'id*, MS. p. 17.

[4] *Khair-u'l-Majalis*, p. 105.

[5] *Durar-i-Nizami*, MS.; *Siyar-u'l-Auliya*, pp. 558–9.

[6] The contemporary literature is replete with the Shaikh's views in this regard. *Durar-i-Nizami*, MS.; *Siyar-u'l-Auliya*, p. 128.

[7] *Maktubat-i-Shaikh Farid-u'd-din Nagauri*, MS. (personal) p. 270.

[8] *Fawa'id-u'l-Fu'ad*, p. 132.

[9] *Siyar-u'l-Auliya*, p. 291.

[10] *Jawami'-u'l-Kalim*, p. 71.

sleep-laden eyes[11] and a big *dastar*[12] over his head—there was an aura of inexpressible spiritual serenity round his face. Yet his awe and prestige were beyond measure. Amir Khusrau was not able to sit in his presence for long. He went out several times to regain his composure. When Maulana Burhan-u'd-din Gharib asked him the reason for it he said: 'When I am in his presence, there is a trembling feeling in me.'[13] He gives the reason in a verse:

چو آئینه که مقابل بآفتاب کنــی

درو چگونه کسی صورتی توان دیدن

(When a mirror is placed before the sun, how can one see one's face in it?)

Even the most senior disciples had to muster courage in order to speak before him.[14] Maulana Husam-u'd-din Multani perspired profusely in his presence.[15] Everyone in his audience kept his eyes fixed on the ground.[16]

But the love and devotion that the disciples had for the Shaikh overrode every other feeling. This was evident in the manner that Maulana Wajih-u'd-din Yusuf came to meet the Shaikh with folded hands. People asked him the reason. 'When I set out for home,' he said, 'the Shaikh appeared in my eyes and I had to show respect to him.'[17] Whenever Khwaja Taj-u'd-din heard the Shaikh's name, tears would flow from his eyes out of love and affection.[18] Khwaja Shams-u'd-din, a nephew of Hasan Sijzi, visualized the face of the Shaikh before he started his prayers.[19] Khwaja Musa Deogiri showed great respect to

---

[11] *Siyar-u'l-Auliya*, p. 128.

[12] *Jawami'-u'l-Kalim*, p. 71; *Durar-i-Nizami*, MS.

[13] *Nafa'is-u'l-Anfas*, MS p. 12.

[14] *Siyar-u'l-Auliya*, p. 305.

[15] Ibid. p. 260.

[16] Ibid. p. 130.

[17] *Qiwam-u'l-'Aqa'id*, MS p. 217; *Ahsan-u'l-Aqwal* MS pp. 49–50.

[18] *Siyar-u'l-Auliya*, p. 312.

[19] Ibid. p. 314.

the Shaikh when he came to see him.[20] The Shaikh was not only the cynosure of the eyes of his disciples but of the people of Delhi also, who were deeply attached to him and looked upon him as a refuge against adversity and misfortune.[21]

The life story of Shaikh Nizam-u'd-din Auliya and his family unfolds itself at four important culture centres of the medieval period: Bukhara, Badaon, Ajodhan, and Delhi. His parents belonged to Bukhara, from where they migrated to India; the saint was born and brought up at Badaon. He came to Delhi to complete his education. There he suffered worse poverty and hunger but he remained determined to face all hardships. He received his spiritual training at Ajodhan where one of the most distinguished saints of the age—Shaikh Farid Ganj-i-Shakar— had set up his mystic centre. The traumatic experience in Bukhara created an otherworldly attitude in his parents and he acquired it through them. Badaon nurtured his emotional life and left indelible impressions on his thought and personality. Ajodhan adorned his spiritual life with a sense of mission and dedication to higher moral and spiritual values. Delhi integrated all these influences and gave him a distinct individuality, charming and charismatic. Though he continued to write *al-Bukhari* and *al-Badaoni* with his name, he imbibed the spiritual and cultural atmosphere of medieval Delhi so thoroughly that he became known as Dehlavi.

LIVING-ROOM

The Shaikh lived in a small room on the roof of his *Jama'at Khanah*. A dangerous wooden staircase was used to go up and climb down. A Lakhnauti[22] rug was spread in his room. The Shaikh and his visitors sat on the floor. The cot was laid in such a way that the Shaikh always faced the Ka'ba.[23] During the summer nights and the rainy season the cot was set on the open roof and a *namgir* (mosquito net) arranged over it.[24]

---

[20] *Qiwam-u'l-'Aqa'id*, MS pp. 69–70.
[21] *Futuh-u's-Salatin*, pp. 455–6; *Diwan-i-Khusrau*, p. 17.
[22] *Siyar-u'l-Auliya*, p. 361.
[23] Ibid. p. 358.
[24] Ibid. p. 146.

DRESS

The Shaikh's usual dress was a long *kurta* (shirt) with broad sleeves, *kulah* and *dastar*. He used night dress (*jama-i-khwab*) also.[25] During the summer days he used a *dastar* measuring seven yards.[26] He tied the *dastar* with a distinct slant, quite different from that of other *silsilah*s, so that one could easily work out from its form the affiliation of the person wearing it.[27] He was always anxious to use the same cloth for his dress that Shaikh Farid had used.[28] However, he used to say that he was unable to act upon three practices of his Shaikh, who took his bath daily, ate bread made of *joar* (a type of millet), and did not take anything at the time of *sahri*.[29]

DIET

The Shaikh's diet was very meagre. At *iftar* time, he ate some bread or rice with some vegetable or *karela* (*Momordica charantia*).[30] The bread hardly weighed seven or eight *dirhams*.[31] While he was at the *ma'idah* (table-spread) he went on passing morsels from his plate to the people present there.[32] One day Maulana Shams-u'l-'Arifin (grandfather of the author of *Qiwam-u'l-'Aqa'id*), asked the Shaikh if his appetite was only that much (i.e. one piece of bread). The Shaikh smiled and said: 'Well, I could eat one more piece but I do not.'[33] When he went upstairs after *iftar* some pomegranate seeds dipped in rose-water were brought. He took very little from this and distributed it to those present.[34] This was the time when people from the city and neighbouring areas, as also his relations, came to meet him.[35] He entertained them with fruits, dried and fresh, light snacks, and delicious sherbet. Amir Khurd

---

[25] *Ahsan-u'l-Aqwal*, MS p. 62.
[26] *Durar-i-Nizami*, MS.
[27] *Ahsan-u'l-Aqwal*, MS p. 58.
[28] Ibid. p. 57.
[29] *Siyar-u'l-Auliya*, p. 386.
[30] Ibid. p. 124.
[31] *Qiwam-u'l-'Aqa'id*, MS p. 616.
[32] *Siyar-u'l-Auliya*, p. 145.
[33] *Qiwam-u'l-'Aqa'id*, MS p. 161.
[34] Ibid. p. 162.
[35] *Siyar-u'l-Auliya*, p. 145.

informs us that the Shaikh himself did not take anything from this: 'It was to entertain the visitors.'[36] At the time of *sahri*, a plate of *tahri* (a rice dish) was brought with a piece of roasted meat of some bird. The Shaikh took only a morsel or two of the rice and then gave it to somebody; sometimes Iqbal distributed it in the morning. 'I never saw the Shaikh,' Shams-u'l-'Arifin once said, 'touching the meat or even the skin of the roasted bird.'[37] Sometimes Khwaja 'Abd-u'r-Rahim, whose duty it was to bring *sahri* to the Shaikh, insisted on his taking more, but the Shaikh would become upset at the thought of those who had gone to sleep hungry, and the food would simply not go down his throat.[38]

The Shaikh habitually concealed his own virtues by attributing to others what was his own practice. One day he told his audience: 'A saintly person said that when people eat food before him, he feels as if it is going down his own throat—he feels as if he is himself taking that food.'[39] He was in fact describing himself. While Amir Khurd has alluded to this briefly, Jamal Qiwam-u'd-din has supplied some interesting details. The Shaikh was fond of certain fruits but instead of eating them himself, he enjoyed watching others do so. He liked sugarcane very much. Once when its season had passed, he wanted to have some. By chance good black sugarcane came to him as a present from some place. He asked Khwaja Karim-u'd-din to peel it; after that, he served it in plates to all those present. He enjoyed seeing them relish it. He did not eat any himself. Jamal Qiwam-u'd-din then remarks: 'Can there be any penitence more than this?'[40]

The Shaikh sometimes chewed betel leaves.[41]

LOVE OF CHILDREN

The Shaikh had great love and affection for children. He kept some food and fruit back for them from his *sahri* and *iftar*.[42] Newborns were

---

[36] Ibid.

[37] *Qiwam-u'l-'Aqa'id*, MS pp. 162–3.

[38] *Siyar-u'l-Auliya*, p. 128.

[39] *Fawa'id-u'l-Fu'ad*, p. 77.

[40] *Qiwam-u'l-'Aqa'id*, MS pp. 159–60.

[41] *Siyar-u'l-Auliya*, p. 142.

[42] Ibid. p. 128.

brought to him, and he blessed them by putting his saliva into their mouths and giving names to them.[43] He performed their *Bismillah* ceremonies.[44] Though a celibate himself, he looked after the children of his sister with the same concern that he would have felt for his own. He talked to them about their pastimes and made them happy in his company.

RESPECT FOR WOMEN

The Shaikh had not married but he had no streak of the misogynist in him. He considered women as important as men and accorded them equal or sometimes higher status.[45] He lauded their religious devotions and said that in prayers the intercession of pious women was sought before that of pious men.[46] It was piety, he said, rather than gender which mattered.[47] 'When a tiger came out of its den, nobody ever asked if it was male or female,' he would say.[48] He particularly appreciated the role of women in building the character of their children.[49] His spiritual mentor Baba Farid owed much to his mother in the shaping of his outlook, and his own mother was a beacon for him.

OPPOSITION TO SLAVERY

Shaikh Nizam-u'd-din Auliya considered slavery an inhuman institution. He appreciated the action of those disciples who emancipated their slaves.[50]

Amir Hasan Sijzi's servant Malih purchased a slave-girl for five *tankas* in Deogir. When the army was leaving, the girl's parents brought ten *tankas* and requested him to return the girl. Hasan Sijzi was so moved

---

[43] Ibid. p. 287; *Fawa'id-u'l-Fu'ad*, p. 197.
[44] *Siyar-u'l-Auliya*, p. 206.
[45] *Fawa'id-u'l-Fu'ad*, p., 22.
[46] Ibid.; *Nafa'is-u'l-Anfas* MS p. 45.
[47] *Fawa'id-u'l-Fu'ad*, p., 22.
[48] Ibid.
[49] Ibid. p. 121.
[50] Ibid. pp. 4–5.

by their appeal that he gave Malih ten *tanka*s from his own pocket, purchased the girl, and returned her to her parents. When the Shaikh heard about this, his eyes filled with tears. 'You have done a good deed,'[51] he said. Contemporary literature records several cases of persons who set free their slaves inspired by the teachings of the Shaikh.

The Shaikh used to say: 'Mysticism knows no slavery or ownership [of persons].'[52]

CONCERN FOR THE SICK

Despite all the demands on his time, and despite his status and position, the Shaikh did not hesitate to visit ailing friends and disciples to enquire about their health.[53] When he learnt from 'Ali Jandar about the illness of Qazi Muhi-u'd-din Kashani, he went to his house and asked after him. After the death of the Qazi, the Shaikh said to 'Ali Jandar: 'If you had not informed me about his illness, and I had not gone there to ask after him, I would have been sorry about it till the Day of Judgement.'[54]

Maulana Zia-u'd-din Sunnami was a critic of Shaikh Nizam-u'd-din Auliya's audition parties (*sama'*). When he fell ill, the Shaikh went to enquire about his condition. On hearing about the Shaikh's visit, Maulana Sunnami gave his *dastar* to those attending on him to spread it in the way of the Shaikh. The Shaikh lifted it and put it on his head. A few days later the Maulana died. The Shaikh remarked: 'Ah! There was one who upheld the *Shari'ah*. He too has expired.'[55]

The Shaikh went even to the graves of persons who were opposed to him and had been a torment to him. Chajju, a resident of Inderpat, always spoke ill of the Shaikh and wished him ill. But when he died, the Shaikh went to his grave and prayed to God for him.[56]

---

[51] Ibid. p. 202.
[52] Ibid. p. 4.
[53] Ibid. p. 44.
[54] *Durar-i-Nizami*, MS.
[55] *Akhbar-u'l-Akhyar*, p. 108.
[56] *Fawa'id-u'l-Fu'ad*, pp. 94–5; *Siyar-u'l-Auliya*, pp. 554–5.

BASIC APPROACH TO PROBLEMS OF SOCIAL RELATIONSHIP

The Shaikh believed in self-discipline and self-criticism as the best methods for reducing tension in society. He would always look for some wrong in him when others wronged him. When treated with insolence by somebody, he would consider it a divine reprimand to himself. He explained his approach in this way:

> If a man finds fault with me or lays some blame on me, I should first of all search my own [heart] and see whether that fault is in me or not. If that fault is in me, I should not be ashamed at being apprised of it by somebody else. If I do not have that fault in me, I should be grateful to God that I have been protected and I should not find fault in others.[57]

Revenge and retribution had no place in the life or thought of Shaikh Nizam-u'd-din Auliya. He believed in forgetting and forgiving evildoers. He hated the sin but not the sinner. He refers to divine admonition to Khwaja Qutb-u'd-din Bakhtiyar Kaki and Qazi Hamid-u'd-din Nagauri that if evil people were neglected by them, who else would look after them?[58] In his view the ideal as enunciated by Caliph 'Ali was, 'to conceal the misdeeds of others'.[59] If anybody offered to retaliate against persons who spoke ill about him, he told them to forgive them.[60]

MODEL OF CONDUCT

Shaikh Nizam-u'd-din Auliya looked upon the Prophet as the model of conduct to be emulated in every detail of life. Jamal Qiwam-u'd-din writes:

> Khwaja Karim-u'd-din . . . whose knowledge of mystic [and religious] literature was unrivalled . . . said on oath that he had watched the

---

[57] *Fawa'id-u'l-Fu'ad*, pp. 226–7.
[58] *Siyar-u'l-Auliya*, p. 52.
[59] *Fawa'id-u'l-Fu'ad*, p. 196.
[60] Ibid. p. 94.

Shaikh for years but never found him to neglect *sunnah* [practice of the Prophet]. [He further said that he himself] had extensively studied Hadith literature and delved deep into it. On the basis of that knowledge he could vow and say that the Shaikh did not neglect any *sunnah* . . . he did not see him at any time doing or saying anything contrary to the practice of the Prophet . . .[61]

The Shaikh's clear and explicit instructions to his disciples were to see that they did not deviate in any matter from the path of the Prophet and the dictates of *Shari'ah*.[62] When his mother, disgusted with the behaviour of her son-in-law, desired divorce of her daughter, the Shaikh advised against it, referring to a Tradition of the Prophet.[63] Amir Khusrau says about him:

راه روئے کو بطریق صفا

رفتہ قدم بر قدم مصطفی[64]

(Itinerant on the path of purity, he walked in the footsteps of Mustafa.)

---

[61] *Qiwam-u'l-'Aqa'id*, MS p. 175.
[62] Ibid. p. 173.
[63] *Siyar-u'l-Auliya*, pp. 103–4.
[64] *Matla'-u'l-Anwar*, p. 21; see also *Majnun Laila*, p. 13.

13

THE SCHOLAR

Shaikh Nizam-u'd-din Auliya was an erudite man,[1] widely read and endowed with a sharp, penetrating intelligence able to comprehend and elucidate intricate problems of theology and mysticism. Among the academic circles of Delhi his stature as a scholar was duly recognized. Delhi was at this time one of the greatest centres of learning in the eastern world of Islam. The Mongol cataclysm had driven the intellectual elite of Muslim lands to Delhi. Writes Barani:

> There were scholars in Delhi, each a master in his subject, the like of whom could not be found in Bukhara, Samarqand, Baghdad, Egypt, Khwarizm, Damascus, Tabriz, Ispahan, Ray, Rum [Constantinople], or anywhere in the inhabited globe. They could split hairs in any subject, traditional or rational, that one can think of—e.g. exegesis, law, jurisprudence, principles of theology, scholastic theology, grammar, lexicography, literary ingenuity, and logic . . . Some of these scholars had attained in learning to the stature of Ghazzali and Razi.[2]

To enjoy academic prestige in a city where such distinguished scholars flourished was to be accorded the highest recognition in the intellectual

---

[1] The author of *Hada'iq-u'l-Hanafiya* (p. 305) says that he was a perfect and erudite scholar of religious sciences—the Qur'an, the Hadith, and *fiqh*—in addition to his command of syntax, semantics and logic.

[2] *Tarikh-i-Firuz Shahi*, pp. 352–3.

world of Islam. Barani has referred to forty-six distinguished scholars who were looked upon as intellectual pillars of Delhi. Several among them, like Qazi Muhi-u'd-din Kashani, Maulana Wajih-u'd-din Pai'li, Maulana Shihab-u'd-din Multani, and Maulana Shams-u'd-din Yahya, were disciples of the Shaikh. When they and others, like Maulana Fakhr-u'd-din Zarradi and Maulana Karim-u'd-din Samarqandi, joined the circle of his disciples, his academic eminence became widely recognized.[3]

Shaikh Nizam-u'd-din Auliya won academic laurels early. His extraordinary skill in debate earned for him the title of *mahfil shikan* (breaker of assemblies) and *bahath* (debator).[4] But as the years rolled on and he joined the discipline of Shaikh Farid Ganj-i-Shakar he wholly renounced casuistry and debate as methods for influencing the outlook of others. Once Maulana Jalal-u'd-din Awadhi, a distinguished scholar and *khalifah* of the Shaikh, sought his permission to arrange debates in the *Jama'at Khanah*. The Shaikh was displeased and told those who had placed this request on his behalf: 'I am so sorry. I expected something different from him, but he is like an onion, all outer and no inner.'[5]

The breadth and depth of the Shaikh's scholarship was evident whenever he was discussing any academic topic.[6] It was a well integrated and thoroughly assimilated knowledge that he presented to the audience. Even when scholarly pedants from Delhi came to embarrass him with difficult queries and questions, he quickly demonstrated his academic superiority.[7]

The Shaikh's elevated conception of knowledge (*'ilm*) transcended all material considerations. He considered it a noble endeavour, an end in itself, that should not be made a means of livelihood. One day a student came to see him and in the course of conversation said that he often went around the court so that he might become affluent. The Shaikh did not like this motive for acquiring knowledge. Similarly,

---

[3] *Qiwam-u'l-'Aqa'id*, MS pp. 25, 35, 113; *Siyar-u'l-Auliya*, p. 223.
[4] Ibid. p. 101.
[5] Ibid. p. 306.
[6] Ibid. p. 130.
[7] Ibid. pp. 223–4.

the Shaikh did not like poetic talent to be wasted in writing panegyrics.[8] He cited in his assembly a remark of Shaikh Jalal-u'd-din Tabrizi that the ambition of the *'Ulama* is confined to getting employment as a teacher, a *qazi*, or a *Sadr-i-Jahan*. 'They aspire to nothing higher; but the dervishes have many stages [of development].'[9]

Both Mir Khurd[10] and 'Ali Jandar[11] have separate sections in their works on the Shaikh's views about the need and value of acquiring knowledge and the status of those who devote themselves to it. The Shaikh once quoted Caliph 'Umar bin 'Abd-u'l-'Aziz to the effect that when a man *acquires* knowledge he becomes respectable in the eyes of the people, but when he *acts* upon it he becomes dear to God.[12] He spoke in his assembly about persons whose salvation was due to their devotion to learning.[13] With the instinct and temperament of the dedicated scholar he used to say that a scholar's pleasure in resolving an academic conundrum was greater than that of a king in conquering a territory.[14] He repeatedly emphasized that one should be an *'alim* with the qualities of a dervish ingrained in him. He referred to three such scholar-saints whom he had the privilege to meet—Maulana Shihab-u'd-din, Maulana Ahmad Hafiz, and Maulana Ahmad Kaithali.[15] Again and again he told his audience that *'ilm* (learning) without a heart full of cosmic emotion was vain and fruitless:[16]

It is said [in Hadith] that God likes high and noble actions and dislikes the low and mean. One should keep his ideals high so that he attains the status of manliness. A scholar should have high ambitions so that he succeeds in acquiring wisdom (*hikmah*).[17]

---

[8] *Fawa'id-u'l-Fu'ad*, p. 182.
[9] Ibid. p. 237.
[10] *Siyar-u'l-Auliya*, pp. 534–40.
[11] *Durar-i-Nizami*, Salar Jang MS fo. 7b *et seq.*
[12] *Siyar-u'l-Auliya*, p. 534.
[13] Ibid. pp. 534–5.
[14] Ibid. p. 535; *Durar-i-Nizami*, MS.
[15] *Siyar-u'l-Auliya*, p. 536.
[16] Ibid. p. 539.
[17] *Durar-i-Nizami*, MS.

For the Shaikh, there were not mere maxims to recommend to others—he had actually practised them in his life.

From his early years the Shaikh was a great lover of books.[18] He retained this interest to the last days of his life. He spent some hours at night in quiet study; made summaries, took down notes, and wrote his comments on books.[19] During his early years in Delhi, when he moved from the house of *Rawat Arz* to a mosque, his only belongings were his books, which were carried to the mosque. The Shaikh later made a *waqf* (endowment) of his library[20] for students. Some of these books were taken to Lakhnauti by Akhi Siraj.[21]

Shaikh Nizam-u'd-in was keenly interested in Qur'anic studies. He emphasized memorization of the Qur'an, and made special arrangements for instruction in it, particularly for his nephews and the grandchildren of Shaikh Farid. Maulana 'Ala-u'd-din Inderpati, an expert *hafiz*, was engaged for this purpose. He taught the Qur'an to the Kirmani family also.[22] Baba Farid had advised Shaikh Nizam-u'd-din Auliya to commit the Qur'an to memory and he faithfully carried out the orders of his master.

The Shaikh used to say that recitation of the Qur'an was more effective for achieving gnosis than *zikr* (recital of Divine Names). *Zikr*, he said, made spiritual progress quicker, but there was always a risk of later loss in progress thus achieved. Progress achieved through recitation of Qur'an was free from such risks of subsequent decline.[23] He said that the Qur'an contained four kinds of instructions: prayer and litanies (*'ibadat*) for the common run of believers; signs and hints (*isharat*) for special categories of believers; spiritual perception and sensation of divine grace (*lata'if*) for the *auliya*, and true maxims (*haqa'iq*) for

---

[18] At one stage in his life he vowed not to buy another book. A man brought *Arba'in* of Imam Ghazzali to sell. The Shaikh wanted to have it, but he could not ignore his vow. He declined to buy it but was deeply grieved at having lost it. A few days later the same book came to him as a present. *Siyar-u'l-Auliya*, p. 145.

[19] Ibid. p. 127.

[20] Ibid. p. 289.

[21] Ibid.

[22] Ibid. p. 316.

[23] Ibid. p. 446.

the Prophet.[24] He advised his disciples to read the Qur'an in such a way that the majesty of God illuminated their hearts.[25]

As a necessary corollary to his interest in the Qur'an, Shaikh Nizam-u'd-din was deeply involved in the study of exegetical literature. A disciple of the Shaikh, Maulana Rukn-u'd-din Chighmar, famed for his skill in calligraphy, wrote out the *Kashshaf* and *Mufassal* for him in excellent hand.[26] Unlike the Multan branch of mystics, he seems to have paid special attention to Zamakhshari's *Kashshaf*.

Shaikh Nizam-u'd-din's special field of interest was, however, Hadith. Shah Ghulam 'Ali, a renowned Naqshbandi saint of Delhi, used to say: 'Sultanji's stature as *muhaddith* was unrivalled.'[27] His cogent and clear elucidation of the traditions of the Prophet was admired by specialists in the subject. Mir Khurd[28] and 'Ali Jandar[29] have given details of some of his discourses on the subject. It appears that he had set apart some days for discussions about Hadith. Qazi Muhi-u'd-din Kashani was a regular participant in these discussions.[30] The Shaikh did not like people to reject anything out of hand with the remark, 'This is not Hadith.' All that one should say is: 'This is not found in standard works of Hadith.'[31] Nevertheless, he clearly distinguished between Hadith and the sayings of Sufis and was prompt to point out the difference.[32] As the Shaikh had committed the *Mashariq-u'l-Anwar* to memory,[33] he may be said to have had on the tip of his tongue more than two thousand traditions of the Prophet.

The Shaikh believed in *ijtihad* (fresh interpretation of law)[34] and did not fasten himself permanently to any juristic opinion. He tried to argue the case for *sama'* in the light of the Traditions of the Prophet.

---

[24] Ibid. p. 435.

[25] Ibid.

[26] Ibid. p. 317.

[27] Muhammad Hasan, *Masha'ikh-i-Naqshbandiya*, p. 323.

[28] *Siyar-u'l-Auliya*, pp. 101–4.

[29] *Durar-i-Nizami*, MS.

[30] For Hadith discussions, see *Qiwam-u'l-'Aqa'id*, MS p. 113.

[31] *Fawa'id-u'l-Fu'ad*, p. 233; *Siyar-u'l-Auliya*, p. 415.

[32] *Fawa'id-u'l-Fu'ad*, p. 175; *Siyar-u'l-Auliya*, p. 326.

[33] Ibid. p. 101.

[34] *Fawa'id-u'l-Fu'ad*, p. 4. See also Siddiq Hasan Khan, *Tiqsar Juyud al-Ahrar min Tizkar Junud al-Abrar* (Bhopal, 1878), p. 136.

The '*Ulama* of Delhi, on the contrary, demanded a verdict of Imam Abu Hanifa and refused to listen to the Traditions of the Prophet.[35] 'You are not a *mujtahid*,' cried the '*Ulama*, 'you are a *muqallid* (follower of the law as laid down by the jurists). You should present the opinion of Abu Hanifa.'[36] The Shaikh was deeply distressed by this passivity of the scholars and fearful that a city where people refused to listen to the Traditions of the Prophet might suffer divine retribution. Indeed, Mir Khurd interpreted Muhammad bin Tughluq's forced transfer of the '*Ulama* from Delhi to Daulatabad as the punishment that the Shaikh had feared for the '*Ulama*.[37]

On account of his erudition and deep insight in the religious sciences, the Shaikh was considered competent to interpret law and perform the functions of a jurist (*mujtahid*). Amir Hasan Sijzi calls him *Khatm-u'l-Mujtahidin*[38] (last of the jurists) and Jamali considered him a second Abu Hanifa.[39] Notwithstanding his views about the need for *ijtihad*, he had great respect for Imam Abu Hanifa. He once reminded an audience that Abu Hanifa had met seven Companions of the Prophet (*sahabah*),[40] a rare distinction for people of his generation.

Apart from Hadith, the Shaikh read extensively on different religious subjects. In his *malfuzat* and accounts references are found to the following works, many of which gained currency in Delhi because of his interest in them:[41]

1. *Ihya-u'l-'ulum* of Imam Ghazzali
2. *Ijaz-u'l-Bayan*
3. *Athar-u'l-Nayyarain*
4. *Adab-u'l-Muhaqqiqin*
5. *Ma'alim-i-Lubab*
6. *Arba'in* of Razi
7. *Arba'in* of Ghazzali

---

[35] *Siyar-u'l-Auliya*, p. 531; p. 89.
[36] Ibid.
[37] Ibid. p. 532.
[38] *Fawa'id-u'l-Fu'ad*, p. 90.
[39] *Siyar-u'l-Auliya*, p. 59.
[40] Ibid. p. 538.
[41] *Tarikh-i-Firuz Shahi*, p. 346.

8.   *Fakhri Namah* of Khwaja Sanai
9.   *Tafsir-i-imam Nasiri*
10.   *Ruh-u'l-Arwah*
11.   *Shafi'i*
12.   *'Umda*
13.   *'Awarif-u'l-Ma'arif* of Suhrawardi
14.   *Qut-u'l-Qulub* of Abu Talib Makki
15.   *Kafi*
16.   *Kashshaf* of Zamakhshari
17.   *Kashf-u'l-Mahjub*
18.   *Lawa'ih* and *Lawama'* of Qazi Hamid-u'd-din
19.   *Mirsad-u'l-'Ibad*
20.   *Mashariq-u'l-Anwar* of Saghani
21.   *Maktubat-i-'Ain-u'l-Quzzat Hamadani*
22.   *Mulakhkhas*
23.   *Nawadir-u'l-Usal* of Hakim Tirmizi
24.   *Hidayah* of Marghinani
25.   *Kimiya-i-Sa'adah* of Ghazzali
26.   *Risalah-i-Qushairiya*
27.   *Sharh Athar-u'l-Nayyarain*
28.   *Jawahir-u'l-Qur'an* of Ghazzali
29.   *Baydawi*
30.   *Tuhfat-u'l-Birra't* of Majd-u'd-din Baghdadi
31.   *Tasrif-i-Maliki*
32.   *Majma'-u'l-Bahrain*
33.   *Tafsir-i Haqq'iq*
34.   *Tamhidat* of Abu Shakur Salmi
35.   *Jami'-u'l-Usul-fi Ahadith-i'r-Rasul Ibn Athir*
36.   *Hizr-i-Yamani*
37.   *Hizr-i-Kafi*

It appears that *Tafsir-i-imam Nasiri* and *Kashshaf* were his favourite books of *tafsir*; *Sahih Muslim* and *Sahih Bukhari* with their summary *Mashariq-u'l-Anwar* were his favourite Hadith compendia; in matters of *'Ilm-i-Kalam* he relied mainly on Ghazzali's *Ihya-u'l-'Ulum* and *Kimiya-i-Sa'adah*. His favourite studies on mystic themes were *Ruh-u'l-Arwah, Qut-u'l-Qulub, Kashf-u'l-Mahjub, Risalah-i-Qushairiya,*

Maktubat-i-'Ain-u'l-Quzzat and works of Qazi Hamid-u'd-din Nagauri; in matters of law, he was guided by *Tamhidat* and *Hidayah*. The Shaikh knew three books by heart—the Qur'an, the *Mashariq-u'l-Anwar*, and the *Maqamat-i-Hariri*. This strengthened the foundations of his literary, religious, and theological knowledge. Shaikh Abu Sa'id Abu'l-Khayr's ethical principles and mystical thought had inspired him deeply. Among the mystic poets he had particular interest in Sana'i, Nizami, Sa'di, Shaikh Auhad-u'd-din Kirmani, and Shaikh Saif-u'd-din Bakharzi. He quoted a remark of Shaikh Saif-u'd-din that every verse of his was as weighty as a book.[42]

The Shaikh had a very mature poetic sensibility. The verses that he quoted were apt and sharp. Once he quoted some verses in a letter to Shaikh Farid Ganj-i-Shakar, who committed them to memory and cited them when he visited Ajodhan.[43] He was immensely fond of the verses of Sa'di. In his audition parties, he appreciated Bibi Fatima Sam's impromptu citation of verses in her conversations.[44] Paying tribute to his Shaikh's vast erudition and learning, Amir Khusrau says:

ز علمش در دو عالم روشنائی[45]

(His knowledge illuminated the two worlds.)

[42] *Fawa'id-u'l-Fu'ad*, p. 35. See also *Durar-i-Nizami*, MS.
[43] *Siyar-u'l-Auliya*, pp. 502–3.
[44] *Fawa'id-u'l-Fu'ad*, pp. 244–5.
[45] *Duwal Rani Khizr Khan*, p. 15.

14

THE MYSTIC

———•◦•———

Shaikh Nizam-u'd-din Auliya carried forward and unified the age-old traditions and ideals of Islamic mysticism. He transformed the ideology of Shaikh Shihab-u'd-din Suhrawardi, Shaikh Muhi-u'd-din Ibn al-'Arabi, and Maulana Jalal-u'd-din Rumi—all distinguished figures of the thirteenth century—into a motive force. Baba Farid Ganj-i-Shakar had initiated the move to convert the mystic movement into a mass movement; Shaikh Nizam-u'd-din Auliya completed the process as Chishti centres came to be established all over the country. Muhammad Ghauthi Shattari says[1] that when Shaikh Nizam-u'd-din Auliya presented himself before his spiritual mentor for the first time, the latter recited a couplet in which he referred to the many eager souls who had been looking forward anxiously to his coming. It meant that he was expected to carry forward the accumulated tradition of Islamic mysticism.

The success of his mystic effort was due to effective use of *'ilm* (knowledge), *'ishq* (cosmic emotion), and *'aql* (practical wisdom combined with intuitive intelligence), as means for the proliferation of ideas. These three faculties had independent development in the persons and work of Shaikh Muhi-u'd-din Ibn al-'Arabi, Maulana Jalal-u'd-din Rumi, and Shaikh Shihab-u'd-din Suhrawardi. Ibn al-'Arabi had constructed ideological bridges for the communication of ideas across world religions; Rumi had made cosmic emotion a motive power in mystic discipline; Shaikh Shihab-u'd-din Suhrawardi had laid down

---

[1] *Gulzar-i-Abrar*, MS.

principles for the organization of *khanqah*s and the dissemination of mystic ways of life. It was now necessary to transform and combine these achievements of the age into a unified programme for the betterment of the individual and society. To Shaikh Nizam-u'd-din Auliya belongs the credit of introducing a principle of movement in the mystic structure with a view to carrying forward its message. As a result of his activity, hundreds of *khanqah*s were established in the country and thousands of disciples became active in propagating the Chishti ideology. It was from his time that spiritual genealogies (*shajra*) were introduced in *khilafat namah*s[2] to articulate the traditions of saints who had gone before and establish historical links with them. According to Amir Khusrau, 'he awakened the elder saints (*shuyukh*) from their sleep.'[3] Contemporaries called him *Junaid-i-Thani*,[4] *Ghauth-u'l-'Azam*,[5] *Shaikh-u'l-Waqt*,[6] etc., and paid eloquent tribute to his spiritual achievements and position. His life was, in fact, a watershed in the history of Islamic mysticism in South Asia, where old traditions crystallized into new social forces. He transformed a discipline for the culture of the individual soul into a social movement for the moral and spiritual uplift of humanity. Amir Khusrau says in a homonymic way that God had created him *payay ghambari* (for lifting the burden of others).[7]

The cornerstone of Shaikh Nizam-u'd-din Auliya's ideology was the formation of God-conscious personalities. He believed that whoever developed love of God in his heart ceased to be vulnerable to sin.[8] For him God was an all-embracing Reality present in his ethical, intellectual, and aesthetic experience. He believed in imitating the moral principles of God. As divine beneficence did not discriminate between one individual and another, so a mystic was also expected to transcend all barriers of cult, race, language, and geography. All human beings are

---

[2] *Siyar-u'l-Auliya*, pp. 230–1. See the *Khilafat Namah* conferred on Shaikh Shams-u'd-din Yahya. Maulana Hujjat-u'd-din Multani versified the *shajra* in Arabic. *Siyar-u'l-Auliya*, p. 317.

[3] *Diwan-i-Amir Khusrau*, p. 17.

[4] *Majnun Laila*, p. 13.

[5] *Nuh Sipihr*, p. 25.

[6] *Maktubat-i-Shaikh Farid Nagauri*, MS p. 270.

[7] There is a pun on the word *payay ghambari*, meaning that he followed the tradition of the Prophet in attending to the problems of the people.

[8] *Durar-i-Nizami*, MS.

the children of God on earth and it was his duty to treat them alike with sympathy and affection. Shaikh Nizam-u'd-din Auliya demonstrated the working of this concept in his social relationships.

The Shaikh believed that one who caused pain to any human heart could not attain spiritual excellence.[9] He cited Shaikh Abu Sa'id Abu'l-Khair's remark that though there were innumerable ways leading to Him, bringing happiness to the human heart was the surest way to gnosis.[10]

In the *khanqah* of Shaikh Ahmad Maghribi in Gujarat, the spiritual qualities of Shaikh Nizam-u'd-din Auliya were once discussed, and it was observed that while other mystics were only 'busy in God', Shaikh Nizam-u'd-din Auliya was also busy in 'bearing the burden of human worries'.[11] All sorts of people brought all sorts of problems to him, and he shared their pains and shouldered their burdens with sympathy and affection.

Shaikh Nizam-u'd-din Auliya's respect and devotion for his spiritual mentor were beyond measure. He fondly remembered the days he had spent at his feet and followed his traditions as best he could. He used to renew periodically his allegiance to his master by having *bay'at* with his garments.[12] He had the garments of his Shaikh buried with him in his grave.[13] He wanted to stop the practice of prostration before him, but he did not do so because it would have meant disrespect to his master, who had not stopped it.[14] One day a visitor asked him about the relative spiritual qualities of Shaikh Farid and Shaikh Baha-u'd-din Zakariya. His reply was: 'Only one like them can explain it.' When the visitor insisted, he said: 'When our Shaikh Farid-u'd-din was overpowered by ecstasy he cried out: *Ya Habib! Ya Habib!* (O Beloved! O Beloved!). When Shaikh Baha-u'd-din was overpowered by ecstasy he used to say: *Ya Ghafur! Ya Ghafur!* (O Forgiving One! O Forgiving One!). Find out the difference from this.'[15]

---

[9] Ibid.

[10] *Siyar-u'l-Auliya*, p. 411.

[11] *Tuhfat-u'l-Majalis*, MS India Office Library, D.P. 977, fo. 24b.

[12] *Siyar-u'l-Auliya*, p. 334.

[13] Ibid. p. 342.

[14] Ibid. p. 340.

[15] *Shawamil-u'l-Jumal*, MS p. 31.

Shaikh Nizam-u'd-din Auliya had developed his own unique and effective method of instructing people. He avoided direct discussion of specific problems. He spoke instead through anecdotes and parables which were extremely apt and went straight to the hearts of people. In his opinion, example taught better then precept.[16] He thought that the most important difference between the approach of the 'Ulama and the dervishes was that, while the former approached people through advice and precept, the Sufis influenced them through example.[17] He concealed his own spiritual qualities so strictly that whenever he had to refer to some such incident of his life, he would say that such and such a thing happened to some dervish. He himself cried out when he heard about the flogging of a person, but referred to Maulana Ahmad Kaithali doing so; he himself enjoyed seeing others take food, but referred to a dervish who felt as if he himself was taking that food. Shaikh Farid also used to refer to 'a certain dervish' whenever he mentioned such incidents.[18] Of the ten pieces of advice which Amir Khurd saw written in the Shaikh's own hand, one was: 'As far as possible, instruct a disciple through hint and suggestion, not explicitly or through statement.'[19]

As a teacher Shaikh Nizam-u'd-din Auliya did not believe in reducing inner life to a continuous struggle with evil. He never performed spiritual exercises meant to over-awe people or establish his superiority as a traveller on the mystic path. He never prescribed an extraordinary number of prayers or penitences to his disciples. His method was to awaken 'the good' in man and make his soul responsive to moral and spiritual obligations. 'The Shaikh's life was,' remarks Professor Muhammed Habib, 'in fact the embodiment of what psychological research shall one day prove to be the deepest principle of our human nature: that salvation, or happiness in its highest form, lies not in war with the attractions of worldly life or in indifference towards them, but in the healthy development of the "cosmic emotion", in a sympathetic identification of the individual with his environment.'[20]

---

[16] *Durar-i-Nizami*, MS chap. II.

[17] *Siyar-u'l-Auliya*, p. 321.

[18] Ibid. p. 336.

[19] Ibid. p. 349.

[20] In *Politics and Society during the Early Medieval Period* (collected works of M. Habib), edited by K.A. Nizami, I, p. 311.

The Shaikh advised his disciples to develop complete reliance upon God (*tawakkul*)[21] and resignation to His will, doing so helped one to break free of entanglements of society and lead a life that one can call one's own. Two other conditions for freedom from social embarrassments were avoidance of debt[22] and refraining from acting as custodian for anyone.[23] These principles had been enunciated to the Shaikh by his spiritual master, Shaikh Farid Ganj-i-Shakar, and he acted upon them throughout his life.

Miracle-working had no place in the spiritual discipline of Shaikh Nizam-u'd-din Auliya, and was considered by him an indicator of spiritual imperfection. In the *Fawa'id-u'l-Fu'ad* there are no references to the miracles of the Shaikh. He did, however, mention the miracles of others—not to demonstrate their spiritual powers but to illustrate some principle or bring home some moral. 'They have divided the mystic path', he once told his audience, 'into a hundred stages of which the capacity of displaying miracles is the seventeenth; if a mystic is stopped at this stage, how will he cross the remaining eighty-three stages?'[24]

Shaikh Nizam-u'd-din Auliya illustrated the ideal practice of principles governing acceptance and distribution of *futuh* (unsolicited gifts). For years he spent his days in penury, starving day in and day out, and living on what people put as charity in the *zanbil* (a dried hollow gourd hung at the door). When fasting and starving had become a part of his nature, the door of *futuh* was opened to him. But he did not consider himself more than a distributing agency for these gifts. Guaranteed payments were never accepted—whether offered by the Sultan or of the *Kotwal*. (The way Malik Nizam-u'd-din, the *Kotwal* of Delhi, fell at his feet with his purse of *tanka*s and begged him to accept it has been recorded by 'Ali Jandar).[25] Though the *Jama'at Khanah* had copious stores—where articles of daily consumption were kept—they were

---

[21] *Fawa'id-u'l-Fu'ad*, pp. 53–4.

[22] *Durar-i-Nizami*, MS. He cited a *hadith* in which the Prophet sought God's protection from *kufr* and debt.

[23] *Siyar-u'l-Auliya*, p. 325.

[24] *Fawa'id-u'l-Fu'ad*, p. 117.

[25] *Durar-i-Nizami*, MS. See also *Fawa'id-u'l-Fu'ad*, p. 125.

cleared of everything every week. The Shaikh lived in the midst of this enormous inflow and outflow of *futuh* as, to use a mystic phrase, the swan lives in water—when it comes out its feathers are dry.

Contemporary mystic circles acknowledged his spiritual excellence in different ways. According to Syed Ja'far Makkial-Husaini his status and that of Shaikh 'Abd-u'l-Qadir Gilani was unique: both were 'the beloved of God'.[26] This was the highest tribute to the Shaikh's spiritual excellence to say that he was the 'beloved of God'. In his *Futuhat-i-Firuz Shahi*, even Firuz Shah Tughluq refers to him as *Mahbub-i-Ilahi*.

---

[26] *Bahr-u'l-Ma'ani*, pp. 85–6.

15

HIS FAMILY

———◆•◆———

Shaikh Nizam-u'd-din Auliya had one elder sister who must have been fairly mature when her mother died, because we hear about her ill treatment by her husband and the mother's worry on that count.[1]

The Shaikh brought up the children of his sister with almost paternal concern and affection. Amir Khurd has particularly referred to the following relations of the Shaikh:

(a) Khwaja Rafi'-u'd-din Harun
(b) Khwaja Taqi-u'd-din Nuh
(c) Khwaja Abu Bakr
(d) Maulana Qasim
(e) Khwaja 'Aziz-u'd-din (son of Khwaja Abu Bakr)

Khwaja Rafi'-u'd-din grew up under the personal supervision of the Shaikh. He put him to memorizing the Qur'an. Out of affection for him the Shaikh did not have his dinner unless he was present. He talked to him pleasantly, and for his sake expressed keen interest in his hobbies, archery and body-building.[2]

---

[1] *Siyar-u'l-Auliya*, pp. 103–4. It is reported that the Shaikh's mother had decided about her divorce as her husband did not treat her well. She told Nizam-u'd-din to arrange divorce. At night the saint saw the Prophet in a dream saying that whoever applied for divorce before the expiry of two and a half years from marriage was doomed. The Shaikh mentioned this to his mother and the divorce was deferred. Shortly after that their relations became pleasant and the idea of divorce was given up.

[2] *Siyar-u'l-Auliya*, p. 203.

Khwaja Rafi'-u'd-din's younger brother, Khwaja Taqi-u'd-din Nuh, had a scholarly temperament and possessed a pious and attractive personality. He too had committed the Qur'an to memory and used to recite the whole of it every Friday night. The Shaikh appreciated his pious ways and academic interests. One day the Shaikh asked him what the purpose was of his prayers and penitences. 'Only for your longevity,' he replied with an affection that touched his uncle's heart. Once the Shaikh fell seriously ill. He called Khwaja Nuh and conferred *khilafah* on him, and advised him thus: 'Whatever comes to you spend it; don't keep anything. If you have nothing, don't be worried about it. God will give it to you. Don't wish ill of anybody. Do not seek God's curse against anybody. Return tyranny and torture with generous rewards and forgiveness. Don't accept any stipend because a dervish cannot be a holder of stipends. If you will act like this, kings will come to your door.'[3] But Khwaja Nuh was not destined to live long. He developed tuberculosis and died during the Shaikh's lifetime and was buried in the Chabutrah-i-Yaran. The Shaikh was deeply grieved at his untimely death.

Khwaja Abu Bakr, whose exact relationship with the Shaikh has not been indicated in *Siyar-u'l-Auliya*, was always in attendance on the Shaikh. He fasted continuously. Sometimes he did not break his fast for several days. On Fridays he carried the Shaikh's prayer-carpet to the Jama' Masjid of Kilugarhi. Fond of audition parties (*sama'*), he was sometimes so overpowered by spiritual ecstasy and exhilaration, that he gave away even his garments to the musicians.[4]

Maulana Qasim bin 'Umar was the son of a nephew of the Shaikh. He committed the Qur'an to memory at the age of twelve. Keenly interested in Qur'anic studies, he wrote a *tafsir* entitled *Lata'if-u'l-Tafsir*.[5] A devoted pupil of Maulana Jalal-u'd-din, he spent nearly fifty years of his life in his company and obtained a certificate from him after receiving instruction in *Hidaya*, *Bazdawi*, *Kashshaf*, *Mashariq*, and *Masabih*.[6]

---

[3] Ibid. p. 204.
[4] Ibid. pp. 204–5.
[5] Ibid. p. 205.
[6] Ibid. p. 207.

Khwaja 'Aziz-u'd-din was the son of Khwaja Abu Bakr and was known for his piety and scholarship. He collected the Shaikh's conversations in his *Majmu'-u'l-Fawa'id*. He recited the whole Qur'an during Friday nights.[7]

Barani has pointed out that one impact of the teachings of Shaikh Nizam-u'd-din Auliya was to encourage interest in committing the Qur'an to memory.[8] Special arrangements for the study of the Qur'an were made by the Shaikh for his nephews and the descendants of Shaikh Farid Ganj-i-Shakar. An experienced and gifted *hafiz* was engaged for this purpose.

GRANDSONS OF HIS SPIRITUAL MENTOR

Besides his nephews, the Shaikh looked after some grandsons of Shaikh Farid-u'd-din Ganj-i-Shakar, with paternal concern. Baba Farid's youngest daughter Bibi Fatimah was married to Maulana Badr-u'd-din Ishaq. Shaikh Nizam-u'd-din was beholden to Maulana Ishaq for the kindness he had shown to him during the days of his stay at the *Jam'at Khanah* of Shaikh Farid. After the death of Maulana Badr-u'd-din, Shaikh Nizam-u'd-din was worried about the education of his two sons—Muhammad Imam and Muhammad Musa. He thought of bringing the family to Delhi, but had no means to arrange it. A Multani merchant once brought two purses of gold coins to him. He accepted the present, called Syed Muhammad Kirmani, handed the purses to him, one to be retained by him and the other to be spent on bringing the family of Maulana Ishaq to Delhi. When the family reached Delhi and was comfortably accommodated in a house, some evil-tempered people circulated the rumour that Shaikh Nizam-u'd-din had called Bibi Fatimah from Ajodhan because he wanted to marry her. When Shaikh Nizam-u'd-din came to know of this, he was shocked and immediately left for Ajodhan. When he came back Bibi Fatimah was already dead. The two sons that she left were now under the charge and supervision

---

[7] Ibid.
[8] *Tarikh-i-Firuz Shahi*, p. 344.

of Shaikh Nizam-u'd-din Auliya. He did his utmost to assure for them the best possible education and training. Khwaja Muhammad Imam[9] committed the Qur'an to memory and distinguished himself as a scholar. The Shaikh had very great affection for him. He was granted authority to enrol disciples during the Shaikh's lifetime. Nobody could sit higher than him in the assembly of the Shaikh, and he often led the prayers in the *Jama'at Khanah*. He collected the conversations of Shaikh Nizam-u'd-din Auliya under the rubric *Anwar-u'l-Majalis*, a work no longer extant. Singers of Persian and Hindi verses were always present in his company. The other brother, Khwaja Musa, also committed the Qur'an to memory. His special field of interest was *fiqh*, in which he had received instruction from Maulana Wajih-u'd-din Pa'ili. He was interested in poetry also and composed verses in Arabic and Persian.

Two other grandsons of Shaikh Farid—Khwaja 'Aziz-u'd-din and Khwaja Qazi—sons of Khwaja Ya'qub, the youngest son of Shaikh Farid—had long been with Shaikh Nizam-u'd-din Auliya, who supervised their education. The Shaikh noticed in Khwaja 'Aziz-u'd-din a desire to travel and so sent him to carry on the teachings of the order in the south. Khwaja Qazi preferred to remain in Delhi. On his death he was buried in Chabutrah-i-Yaran.

Shaikhzada Kamal-u'd-din was also related to Shaikh Farid. When Shaikh Nizam-u'd-din sent Shaikhzada 'Aziz-u'd-din off to Deogir and Shaikhzada Kamal-u'd-din to Malwa, he gave a *Jalali* to each of them. On retiring from the Shaikh's *majlis*, 'Aziz-u'd-din asked Kamal-u'd-din: 'What will this single *Jalali* do for us?' 'This is symbolic of the *jalal* (prestige) which the Shaikh has conferred on us,' said Kamal-u'd-din and left for Malwa.

Khwaja 'Aziz-u'd-din bin Khwaja Ibrahim bin Khwaja Nizam-u'd-din was also brought up under the care of Shaikh Nizam-u'd-din Auliya. So too was Khwaja 'Aziz-u'd-din Sufi, son of Bibi Masturah, daughter of Shaikh Farid Ganj-i-Shakar. He compiled the Shaikh's *malfuzat* in *Tuhfat-u'l-Abrar fi-Karamat-u'l-Akhyar*. His younger brother

---

[9] *Siyar-u'l-Auliya*, p. 200.

Shaikhzada Kabir-u'd-din also received education under the care of Shaikh Nizam-u'd-din Auliya. He was always in the presence of the Shaikh and his pious ways were appreciated by him. He too was buried in the Chabutrah-i-Yaran.

In fact it was Shaikh Nizam-u'd-din Auliya who looked after the education of many of the descendants of Shaikh Farid Ganj-i-Shakar and provided the affection and paternal support they needed.

THE KIRMANI FAMILY

Among those close to Shaikh Nizam-u'd-din Auliya from the very beginning of his career as a mystic teacher was the Kirmani family.[10] The Shaikh first came into contact with this family in Ajodhan at the *Jama'at Khanah* of his spiritual master. As stated earlier, Syed Muhammad Mahmud was a businessman from Kirman, who used to visit India frequently in connection with his trade. His uncle was a mint officer in Multan, whose daughter, Bibi Rani, he married. During his stay in India he used to visit Shaikh Farid Ganj-i-Shakar. He became so enamoured of the spiritual atmosphere that prevailed in the *Jama'at Khanah* that he decided to settle there with his wife. He adopted the life of a mystic and preferred penitence and poverty to affluence and prosperity. When Shaikh Nizam-u'd-din Auliya reached the *Jama'at Khanah* of Shaikh Farid, Bibi Rani looked after him like a sister. After the death of Shaikh Farid, Syed Muhammad Mahmud came to Delhi with his family and started living with Shaikh Nizam-u'd-din Auliya. This contact developed into close personal friendship and identity of views on both spiritual and material affairs. He left four sons—the eldest, Syed Nur-u'd-din Mubarak, was the father of Amir Khurd, the author of *Siyar-u'l-Auliya*. He was a disciple of Shaikh Farid and was a man of otherworldly attitude. Generous and hospitable, he was a lovable figure. Amir Khurd tells us that he had joined the discipleship of Khwaja Qutb-u'd-din Maudud at Chisht and had also received *khilafat* from him. Syed Nur-u'd-din Mubarak, however, did not admit anyone to his discipline.

---

[10] Our only source of information on the members of the Kirmani family is *Siyar-u'l-Auliya*.

Syed Kamal-u'd-din Amir Ahmad, the second son of Syed Mahmud, was a landlord and a soldier. He was brought up in the company of Shaikh Nizam-u'd-din Auliya. He was thrown in prison at Bhaksi, near Deogir, by Sultan Muhammad bin Tughluq but was released and ordered to appear at the court. He went there in his Sufi dress. 'Why this dress?' asked the Sultan. 'I used to have an external likeness with the descendants of the Prophet [i.e. by wearing the mystic dress],' he replied, 'But when I gave that up, I was punished as I deserved.' The Sultan said that this was a pretext to avoid government service. 'I want to run the government of the country with your advice,' remarked the Sultan and appointed him to a high post.

Syed Qutb-u'd-din Husain, the third son, was learned, pious, and generous. He was a pupil of Maulana Fakhr-u'd-din Zarradi and was brought up under the care and supervision of Shaikh Nizam-u'd-din Auliya, who called him his son. He was always present in the assembly of the Shaikh at the time of the *zuhr* (afternoon) prayers. Many visitors to the Shaikh came to see him also at his house. Khwaja Jahan Ahmad Ayaz took him to Deogir against his wishes. He did not live long and died of a stroke.

Shams-u'd-din Syed Khamosh, the fourth son of Mahmud Kirmani, was also brought up in the society of the Shaikh and read the *Khamsa-i-Nizami* with him. Many disciples of the Shaikh who came from the city stayed with him at night. He received them with kindness. It was this long association of his elders with the Shaikh that led Amir Khurd to compile a comprehensive biography of the saint.

16

HIS *KHALIFAHS*

————•◦•————

Shaikh Nizam-u'd-din Auliya's efforts transformed the Chishti *silsilah* into an all-India movement for the spiritual culture of man. He sent his *khalifah*s to all parts of the country with instructions to invite people to the path of rectitude, honesty, and piety and check immoral and unethical trends. According to Muhammad Ghauthi Shattari he sent seven hundred spiritually gifted *khalifah*s to different cities of the country.[1] Effective centres of the *silsilah* thus sprang up in Haryana, Malwa, Gujarat, the Deccan, and Bengal. In the centuries that followed, particularly during the period when provincial kingdoms arose, these branches of the Chishti order played a very prominent role in the cultural life of the region.

It appears that during the last illness of the Shaikh a list of persons eligible for appointment as *khalifah*s was drawn up after mutual consultation among Syed Husain Kirmani, Shaikh Nasir-u'd-din Mahmud, Maulana Fakhr-u'd-din Zarradi, Khwaja Mubashshir, and Khwaja Iqbal. It contained thirty names of persons qualified for this honour. A *mahzar* (petition) was drafted by Amir Khusrau on behalf of some senior disciples of the Shaikh and submitted to him. 'What is the need for selecting so many people for *khilafat*?', remarked the saint. The proposers narrowed the selection and presented it again to the Shaikh for approval. Finding the name of Akhi Siraj in the list, the Shaikh remarked: 'The first requisite for this work is learning.'

---

[1] *Gulzar-i-Abrar*, MS.

He then ordered Syed Husain Kirmani to write out the *khilafat namah*s. These documents were drafted by Maulana Fakhr-u'd-din Zarradi and the name of the grantee was, at the instance of the Shaikh, entered by Syed Husain Kirmani, whose name also was mentioned as scribe. The Shaikh added the words 'From the poor Muhammad bin Ahmad 'Ali-al-Badaoni al-Bukhari',[2] and handed it over to those concerned. Maulana Shams-u'd-din Yahya and Maulana 'Ala-u'd-din Nili were in Awadh at that time. The Shaikh entrusted their documents and *Khil'at*s to Shaikh Nasir-u'd-din Mahmud to be handed over to them. These documents were drafted on 20 Zu'l-Hijah 724/1324,[3] nearly four months before his death.[4]

1. Maulana Shams-u'd-din Yahya[5] entered the discipline of the Shaikh during his student days. With the characteristic arrogance of young scholars of promise, he came to the Shaikh to test his scholarship, but was so impressed by the Shaikh's erudition that he decided to become his disciple. Like his spiritual master he passed his life in celibacy. Though he received the *khilafah* from the Shaikh, he did not admit many people to the discipline. Whatever came to him as *futuh* he distributed among his visitors and retained nothing for himself. He was distinguished as a scholar and a large number of the scholars of Delhi were among his pupils. Shaikh Nasir-u'd-din Chiragh, also a pupil of his, wrote about him:

سـألت العــلم من أحياك حقًّا

فقال العلم شمس الدين يحيى

(I asked Knowledge: Tell me truthfully who has revived thee? Knowledge replied: Shams-u'd-din Yahya).[6]

---

[2] *Siyar-u'l-Auliya*, p. 222.
[3] Ibid.
[4] The Shaikh expired on 18 Rabi'-u'l-Akhir 725 AH.
[5] For biographical references, see *Siyar-u'l-Auliya*, pp. 223–36; *Akhbar-u'l-Akhyar*, pp. 96–7; *Gulzar-i-Abrar*, MS; *Ma'arij-u'l-Walayat*, MS I, pp. 326–9.
[6] *Akhbar-u'l-Akhyar*, p. 97.

He wrote a commentary on the *Mashariq-u'l-Anwar*. Sultan Muhammad bin Tughluq summoned him to the court and said: 'What is a man of your erudition and sagacity doing here?' He then ordered him to proceed to Kashmir and work there for the spread of Islam. He deputed some persons also to take him to Kashmir. Shams-u'd-din returned home and told people that he had dreamt that his Shaikh was calling him to his presence. He fell seriously ill and a boil appeared on his chest. The Sultan considered it a trick to evade going to Kashmir. He called him to the court and after personally inspecting the wound allowed him to go back home. He died soon after and was buried in the graveyard of Chabutrah-i-Yaran.

2.   Shaikh Nasir-u'd-din Chiragh,[7] was another very distinguished disciple of Shaikh Nizam-u'd-din Auliya who played an important part in keeping alive the traditions of his master. He was looked upon as his chief successor and, according to Amir Khurd, his mystic gatherings had the same fragrance as the *majalis* of Shaikh Nizam-u'd-din Auliya.[8] He continued with devotion and meticulous care the programmes and procedures of his Shaikh.[9] At a time when Sultan Muhammad bin Tughluq was zealously propagating the ideology of Ibn Taimiyyah,[10] he saved the mystic organization from criticism by bringing it closer to the traditions of the Prophet and declared: 'No practice of a spiritual teacher is binding unless it is supported by the Qur'an and the Hadith.'[11]

Shaikh Nasir-u'd-din originally belonged to a rich merchant family of Awadh. Attracted by the reputation of Shaikh Nizam-u'd-din Auliya, he came to Delhi and joined his discipline. Used to contemplation and meditation in the lonely jungles of Awadh, he approached the

---

[7] For biographical references, see *Siyar-u'l-Auliya*, pp. 236–47; *Akhbar-u'l-Akhyar*, pp. 80–6; *Gulzar-i-Abrar*, MS; *Ma'arij-u'l-Walayat*, MS I, pp. 121–40. See also the life of the Shaikh in Introduction to *Khair-u'l-Majalis*, pp. 35–62.

[8] *Siyar-u'l-Auliya*, p. 41.

[9] Ibid. pp. 237–41.

[10] For details, see Nizami, 'The Impact of Ibn Taimiyya on South Asia', in *Journal of Islamic Studies* (Oxford, 1990), i. 125–34.

[11] *Akhbar-u'l-Akhyar*, p. 81.

Shaikh through Amir Khusrau for permission to move away from the city. 'Amir Khusrau!' the Shaikh replied, 'Tell Nasir-u'd-din that he should live in society and bear the blows and buffets of the people.' The future course of his life was thus decided and he stuck to Delhi under circumstances that would have shaken any person of lesser stature and inferior mettle. After the death of his Shaikh, he had to face great hardships at the hands of Sultan Muhammad bin Tughluq. The Sultan wanted the mystics to settle in different areas according to his directions. This clearly contravened the concept of *walayah*, which meant allocation of spiritual territories by the Shaikh. According to some accounts the Sultan put him to severe tortures but Shaikh Nasir-u'd-din did not budge from his principles. He died on 18 Ramadan 757/1356.

3. Shaikh Qutb-u'd-din Munawwar,[12] grandson of Shaikh Jamal-u'd-din of Hansi, lived in a secluded corner where his ancestors had passed their lives. Except for offering Juma' prayers or for visiting the graves of his elders, he never stepped out of his *khanqah*. Shaikh Nizam-u'd-din Auliya bestowed upon him a copy of the *'Awarif-u'l-Ma'arif*, given to him by his grandfather, who had received it from Shaikh Farid Ganj-i-Shakar. Sultan Muhammad bin Tughluq sent to him a grant of two villages through Qazi Kamal-u'd-din Sadr-i-Jahan. He convinced the Sadr-i-Jahan that it was not proper for him to accept the grant and deviate from the traditions of his elders. The Sadr-i-Jahan conveyed his refusal to the Sultan in such a way that he did not react to this refusal with anger. Once the Sultan passed through Hansi. He summoned Shaikh Qutb-u'd-din but soon after left the city. When the two finally met in Delhi the Sultan complained that the Shaikh had shown disrespect by not visiting him when he was camping in Hansi. The saint explained the matter in such a humble way that the Sultan was pleased with him and shook hands with him. The Shaikh clasped the Sultan's hand so firmly that he was impressed by his confidence and poise. The Sultan later sent one lakh *tanka*s to him through Firuz (future Sultan Firuz Shah) and Zia-u'd-din Barani.

---

[12] For biographical references, see *Siyar-u'l-Auliya*, pp. 247–56; *Akhbar-u'l-Akhyar*, pp. 87–8; *Gulzar-i-Abrar*, MS; *Ma'arij-u'l-Walayat*, MS I, pp. 278–303.

The Shaikh accepted only two thousand *tanka*s after great persuasion. Most of this amount he distributed at the tombs of Shaikh Nizam-u'd-din Auliya and Khwaja Qub-u'd-din Bakhtiyar Kaki and presented some to Shaikh Nasir-u'd-din Chiragh.[13] He died on 16 Zul-Qa'dah 757/1356.[14]

4. Maulana Husam-u'd-din Multani,[15] another distinguished *khalifah* of Shaikh Nizam-u'd-din Auliya, was known for his insight into literature on *fiqh*. He knew by heart large parts of *Hidayah*. He was also well-versed in *Qut-u'l-Qulub* and *Ihya-u'l-'Ulum*. Jamal Qiwam-u'd-din says that in his erudition he had no peer in Delhi.[16] The Shaikh advised him to reject the material attractions of the world (*tark-i-dunya*). He sought his permission to give up residence in the city and settle at some place near the river. 'No,' instructed the Shaikh, 'live in the city and live as others live.' When Muhammad bin Tughluq embarked upon his project to force the *'Ulama* and *masha'ikh* to migrate to Deogir, the Shaikh went to Gujarat, where he died on 8 Zu'l-Qa'dah 736/1336. His grave is in Pattan.

5. Maulana Fakhr-u'd-din Zarradi,[17] another distinguished *khalifah* of the Shaikh, was an erudite, pious, and dedicated scholar. Though an externalist scholar by training, he was so impressed by the Shaikh's learning and piety, that he became his disciple and constructed a house for himself in the *khanqah* town. After the death of the Shaikh he lived for some time at Basnala, then moved to Loni and finally settled near the *Hauz-i-'Alai*. He wrote two pamphlets[18] in defence of the mystic practice of *sama'* at a time when Sultan Ghiyas-u'd-din Tughluq, under the influence of the *'Ulama*, objected to it and convened a *mahzar* to consider

---

[13] *Siyar-u'l-Auliya*, pp. 254–5.

[14] 'Afif, *Tarikh-i-Firuz Shahi*, p. 87.

[15] For biographical references, see *Siyar-u'l-Auliya*, pp. 256–62; *Akhbar-u'l-Akhyar*, pp. 89–90; *Gulzar-i-Abrar*, MS; *Ma'arij-u'l-Walayat*, MS I, pp. 303–6.

[16] *Qiwam-u'l-'Aqa'id*, MS pp. 29–30; 33–4.

[17] For biographical references, see *Siyar-u'l-Auliya*, pp. 262–75; *Akhbar-u'l-Akhyar*, pp. 90–2; *Gulzar-i-Abrar*, MS; *Ma'arij-u'l-Walayat*, MS I, pp. 303–6.

[18] One pamphlet, entitled *Usul al-Sama'*, was published by Muslim Press Jhajjar in 1311 AH.

its legality. His confrontation with Muhammad bin Tughluq has been recorded by Mir Khurd in some detail. The Sultan called him to his presence and said that he wanted to wage *jihad* against the Mongols and would like to have his cooperation in this venture. The Shaikh said: *'Insha Allah* (God willing).' 'This is a phrase of doubt and indecision,' remarked the Sultan. He then ordered food to be served and himself began to give meat from his own dish to the Shaikh, who ate very little and reluctantly. He then gave a bag of *tanka*s and some cloth as a present to Shaikh Fakhr-u'd-din Zarradi, Shaikh Nasir-u'd-din Mahmud, and Shaikh Shams-u'd-din Yahya—who were all there at the summons of the Sultan. Qutb-u'd-din Dabir,[19] a pupil of Maulana Fakhr-u'd-din Zarradi, showed great respect to the Shaikh—carrying his shoes under his arm and lifting his bag of money. The Sultan was peeved at this and threatened to punish him. Maulana Zarradi later migrated to Daulatabad and from there he proceeded on Hajj pilgrimage. On his return from Hajj he visited Baghdad, where the academic circles were deeply impressed by his erudition. He was shipwrecked on the return journey.

6. Another *khalifah* of the Shaikh, Maulana 'Ala-u'd-din Nili,[20] was a *hafiz* known for his mastery over the religious sciences. He was a powerful orator and his lectures on *Kashshaf* were appreciated for their clear analysis of exegetical problems. The Shaikh was particularly impressed by his recitation of the Qur'an while leading the prayers. Once he was so pleased with his recitation that he granted his prayer-carpet to him. He had transcribed *Fawa'id-u'l-Fu'ad* with his own hand and busied himself most of the time in reciting it. Ibn Battuta, who attended his Friday sermons, says: 'Many listeners to his sermons repent at his hand, shave their heads and become men of ecstasy.'[21] He did not enrol any disciples. He lies buried in Chabutrah-i-Yaran.

---

[19] For the straitened circumstances of Qutb-u'd-din Dabir's descendants, see *Insha-i-Mahru*, p. 56.

[20] For biographical references, see *Siyar-u'l-Auliya*, pp. 275–8; *Akhbar-u'l-Akhyar*, pp. 93–4; *Gulzar-i-Abrar*, MS; *Ma'arij-u'l-Walayat*, MS I, pp. 312–13.

[21] *Rihla*, II, p. 19.

7. Maulana Burhan-u'd-din Gharib[22] was another very devoted *khalifah* of Shaikh Nizam-u'd-din Auliya. He was particularly fond of audition parties and his disciples used to dance in a particular way which came to be called the *Burhani* way of ecstasy. Shaikh Nasir-u'd-din Chiragh, Amir Khusrau, and Amir Hasan were among his close friends and had great regard and affection for him. He migrated to Deogir, perhaps under the orders of Muhammad bin Tughluq. He played a very distinguished role in disseminating the Chishti mystic ideology in the Deccan. His *malfuzat* were compiled by his disciples under the rubrics *Ahsan-u'l-Aqwal, Nafa'is-u'l-Anfas, Shama'il-u'l-Atqiya,* and *Ghara'ib-u'l-Karamat.* These conversations reveal his anxiety to propagate the ideology of Shaikh Nizam-u'd-din Auliya in the Deccan. He lies buried in Daulatabad.

8. Maulana Wajih-u'd-din Yusuf,[23] one of the early *khalifah*s of the Shaikh, was known for his urbanity and culture. Shaikh Nizam-u'd-din Auliya sent him to Chanderi long before 'Ala-u'd-din Khalji's armies reached there. When Chanderi was annexed to the Khalji Empire a large number of soldiers, associated in some way with Shaikh Nizam-u'd-din Auliya, gathered round him for spiritual guidance and blessing. He lies buried in Chanderi.

9. Maulana Siraj-u'd-din 'Usman,[24] popularly known as Akhi Siraj, belonged to Bengal and had come to Delhi attracted by the spiritual fame of Shaikh Nizam-u'd-din Auliya. The Shaikh used to call him 'Mirror of India' (*A'ina-i-Hindustan*). Every year he used to go to Lakhnauti to see his mother. He spent time in a corner of the *Jama'at Khanah* and had no belongings except for some books and papers. Initially, when his name was mentioned for the conferment of *khilafah*, Shaikh Nizam-u'd-din Auliya quietly observed that education up to the recognized standard was

---

[22] For biographical references, see *Siyar-u'l-Auliya*, pp. 278, 282; *Akhbar-u'l-Akhyar*, pp. 93–4; *Gulzar-i-Abrar*, MS; *Ma'arij-u'l Walayat*, MS I, 313–8.

[23] For biographical references, see *Siyar-u'l-Auliya*, pp. 282–8; *Akhbar-u'l-Akhyar*, p. 198; *Gulzar-i-Abrar*, MS; *Ma'arij-u'l Walayat*, MS I, pp. 318–20.

[24] For biographical references, see previous note. *Siyar-u'l-Auliya*, pp. 288–90; *Akbar-u'l-Akhyar*, p. 86–7; *Gulzar-i-Abrar*, MS; *Ma'arij-u'l Walayat*, MS I, pp. 296–8.

the first requisite for spiritual work. Maulana Fakhr-u'd-din Zarradi
undertook to educate him and wrote a book, *Tasrif-i-'Usmani*,
for him. In very short time he became qualified for the grant
of *khilafah*. When people were forced to migrate to Daulatabad,
Akhi Siraj went to his home town, Lakhnauti, and took with
him some books from the library which the Shaikh had turned
into a public *waqf*. He popularized the Chishti order in Bengal
and Bihar and all sorts of people came to him in search of spiritual
bliss. He lies buried at Pandua.

10. Maulana Shihab-u'd-din[25] was the leader of prayers in the *Jama'at
    Khanah* mosque. He had a very attractive intonation and his
    recitation thrilled the congregation. He also went to Daulatabad,
    perhaps with the mass exodus demanded by Muhammad bin
    Tughluq. But he later returned to Delhi and died there.

11. One other very eminent scholar and *khalifah* of the Shaikh was
    Qazi Muhi-u'd-din Kashani.[26] An account of him is given by
    Amir Khurd under the caption *Yaran-i-A'la* (high placed
    disciples). The Shaikh had great regard and consideration for
    him and stood up to receive him. It appears that he was particu-
    larly keen to attend the Shaikh's lectures on Hadith. He died
    during the Shaikh's lifetime.

The above list is in no way complete. Amir Khurd selected only those
*khalifah*s for brief biographical notices who were either pre-eminent
or had long contact with the *khanqah* and the Kirmani family. He
has, however, given three separate accounts of the disciples of the
Shaikh under three different categories: (*a*) nine *khalifah*s, (*b*) nineteen
Yaran-i-A'la (senior disciples), and (*c*) nineteen disciples. Under the
first category he has mentioned Maulana Shams-u'd-din Yahya, Shaikh
Nasir-u'd-din Mahmud, Shaikh Qutb-u'd-din Munawwar, Maulana
Husam-u'd-din, Maulana Fakhr-u'd-din Zarradi, Maulana 'Ala-u'd-din

---

[25] For biographical references, see *Siyar-u'l-Auliya*, pp. 290–2; *Ma'arij-u'l Walayat*, MS I,
pp. 320–2.

[26] For biographical notices, see *Siyar-u'l-Auliya*, pp. 294–6; *Akhbar-u'l-Akhyar*, pp. 97–8;
Gulzar-i-Abrar, MS; *Ma'arij-u'l Walayat*, MS I, pp. 322–6. Interesting references to him are
also found in *Durar-i-Nizami*, MS, and *Qiwam-u'l-'Aqa'id*, MS pp. 34–5, 113–14, 172.

Nili, Maulana Wajih-u'd-din Yusuf, Maulana Siraj-u'd-din, and Maulana Shihab-u'd-din Imam. The following names occur in the second category:

1.   Khwaja Abu Bakr Manda
2.   Qazi Muhi-u'd-din Kashani
3.   Maulana Wajih-u'd-din
4.   Maulana Fakhr-u'd-din Maruzi
5.   Maulana Fasih-u'd-din
6.   Amir Khusrau
7.   Maulana Jamal-u'd-din
8.   Maulana Jalal-u'd-din Awadhi
9.   Khwaja Karim-u'd-din Samarqandi
10.   Amir Hasan Sijzi
11.   Qazi Musharraf Firuz
12.   Maulana Baha-u'd-din Adhami
13.   Shaikh Mubarak Gopamavi
14.   Khwaja Muiyyid-u'd-din Ansari
15.   Khwaja Zia-u'd-din Barani
16.   Khwaja Muyyid-u'd-din Ansari
17.   Khwaja Shams-u'd-din
18.   Maulana Nizam-u'd-din Shirazi
19.   Khwaja Salar Nahin.[27]

Under the third category the following names are given:

1.   Maulana Fakhr-u'd-din of Meerut
2.   Maulana Mahmud Nu-Haiyat
3.   Maulana 'Ala-u'd-din Inderpati
4.   Maulana Shihab-u'd-din Kastori
5.   Maulana Hujjat-u'd-din Multani
6.   Maulana Badr-u'd-din
7.   Maulana Rukn-u'd-din Chighmar
8.   Khwaja 'Abd-u'r-Rahman Sarangpuri

---

[27] According to Khwaja Hasan Nizami (*Nizami Bansari*, 4th edn, p. 439) his name was Hum Yun and he was of Chinese origin. See also *Lata'if-i-Ashrafi*, p. 364.

9.   Khwaja Ahmad Badaoni

10.   Khwaja Latif Khandsali

11.   Maulana Najm-u'd-din Mahbub known as Shakar Khani Thanesari

12.   Khwaja Shams-u'd-din Vihari

13.   Maulana Yusuf Badaoni

14.   Maulana Siraj-u'd-din Hafiz Badaoni

15.   Maulana Qazi Pa'ili

16.   Maulana Qiwam-u'd-din Yak dana

17.   Maulana Burhan-u'd-din Sawi

18.   Khwaja 'Abd-u'l-Aziz Banarmodi

19.   Maulana Jamal-u'd-din Awadhi

Mir Khurd has not stated the reason for giving these names under different categories. Perhaps he had in mind some significant difference of spiritual status and position that he has not explicitly indicated.

Ghulam Mu'in-u'd-din 'Abdullah, the author of *Ma'arij-u'l-Walayat*, an encyclopaedia of Chishti saints, has given notices of fifty-seven *khalifah*s of the Shaikh. It appears that he did not distinguish among those associated with the Shaikh—different categories such as *khalifah*s, senior disciples, eminent figures, disciples, relatives. The Shaikh was very strict in the appointment of *khalifah*s and not every person referred to by Ghulam Mu'in-u'd-din was in the category of *khalifah*. Similarly, the author of *Mir'at-u'l-Asrar* has not made any clear distinction between the different categories of the disciples of the Shaikh.

Among the disciples there were many celebrities of the age—saints, scholars, poets, historians, etc. The greatest historian (Barani) and the most outstanding Persian poet (Amir Khusrau) of the times were among his disciples. The Shaikh treated them with affection but did not confer *khilafah* on them because they could not concentrate exclusively on the work involved in providing spiritual guidance to people. The Shaikh never asked them to forsake association with the court or renounce *shughl* for the simple reason that these restrictions applied to the *khalifah*s alone. One day Amir Khusrau raised his hands and stood up in ecstasy in an audition party. The Shaikh called him nearer and said that, as he was associated with the world, it was not permitted for him to raise his hands in that manner.[28] Short of granting of *khilafah*, the Shaikh showed great affection for Amir Khusrau, whom he called 'My Turk', and composed verses about him.[29] The Shaikh used to say that there were moments when he got fed up even with his own self, but never felt disgusted with Amir Khusrau.[30] Knowing the Shaikh's affection for him, other disciples sought his intercession in different matters. Shaikh Nasir-u'd-din Chiragh appealed through him to obtain the Shaikh's permission to live in some secluded place.[31] When the Shaikh was displeased with Maulana Burhan-u'd-din Gharib, it was Amir Khusrau who secured his pardon.[32]

Amir Hasan Sijzi enjoyed the Shaikh's affection on account of his literary interests and his sincere dedication to the Shaikh. He even allowed him to record his conversations but no *khilafat namah* was granted to him as he was employed in the army.

Zia-u'd-din Barani belonged to an aristocratic family which was closely associated with the Sultans of Delhi. A brilliant conversationalist with vast knowledge of history, he was a prominent figure among the literary circles of Delhi. He visited the Shaikh often but was never granted *khilafah*. During the reign of Firuz Shah Tughluq, when evil days fell on him and he was deprived of his position and property, he spent his days at the mausoleum of the Shaikh.

17

EVALUATION

————◆◆◆————

Shaikh Nizam-u'd-din Auliya was one of the most charismatic personalities of South Asia. A scholar with deep insight in the religious sciences, particularly the Qur'an and the *Hadith*; a saint whose vigils and fasts cast an aura of serene spirituality round his face; a humanitarian who spent his time attending to the problems of the weak and the worried; a pacifist who believed in non-violence and returned evil with good—the Shaikh represented in his person the highest traditions of religion and morality. According to Jamali, in his inner life he was the 'Bayazid of the time' and in adherence to the externals of religion he was a 'second Abu Hanifa'.[1] For more than half a century his *khanqah* in Delhi was a sanctum of peace for people in search of spiritual solace. His mission in life was to cultivate cosmic emotion by restoring man's relations with his Creator and by developing a worldview that raised man above all narrow and parochial motivations in life. He believed in building up morally autonomous personalities of his disciples in consonance with the noblest principles of religion. His concept of religion gave a revolutionary direction to religious activism by identifying it with the service of humanity. His deep and abiding concern for the poor and the downtrodden sections of society endeared him to all people. During his lifetime his name and fame reached different parts of the country,[2] and people flocked to him from every direction in search of blessings and benedictions.

---

[1] *Siyar-u'l-'Arifin*, p. 59.
[2] *Qiwam-u'l-'Aqa'id*, MS pp. 3–4.

These visitors came from different strata of society and included high and low, rich and poor, villagers, and townsfolk. For him all were children of God and he loved them all. The contemporary historian Zia-u'd-din Barani informs us that Shaikh Nizam-u'd-din,

opened wide the doors of his discipleship . . . and admitted [all sorts of people into his discipline] nobles and plebeians, rich and poor, learned and illiterate, citizens and villagers, soldiers and warriors, free-men and slaves and these people refrained from many improper things, because they considered themselves disciples of the Shaikh: if any of the disciples committed a sin, he confessed it [before the Shaikh] and vowed allegiance anew. The general public showed an inclination to religion and prayer; men and women, young and old, shop-keepers and servants, children and slaves, all came to say their prayers. Most of them who visited the Shaikh frequently, offered their *chasht* and *ishraq*[3] prayers regularly. Many platforms, with thatched roofs over them, were constructed on the way from the city to Ghiyaspur. Wells were dug, water-vessels were kept, carpets were spread, and a servant and a *hafiz* were stationed at every platform so that the people going to the Shaikh might have no difficulty in saying their supererogatory prayers. Due to regard for the Shaikh's discipleship all talk of sinful acts had disappeared from the people. There were no topics of conversation among most people except inquiries about the prayers of *chasht*, *awwabin*, and *tahajjud*. How many *rak'ah*s did they contain? What *surah* of the Qur'an should be recited in each *rak'ah*? What invocations (*du'a*) should follow each prayer? How many *rak'ah*s does the Shaikh say every night and what part of the Qur'an in every *rak'ah* and what *darud*s [blessings on the Prophet]? What was the custom of Shaikh Farid and Shaikh Bakhtiyar? Such were the questions which the new disciples asked from the old. They enquired about fasting and prayer and about reducing their diet. Many persons took to committing the Qur'an

---

[3] In addition to the five compulsory (*farz*) prayers—*fajr*, *zuhr*, *'asr*, *maghrib*, and *'isha*—there are five recommended prayers (i) *ishraq*, offered after sunrise; (ii) *chasht*, offered at forenoon; (iii) *zawwal*, offered at midday; (iv) *awwabin*, offered at twilight; and (v) *tahajjud*, offered between midnight and early dawn.

to memory. The new disciples of the Shaikh were entrusted to the old. And the older disciples had no other occupation but prayer and worship, aloofness from the world, the study of books on devotion and the lives of saints. And God forbid that they should ever talk or hear about worldly affairs or turn towards the houses of worldly men, for such things they considered to be entirely sinful and wrong. Interest in supererogatory prayers alone had developed to such an extent that at the Sultan's court many nobles, clerks, guards, and royal slaves had become the Shaikh's disciples. They said their *chasht* and *ishraq* prayers and fasted on the 13th, 14th, and 15th of every lunar month (*Ayyam-i-Biz*) as well as during the first ten days of Zu'l-Hijjah. There was no quarter of the city in which a gathering of the pious was not held every month or after every twenty days with mystic songs that moved them to tears. Many disciples of the Shaikh finished the *tarawih*[4] prayers in their houses or in the mosques. Those with greater perseverance passed the whole night standing in their prayers throughout the month of Ramadan, on Fridays and during the days of the Hajj. The higher disciples stood in prayers for a third or three-fourths of the night throughout the years, while others said their morning prayers with the ablution of their *'isha* prayer. Some of the disciples had, by now, reached to eminence in spiritual power through this training. Owing to the influence of the Shaikh, most of the Mussalmans of this country developed an interest in mysticism, prayers, and aloofness from the world, and came to have a faith in the Shaikh. The hearts of men having become virtuous by good deeds, the very name of wine, gambling, and other forbidden things never came to any one's lips. Sins and abominable vices appeared to people as bad as unbelief. Out of regard for one another the Muslims refrained from open usury and regrating (*ihtikar*), while the shop-keepers, from fear, gave up speaking lies, using false weights, and deceiving the ignorant. Most of the scholars and learned men, who frequented the Shaikh's company, applied themselves to books on devotion and mysticism. The books *Qut-u'l-Qulub*,[5] *Ihya-u'l-'Ulum*[6]

---

[4] The prayers of usually twenty *rak'ahs*, recited at night during the month of Ramadan.
[5] By Maulana Abu Talib Makki (d. 996), published in Cairo in 2 volumes, 1310/1882.
[6] By Imam Ghazzali (d. 1111), published in Cairo, 1311/1893.

and its translation,[7] *'Awarif,*[8] *Kashf-u'l-Mahjub,*[9] *Sharh-i-Ta'arruf,*[10] *Risalah-i-Qushairi',*[11] *Mirsad-u'l-'Ibad,*[12] *Maktubat-i-'Ain-u'l-Quzzat,*[13] and the *Lawa'ih* and *Lawama'* of Qazi Hamid-u'd-din Nagauri found many purchasers, as also did the *Fawa'id-u'l-Fu'ad* of Amir Hasan owing to the sayings it contains of the Shaikh. People asked the booksellers about books on devotion. No handkerchief was seen without a toothbrush (*miswak*) or a comb tied to it. Owing to the great number of purchasers, the price of water and eathern vessels became high. In short, God had created the Shaikh as a peer of Shaikh Junaid[14] and Shaikh Bayazid[15] in these later days and a man of wisdom. The virtues of a Shaikh—and the art of leading men (in the mystic path)—found their fulfilment and their final consummation in him.

Do not try to obtain eminence in this art,
For it has come to an end with Nizami.[16]

Before the close of the thirteenth century the mystic organization of the Shaikh had reached the zenith of its prestige and influence. The two decades of Sultan 'Ala-u'd-din Khalji's reign (1296–1316) saw the Shaikh at the helm of brisk spiritual activity. In the political sphere, the Sultan had embarked on his imperialistic adventures and was anxious to control the totality of the life of the people—social, economic, and religious. In the spiritual realm the Shaikh had opened wide the door

---

[7] *Kimiya-i-Sa'adah* (Nawal Kishore, Lucknow 1324/1907).

[8] By Shaikh Shihab-u'd-din Suhrawardi (d. 1234 AD), first published in Cairo in the margins of *Ihya* of Imam Ghazzali. See Beirut Edition, Dar-u'l-Kitab al-'Arabia, 1966.

[9] By Shaikh 'Ali Hujweri (d. after 1074); Persian text (*Gulzar-i-Hind*, Steam Press, Lahore); English trans. by R. A. Nicholson, Luzac 1936.

[10] *Kitab-i-Ta'arruf* was written by Abu Bakr Muhammad bin Ibrahim Bukhari (d. 999). It is one of the classics on Islamic mysticism. The author of *Kashf-u'z-Zunun* quotes a saying of the mystics about his book: 'One who does not know *Ta'arruf* does not understand mysticism.'

[11] By Abu'l-Qasim 'Abd-u'l-Karim Qushairi (d. 1072). Published in Cairo, 1346/1927.

[12] By Najm-u'd-din Razi in 1123.

[13] 'Ain-u'l-Quzzat Hamadani (d. 1131), says Jami, showed a unique power of expressing subtle mystic ideas. His works include: *Zubdat al-Haqa'iq* and *Tamhidat.*

[14] Abu'l-Qasim bin Muhammad bin Junaid (d. 910) See *Kashf-u'l-Mahjub* (trans.), pp. 128–30.

[15] Bayazid Taifur Bistami (d. 875). See Ibid. pp. 106 *et seq.*

[16] *Tarikh-i-Firuz Shahi*, pp. 343–7.

of spiritual training for all and had transformed the mystic movement into a mass movement. One day Zia-u'd-din Barani found the Shaikh admitting all sorts of people into his discipline for several hours continuously and wanted to ask the Shaikh the reason for mass admission into spiritual discipline, but the Shaikh himself addressed him and said that every age had its own needs and that what he was doing was the need of the hour.[17]

Never before had political and spiritual activities come up in such sharp contrast, running almost parallel to each other. Noble streaks of altruism running side by side with grim and sordid trails of militarism: one anxious to conquer territories, the other out to win the hearts of men. Barani's historical vision caught a glimpse of this phenomenal development,[18] but he did not attempt any analysis of it.

II

Inexorable in his judgement and unsurpassable in his pomp, 'Ala-u'd-din Khalji ruled the country with an iron hand. He consolidated his power effectively and forced all contumacious elements to submit to his authority. The north-western frontier was so garrisoned that the Mongols, who had devastated flourishing centres of Muslim culture in 'Ajam, had to think twice before stepping into his territory.[19]

To demonstrate his might and strike awe and terror into his enemies' hearts, he built victory towers with the heads of massacred Mongols.[20] The Sultan called himself 'Second Alexander'[21] and was anxious to excel the achievements of the preceding sultans in public works, in administration, and in conquests. If Aibek and Iltutmish had built the Qutb Minar, he must have another, bigger minaret[22] to commemorate his achievements; if Iltutmish had constructed the Hauz-i-Shamsi,

---

[17] *Hasrat Namah* as cited by Mir Khurd (see above).

[18] *Tarikh-i-Firuz Shahi*, pp. 339 *et seq.*

[19] *Nabhinandana-Jinodhara-Prabandh*, a Jain treatise, says: 'He dealt with them in a manner that prevented their return.' *Proceedings of the Indian History Congress* (1954), p. 241.

[20] *Khaza'in-u'l-Futuh* (Calcutta, 1953), p. 28; Ferishta, I, p. 116.

[21] *Tarikh-i-Firuz Shahi*, p. 263.

[22] *Khaza'in-u'l-Futuh*, p. 25.

he must have a more extensive Hauz-i-'Alai;[23] if other sultans had consolidated their power in the north alone, he would extend his authority to the south also. His predecessors were reluctant to touch the structure of agrarian administration, but he would liquidate the intermediaries and bring the state into direct contact with the peasants. Other rulers had controlled the actions of the people, why should he not control their conscience also and promulgate a new religion?[24]

'Ala-u'd-din dealt sternly with all hoarders and black-marketeers, and through control of the market brought down the price of all essential commodities.[25] Fear of draconian punishments made it impossible for merchants and traders to charge a *jital* more than the price fixed by the Sultan.[26] Sources of both supply and demand were effectively controlled and a rare coordination was brought about in rural and urban economies through the control of *banjara*s, realization of land tax in kind, and the control of *khut*s, *muqaddam*s and *chaudhari*s. Anti-social elements were brought to book. Magicians, *ibahatis*,[27] gamblers, and astrologers were either forced to give up their vocations or ruthlessly executed.[28] Prohibition was introduced[29] and prostitutes (whom even Iltutmish[30] had not been able to stop from carrying on their profession) were forced to marry.[31] Social contacts between the nobles were controlled[32] and a highly efficient espionage system kept the argos-eyed Sultan fully informed of the activities of the high and the low, and what went on in the houses and in the markets. People attributed his knowledge about every happening in the city to his miraculous powers.[33] There was hardly any aspect of life—public or private—which was not controlled by the Sultan. His successful banners reached distant

---

[23] Ibid. p. 30.

[24] *Tarikh-i-Firuz Shahi*, p. 263.

[25] *Khaza'in-u'l-Futuh*, pp. 21–2; *Tarikh-i-Firuz Shahi*, p. 307.

[26] *Tarikh-i-Firuz Shahi*, p. 309; *Khaza'in-u'l-Futuh*, pp. 20–1.

[27] Those who considered illegal things, like incest, as legal. See Khusrau, Ibid. p. 20; *Futuhat-i-Firuz Shahi*, p. 7. See also Nizami, *Salatin-i-Dehli Kay Mazhabi Rujhanat*, pp. 246–9.

[28] *Khaza'in-u'l-Futuh*, pp. 19–20; *Tarikh-i-Firuz Shahi*, p. 336.

[29] *Khaza'in-u'l-Futuh*, pp. 17–18; *Tarikh-I-Firuz Shahi*, p. 284.

[30] Ibid. p. 43.

[31] *Khaza'in-u'l-Futuh*, p. 18.

[32] *Tarikh-i-Firuz Shahi*, p. 286.

[33] Ibid. pp. 324–5.

Warangal and his coffers overflowed with the wealth of the south—
where the arm of no north-Indian ruler had reached for centuries.

III

In Delhi, however, there was a *khanqah* which, though within the
political confines of the Sultanate, was not a part of the Delhi Empire.
In the midst of a world of ceaseless political and military activity, it
stood like an oasis of love. The writ of the Sultan did not run here
and could not interfere with its functioning; neither could its inmates
be forced to serve the government, nor the presiding saint be persuaded
to visit the court. A serene spiritual atmosphere pervaded it, free from
the contamination of political life. Both high and low rubbed their
shoulders here; the spy ring of the Sultan could not encircle it.[34] It
was a world to itself. This was the *khanqah* of Shaikh Nizam-u'd-din
Auliya. The Shaikh had taken upon himself the stupendous task of
inculcating in people respect for moral values and dedication to the
service of man. It was an antidote to the imperialistic enterprise of
the Khalji state. He checked materialistic ambitions and preached a
life of contentment, self-respect, and self-control.

On Muharram 24, 710/26 May 1310, Malik Kafur returned from
his southern campaigns and brought with him enormous booty. This
wealth was displayed at *Chabutrah-i-Nasiri* and whoever looked at it
was duly dazzled.[35] The next day, on Muharram 25, 710/27 May 1310,
Shaikh Nizam-u'd-din Auliya addressed his audience about the use
of wealth and said that it should be used for general welfare.[36] In his
own unobtrusive but effective manner he gave advice that must have
reached the ears of all in Delhi.

Sultan 'Ala-u'd-din Khalji was on his deathbed. The Shaikh referred
in his assemblies to Iltutmish[37] and said that his salvation was due to
the construction of Hauz-i-Shamsi, which supplied water to Delhi.
The Shaikh's practice was that, instead of giving direct advice to anybody,

---

[34] See *Qiwam-u'l-'Aqa'id* for early efforts of the spies to probe into its affairs (MS p. 177
et seq.)

[35] *Khaza'in-u'l-Futuh*, p. 112.

[36] *Fawa'id-u'l-Fu'ad*, p. 49.

[37] Ibid. p. 119.

he spoke his mind through stories and parables. When 'Ala-u'd-din Khalji died, Amir Khusrau made the most pungent comment on his imperialistic ambitions and said:[38]

چـــرا باید گرفت کـشـور وشهر

کزاں ندهند بیش از چهار گز بهر

(Why conquer so many realms and cities when you cannot get more than four yards of land after your death.)

It was Khusrau, the disciple of Shaikh Nizam-u'd-din Auliya, who could express such sentiments, which neatly represent the viewpoint of his spiritual master.

The contemporary historian, Zia-u'd-din Barani, has summed up the tremendous impact of the Shaikh on public life in one pithy observation: 'As a result [of his teachings] sin among people had been reduced.'[39]

This was the *summum bonum* of all his mystic activity—the creation of a better order of society, in which people respect moral and spiritual values. As a result of his efforts wine-drinking, gambling, regrating, and other anti-social activities had stopped.[40] The Sultan had muzzled freedom of action; the Shaikh concentrated on building independent and self-reliant personalities, capable of thinking and acting independently of the Sultan. He did not enter into any conflict with the state but, on his part, never allowed the state to fetter his soul.

IV

The Shaikh was like a living fountain of light, a comfort to be near, and enlightening to everyone who did come near him. Those nearest of all, his disciples, were so enamoured of him that their respect and devotion knew no bounds.

---

[38] *Duwal Rani Khizr Khan*, p. 260.
[39] *Tarikh-i-Firuz Shahi*, p. 344.
[40] See above.

A wandering mendicant came to the Shaikh during the early years of his stay in Delhi and asked for some monetary help. The Shaikh had nothing to offer at that time, and so he asked him to stay for a few days and wait for some *futuh*. As no *futuh* came for several days, the dervish decided to leave the *khanqah*. While permitting him to go, the Shaikh gave him his pair of shoes. The dervish set out and on his way met Amir Khusrau, who was on his annual visit to Delhi from Multan. He had several lakh *tankas* with him. When the two met, Amir Khusrau enquired about his spiritual master. The dervish informed him about his financial difficulties and narrated all that had happened with him. Khusrau offered his whole wealth to him in exchange for the slippers. With these slippers on his head he reached his master. The Shaikh looked at him and remarked: 'Khusrau! You have purchased them very cheap.'[41] Malikzada Ahmad had so great a faith in the Shaikh and was so overwhelmed by his spiritual prestige that he did not have the courage to place his hand on his hand, as the custom is when being admitted into the discipline.[42]

Even after the death of the Shaikh, his disciples continued to show the same love and respect to his memory. When Shaikh Qutb-u'd-din Munawwar and Shaikh Nasir-u'd-din Chiragh met after the death of the Shaikh they cried in pain, remembering him.[43]

Maulana Siraj-u'd-din 'Usman, popularly known as Akhi Siraj, had all the garments that the Shaikh had bestowed on him on different occasions buried above his head;[44] Amir Khusrau had the letters he had received from the Shaikh buried with him in his grave.[45] Shaikh Burhan-u'd-din Gharib, who had to migrate to Daulatabad under the orders of Muhammad bin Tughluq, never turned his back towards the tomb of his spiritual mentor in Delhi.[46]

Even in times of distress and despondency, when death loomed large before them, they did not forget the Shaikh. When Khwaja Jahan was

---

[41] Dara Shukoh, *Safinat-u'l-Auliya*, p. 100.
[42] *Shawamil-u'l-Jumal*, MS p. 65.
[43] 'Afif, *Tarikh-i-Firuz Shahi*, p. 83.
[44] *Siyar-u'l-Auliya*, p. 289.
[45] Ibid. p. 303.
[46] Ibid. p. 278.

brought to the scaffold, he put the cap of the Shaikh on his head and tied on the *dastar* he had received from him, and surrendered to the executioner.[47]

Pledges made at the shrine of the Shaikh were considered so sacrosanct that no one ever thought of breaking them. When Firuz Shah assigned the government of Gujarat to Shams-u'd-din Damghani, he ordered him to produce a surety for his good conduct. 'Whatever be your Majesty's order,' said Damghani. Firuz Shah asked him to make Shaikh Nizam-u'd-din Auliya his surety. Damghani agreed. Next day he went with the Sultan to the grave of the Shaikh, 'lifted the cover-sheet of the grave in his hand and standing in the direction of Ka'ba, made the Shaikh his surety.'[48]

Shaikh Farid Ganj-i-Shakar had conferred on Shaikh Nizam-u'd-din Auliya the spiritual kingdom of Hindustan[49] and had ordered him to go and take it. He had also predicted that he would be like a shady tree,[50] providing shade and shelter to the people. The Shaikh's life was one long illustration of the way he had lived up to the expectations of his master, established his spiritual authority, and earned the sobriquet of *Sultan-u'l-Masha'ikh*, with *khanqahs* owing allegiance to him spread all over the country. He attended to the problems of the people who were secretly tormented by mundane ambitions, assuaged their wounds, raised their drooping spirits, and infused in them courage and confidence by inculcating respect for moral and spiritual values. Whenever a problem was brought to him, he felt it as if it was his own, and the worries of the sufferer were transferred to him.[51] The effect of the constant flow of tears from his eyes was visible on his cheeks.[52]

For more than five decades Shaikh Nizam-u'd-din Auliya provided spiritual guidance and shelter to the people of South Asia. Three dynasties and a dozen rulers appeared on the throne and disappeared like

---

[47] 'Afif, *Tarikh-i-Firuz Shahi*, p. 77.
[48] Ibid. p. 500.
[49] *Qiwam-u'l-'Aqa'id*, MS p. 18.
[50] *Siyar-u'l-Auliya*, p. 11; *Qiwam-u'l-'Aqa'id*, MS p. 17.
[51] *Khair-u'l-Majalis*, p. 105.
[52] *Jawami'-u'l-Kalim*, p. 63.

iridescent bubbles, but he remained unshaken and undisturbed by any political change. Empires rose and fell, but he went on inculcating his moral principles regardless of change in the political scenario of the period.

VI

Contemporary assessments of Shaikh Nizam-u'd-din Auliya reveal the nature and extent of the veneration and esteem with which he was regarded by the people and the place they assigned to him in the mystic hierarchy. They saw in him an image of the eminent mystic masters, Junaid[53] and Bayazid,[54] and considered him to be the 'the last of the saints as the Prophet Muhammad was the last of the Prophets'.[55] Amir Khusrau claimed that his disciples trod the same path that Shibli and Ibrahim Adham had traversed.[56] Whoever joined his discipline immortalized himself.[57] People looked upon him as the *Qutb* of the times.[58] As sovereign of the spiritual realm he was deemed to have bestowed spiritual territories on his disciples.[59] He was the refuge and asylum of people against calamities and misfortunes.[60] Khusrau said about him:

بهر سو کز دمش بادے رسیده

هزاراں کـــوه رنج از جا پریده

(Wherever his breath has reached, thousands of mountains of grief have melted away.)

---

[53] *Majnun Laila*, p. 13.
[54] Barani, p. 346.
[55] *Futuh-u's-Salatin*, p. 456.
[56] *Nuh Sipihr*, p. 24.
[57] *Matla'-u'l-Anwar*, p. 22.
[58] *Hasht Bihisht*, p. 12; *Duwal Rani Khizr Khan*, p. 227; *Sirat-i-Firuz Shah*, MS fo. 85ᵃ.
[59] *Matla'-u'l-Anwar*, p. 23.
[60] *Futuh-u's-Salatin*, pp. 456–7.

The Shaikh's close adherence to the *sunnah* of the Prophet was lauded in different ways.[61] He was called 'the right arm of the Prophet'[62] and a medieval saying—

فإن الشيخ في القوم كالنبي في أمته

(A *Shaikh* is for his *qaum* what a prophet is for his *ummah*)

—was cited by a number of contemporary writers as a way to measure the special nature of his status and contribution.[63] What inspired this maxim was the conviction that though apostolic succession had come to an end with the Prophet, the prophetic mission (*kar-i-nabuwwat*) was an obligation of the mystic teachers to carry forward. Barani calls sainthood 'deputyship of the Prophet',[64] and Khusrau considered the character of the Shaikh to be the *nuskha-i-dibacha-i-payghambari*.[65]

A significant aspect of contemporary and later assessments of the Shaikh was the belief that he combined in his person the virtues and qualities of Jesus and Khizr. From Amir Khusrau to Dr Mohammed Iqbal, all writers of mature religious sensitivity have referred to it. As Jesus cured people of disease, so Shaikh Nizam-u'd-din Auliya cured the ailing hearts;[66] as Khizr showed people the way to truth and virtue, so Shaikh Nizam-u'd-din Auliya guided men on the path of piety and rectitude. Khusrau declared:[67]

وجود خواجه نه از آب وگل گشته مرتب

که جان خضر ومسیحا بهم شد مرکب

---

[61] *Duwal Rani Khizr Khan*, p. 16.

[62] *Shirin Khusrau*, p. 12; *Matla'-u'l-Anwar*, p. 22; *Hasht Bihisht*, p. 13.

[63] *Qiwam-u'l-'Aqaid*, MS p. 8; *Shawamil-u'l-Jumal*, MS p. 25; *Siyar-u'l-Auliya*, p. 360.

[64] *Tarikh-i-Firuz Shahi*, p. 341.

[65] *Matla'-u'l-Anwar*, p. 21.

[66] *Diwan*, p. 37; *Matla'-u'l-Anwar*, pp. 20, 22; *A'ina-i-Sikandari*, p. 12; *Duwal Rani Khizr Khan*, p. 15; *Majnun Laila*, p. 17; *Qiwam-u'l-'Aqaid*, MS p. 8.

[67] *Siyar-u'l-Auliya*, p. 19.

(The person of the Khwaja is not made of water and clay. The lives of Khizr and Jesus have been mixed to give form to his being.)

Dr Muhammad Iqbal said:[68]

تری لحد کی زیارت ہے زندگی دل کی

مسیح وخضر سے اونچا مقام ہے تیرا

(Pilgrimage to your grave gives life to the heart; your station is higher than that of Christ and Khizr).

VII

Throughout the centuries that followed the Shaikh's death his tomb was visited alike by kings, nobles, scholars, Sufis, the rich, and the poor. Muhammad bin Tughluq, who had carried the Shaikh's bier on his shoulders,[69] constructed a mausoleum over his grave.[70] Firuz Shah Tughluq made several additions to it. He writes in his *Futuhat*:

The doors of the domed chamber and the latticed screens of the mausoleum of Sultan-u'l-Masha'ikh Nizam-u'l-Haqq wa'd-din Mahbub-i-Ilahi (may God hallow his holy grave), were also made with sandalwood. Golden chandeliers were hung by gold chains in the four corners of the hall and a new *Jama'at Khanah*, such as had not existed there before, was built.[71]

When Babur reached Delhi he 'made a circuit of the luminous mausoleum of Shaikh Nizam-u'd-din Auliya' . . . and then encamped on the bank of the river Jumna.'[72] Akbar selected for his father's burial

---

[68] *Kulliyat*, p. 96.
[69] Ibn Battuta, *Rihla*, II, p. 33.
[70] *Siyar-u'l-Auliya*, p. 154.
[71] *Futuhat-i-Firuz Shahi*, p. 17 tr. 118.
[72] *Tabaqat-i-Babari*, p. 92; *Babur Namah*, tr. Beveridge, II, p. 475.

a place near the *khanqah* of the Shaikh.[73] All the Mughal rulers from Akbar to Bahadur Shah Zafar visited his tomb for blessing and benediction. When an attempt on Akbar's life in Delhi failed, he attributed it to the blessings of the Shaikh whose grave he had visited just before the incident.[74] When facing Khusrau's rebellion, Jahangir visited the tomb of the Shaikh.[75] Muhammad Shah was buried at the foot of the Shaikh's tomb.[76]

The rulers of the South also displayed great respect and veneration for Shaikh Nizam-u'd-din Auliya. As already stated, the founder of the Bahmani kingdom, 'Ala-u'd-din Hasan Gangu, came to Delhi during the days of his adversity. One day he went to see the Shaikh. Just before him Ulugh Khan (the future Muhammad bin Tughluq) had left the hospice. The Shaikh told an attendant: 'One king has left and another is waiting at the door. Bring him in.' The Shaikh received the visitor with affection and prophesied a bright future for him in the Deccan. He pressed a piece of bread on one of his fingers and offered it to him with the prophesy: 'This will be the standard of your kingdom.' The visitor took it as a happy omen and left.[77] When better days dawned and Hasan Gangu became the Sultan, he sent five *maund*s of gold and ten *maund*s of silver to Shaikh Burhan-u'd-din Gharib for distribution among the needy and the poor, in order to bless the soul of Shaikh Nizam-u'd-din Auliya.[78]

The Shaikh was held in high esteem by the saints of different *silsilah*s. Shaikh Rukn-u'd-din Abu'l-Fath, the famous Suhrawardi saint of Multan, referred to him as 'king of religion'.[79] Shaikh Sharaf-u'd-din Yahya Maneri used to say that Shaikh Nizam-u'd-din Auliya had reached that stage of mystic consciousness where sleep and wakefulness have equal significance.[80]

---

[73] Bayazid, *Tazkirah-i-Humayun wa Akbar*, p. 234.

[74] *Akbar Namah*, tr. II, p. 313; Badauni, II, p. 60.

[75] *Tuzuk-i-Jahangiri*, p. 27.

[76] It is said that Muhammad Shah had purchased this piece of land for his grave in his lifetime from the *khanqah* people for one lakh rupees. See Bashir-u'd-din, *Waqi'at-i-Darul Hakumat Delhi*, II, p. 797.

[77] *Burhan-u'l-Ma'asir*, p. 12; *Tabaqat-i-Akbari*, III, p. 6; *Ferishta*, I, p. 274.

[78] *Ferishta*, I, p. 277.

[79] *Siyar-u'l-Auliya*, p. 139.

[80] *Ma'dan-u'l-Ma'ani*, p. 405.

Later saints and Sufis visited the grave of Shaikh Nizam-u'd-din Auliya for spiritual blessings; they sat in meditation there and considered its atmosphere efficacious in integrating their spiritual personalities. Syed Muhammad Gisu Daraz of Gulbarga once told his audience that, after the exodus from Delhi demanded by Sultan Muhammad bin Tughluq, all *khanqah*s and mausoleums became desolate except a few that included those of Khwaja Qutb-u'd-din Bakhtiyar Kaki and Shaikh Nizam-u'd-din Auliya where candles could be seen burning.[81]

Scholars, poets, and men of letters visited the mausoleum in large numbers. Before leaving for Europe for higher education, Dr Muhammad Iqbal prayed at his grave for his spiritual blessing in the shaping of his intellectual life.

The graveyards round the tomb of the Shaikh are a testimony to the respect in which the Shaikh was held by posterity. Finding a place for burial in the vicinity of the Shaikh's tomb was regarded as a special blessing. From Amir Khusrau to Ghalib, from Khan-i-Jahan Maqbul to 'Aziz Kokaltash, from Zia-u'd-din Barani to Sir Shah Sulaiman, many celebrities lie buried in and around the complex. Historical knowledge will always be beholden to Khwaja Hasan Nizami, himself a renowned Sufi and man of letters, for the sincere efforts that he made to identify and preserve the graves in the area. The Chabutra-i-Yaran was exclusively for the disciples and descendants of the Shaikh, and eminent *khalifah*s lie buried there. The graves that have sprung up from 1325 to the present day round the mausoleum of the Shaikh are like seals of history attesting to the feelings of love and faith which the Shaikh has enjoyed throughout the six and a half centuries that have passed since his death. Today both Hindus and Muslims pay homage to his memory and with his name a world of historic visions and memories glows into consciousness. His lifestory, dedicated as it was to human love and sympathy, provides a happy diversion from the pomp and panoply of the medieval courts and the din and clatter of the battlefields.

---

[81] *Jawami'-u'l-Kalim*, p. 143.

APPENDIX - I

NAME AND TITLES

What was the original name of Shaikh Nizam-u'd-din Auliya? What other titles or *kunya*s were added to it later? Why does the word *Auliya* (plural of *wali*) appear with his name?

1. In *Fawa'id-u'l-Fu'ad* the Shaikh's name appears as *Shaikh Nizam-u'd-din* (pp. 1, 41, 90, 114, 218, etc.) along with honorific epithets like *Malik-u'l-Fuqara, Qutb-u'l-Aqtab, Khatm-u'l-Masha'ikh, Khatm-u'l-Mujtahidin,* and *Sultan-u'l-Auliya.*

2. *Siyar-u'l-Auliya* generally refers to him as *Sultan-u'l-Masha'ikh.* The printed text has, however, some interpolations. The writer of these lines had a very reliable manuscript copy, made for his great-grandfather M. Irshad 'Ali Sahib of Amroha, of *Siyar-u'l-Auliya,* collated and corrected by Diwan Allah Jiwaya of Pakpattan. Page 92 of the printed text of *Siyar-u'l-Auliya* gives the following titles and epithets:

   > Sultan-u'l-Masha'ikh Nizam-u'l-Haqq wa'l-Haqiqat wa'l-Sharh wa'd-Din Warith al-Auliya-wa'l-Mursilin *Syed Sultan-u'l-Auliya Nizam-u'd-din* Muhammad *Mahbub-i-Ilahi bin Syed* Ahmad bin *Syed* 'Ali al-Bukhari *al-Chishti al-Dihlawi.*
   >
   > The manuscript (p. 170), however, does not give the epithets shown in italics. The genealogical table of the Shaikh as given in the printed edition is also an interpolation and does not appear in the manuscript.

3. Firuz Shah Tughluq refers to him as *Sultan-u'l-Masha'ikh* and *Mahbub-i-Ilahi* (*Futuhat-i-Firuz Shahi,* p. 17).

4. *Durar-i-Nizami* (Salarjang Museum MS fos. 1^b, 2^a), refers to him as *Nizam-u'l-Haqq wa Sharh wa'd-Din Muhammad bin Ahmad bin 'Ali al-Bukhari.*

5. *Khair-u'l-Majalis* refers to him as Shaikh Nizam-u'l-Haqq wa'l-Sharh wa'd-Din (pp. 5, 9, etc.) with various honorific epithets like *Qutb-u'l-Aqtab*, and *Shaikh-u'l-'Alam*. *Ahsan-u'l-Aqwal* refers to him as *Shaikh-u'l-Islam* (MS p. 13); and *Jawami'-u'l-Kalim* calls him 'Shaikh' or 'Shaikh-u'l-Islam' Nizam-u'd-din (p. 31, etc.).

6. Among the early historians, Zia-u'd-din Barani (*Tarikh-i-Firuz Shahi*, p. 341) and Shams-i-Siraj 'Afif (*Tarikh-i-Firuz Shahi*, pp. 28, 83, 500, etc.) refer to him as *Shaikh-u'l-Islam*. Ibn Battuta (*Rihla*, II p. 33) calls him *Nizam-u'd-din Badaoni*.

7. Among the mystic *tazkirah* writers, Maulana Jami was perhaps the first to refer to him as *Shaikh Nizam-u'd-din Auliya* (*Nafahat-u'l-Uns*, p. 452). Jamali refers to him (*Siyar-u'l-'Arifin*, earliest available MS in John Rylands Library) as *Malik-u'l-Masha'ikh wa'l-Auliya* (fo. 91[b]) or generally as *Sultan-u'l-Masha'ikh* (fos. 46[b], 19[b] etc.). On f. 80[b] of the John Rylands manuscript someone has deleted *Sultan-u'l-Auliya* and substituted *Sultan-u'l-Masha'ikh Mahbub-i-Ilahi*. *Siyar-u'l-'Arifin* gives his name as Nizam-u'd-din Muhammad (fo. 80[b]).

Shaikh 'Abd-u'l-Haqq Muhaddith Dihlawi says: 'His title is *Sultan-u'l-Masha'ikh* and *Nizam-i-Auliya*' (*Akhbar-u'l-Akhyar*, p. 57).

8. It is clear that his original name was 'Muhammad'. The certificate granted to him by Maulana Kamal-u'd-din Zahid refers to him as 'Nizam-u'd-din Muhammad bin Ahmad bin `Ali' (*Siyar-u'l-Auliya*, p. 104). In the *Khilafat Namah* conferred on him by Shaikh Farid Ganj-i-Shakar his name occurs as Nizam-u'l-Millat wa'd-Din Muhammad bin Ahmad (*Siyar-u'l-Auliya*, p. 117). In the *Khilafat Namah*, which the Shaikh himself granted to Maulana Shams-u'd-din Yahya, he mentions his own name as Nizam-u'd-din Muhammad (*Siyar-u'l-Auliya* p. 449). We find a teacher in Badaon addressing him as *Baba Muhammad* (*Qiwam-u'l-'Aqa'id* MS p. 13).

It seems that *Nizam-u'd-din* was his *kunya* and had been adopted very early. Jamal Qiwam-u'd-din says that early in his life a man, whose identity has not been traced, was heard calling him at his house door as *Maulana Nizam-u'd-din*. The Shaikh himself was surprised at this but felt that some mysterious voice had called him as such. (*Qiwam-u'l-'Aqa'id*, MS p. 15). Thereafter everybody started calling him *Nizam-u'd-din*. Even his mother called him so. Amir Khusrau (as quoted earlier) says that since he gathered and organized the disciples of Shaikh Farid-u'd-din Ganj-i-Shakar, his title became Nizam:

شد سلک فرید از تو منظوم

زانست که شد لقب نظامت

Jamal Qiwam-u'd-din himself refers to him as *Qutb-i'Alam Nizam-u'l-Haqq wa'd-Din* (MS p. 2).

9. The suffix *Auliya* has led to a number of speculations. The view that it is part of some larger title—*Sultan-u'l-Auliya* or *Nizam-i-Auliya*—does not appear very convincing because retaining part of the title and dropping the rest is not at all common practice.

Some writers have expressed surprise at the use of the plural where the singular is expected. The fact is that in the Arabic language the plural is used where some particular quality or characteristic of an individual is emphasized. Shah 'Abd-u'l-'Aziz, son of Shah Waliullah of Delhi, a distinguished scholar of Arabic, says that it conforms to the Arabic semantics. The precedents being: (*a*) the Prophet Abraham has been called *ummah* in the Qur'an, (*b*) Khwaja 'Ubaidullah came to be known as *Ahrar*, and (*c*) Ka'b was called *Ahbar*. (*Shifa al-'Alil*, being translation with commentary of Shah Waliullah's *Qaul-u'l-Jamil*, Matba'-i-Nizami, Kanpur 1291 AH, p. 135).

The title *Mahbub-i-Ilahi* came to be used for him during his lifetime, as is evident from the statement of Amir Khusrau and Firuz Shah Tughluq. Amir Khusrau says:

بجن وانس راند پادشاهی

نظام الدین محبوب الهی

The title *Sultan-u'l-Masha'ikh* also found currency during his lifetime (*Siyar-u'l-Auliya, Futuhat-i-Firuz Shahi*). The word *Auliya* appears with his name from the sixteenth century. It appears that a number of epithets and sobriquets were given to him during his lifetime and after his death. The two that stuck with his name and survived were *Sultan-u'l-Masha'ikh* and *Mahbub-i-ilahi*. The first fixed his position with reference to saints; the second indicated his place in the eyes of God.

It was Amir Khusrau who called himself *Nizami* for the first time.

مفتخــــر از وے بغلامی منم

خواجه نظام است ونظامی منم

Appendix - II

---•◦•---

THE *KHUTBAH*

The following introductory lines of an Arabic *khutba* written by Shaikh Nizam-u'd-din Auliya have been rendered into English by Dr. M. G. Zubaid Ahmad in his book *The Contribution of India to Arabic Literature* (pp. 185–6).

All praise is due to Him, of the vision of Whom the eyes of beholders have fallen short and Whom the imaginations of those who have communion with Him have failed to describe. He has created creatures with His power and brought them out of absolute nothingness into existence by His will. He has made the tongue of the Divine praisers recite *La ilaha illa-llah* and has deposited in the breasts of the learned the keys to lights known to none but God. He has animated the souls of those who are longing for the Divine vision, with the spirit of longing to behold the Beauty of God, and has shed the blood of the lovers [of God] with the sword of His majesty in the desert of communion with God, and has burnt the hearts of the Divine lovers with the fire of love in their longing to meet God. He has created Paradise and Hell for the believers and the infidels in order to repay the wicked for what they have done, and to compensate the righteous for their good deeds. If Paradise be the lot of gnostics, but without the vision of, and communion with, Him, woe betide them; and if Hell, accompanied with the Beauty of God and with communion with Him, be allotted to those who long [for God], how great will be their longing!

APPENDIX - III

LETTERS OF THE SHAIKH

It appears that despite his heavy preoccupations Shaikh Nizam-u'd-din Auliya regularly corresponded with his friends and disciples. References are also found to his letters to Baba Farid Ganj-i-Shakar (*Durar-i-Nizami*, MS). The *Tuhfat-u'l-Majalis*, conversations of Shaikh Ahmad Maghribi, refers to Shaikh Nizam-u'd-din Auliya's correspondence with Syed Mu'in-u'd-din (MS India Office fos. 24ᵃ⁻ᵇ). With his *khalifah*s spread all over the country, he could not avoid corresponding on different matters of personal and organizational significance. He wrote as many as one hundred letters to Shaikh Mubarak Gopamavi (*Siyar-u'l-Auliya*, p. 310). A letter written to Maulana Fakhr-u'd-din Maruzi has been quoted in *Siyar-u'l-Auliya* (p. 299). Copies of a letter written to Maulana Husam-u'd-din regarding monotheism are found in manuscript (MSS, Aligarh Muslim University, *Farsiya Mazhab* 129 and Ahsan collection no. 297.71). Amir Khusrau received numerous letters from him on different mystical matters (*Siyar-u'l-Auliya*, p. 302). Substantial points of some of these letters have been referred to by Amir Khurd in *Siyar-u'l-Auliya* (p. 302). Amir Khusrau had all these letters buried with him in his grave (*Siyar-u'l-Auliya*, p. 303).

Later *tazkirah* writers, like Rahim Bakhsh Fakhri, have quoted the Shaikh's letters to Amir Khusrau and Maulana Fakhr-u'd-din Maruzi (*Shajrat-u'l-Anwar*, MS fo. 253ᵃ). An Urdu translation of a letter entitled *Tuhfat-u'l-Mahbub* was published by Khwaja Muhammad Abu'l-Hasan Muhi-u'd-din Khan of Hyderabad from Agra in 1902.

These letters deal mostly with matters of spiritual significance, e.g. cosmic emotion, adherence to *Shari'ah* (*Siyar-u'l-Auliya*, p. 385), and being continually in a state of *wuzu* (ablution) (*Siyar-u'l-Auliya*, p. 371). In a letter to Amir Khusrau, the Shaikh refers to his having sent a comb to him (*Siyar-u'l-Auliya*, p. 371). It may be noted in passing that the Shaikh had presented a comb to

Shaikh Rukn-u'd-din of Multan (*Siyar-u'l-Auliya*, p. 139). The present of a comb had special significance in mystic practice. For Shaikh Farid's refusal to give a comb to a dervish, see *Khair-u'l-Majalis* p. 202.

Appendix - IV

KHILAFAT NAMAH GRANTED TO SHAIKH NIZAM-U'D-DIN AULIYA BY SHAIKH FARID-U'D-DIN MAS'UD GANJ-I-SHAKAR

The following is an abridged English translation of the Arabic *Khilafat-cum-Ijazat-Namah* granted to Shaikh Nizam-u'd-din Auliya by his spiritual mentor Shaikh Farid-u'd-din Mas'ud Ganj-i-Shakar. It confers spiritual authority on Shaikh Nizam-u'd-din Auliya and accords permission to teach *Tamhidat* of Abu Shakur Salimi, a book dealing with the fundamentals of faith.

In the name of God, the Compassionate and the Merciful . . . He is the First and the Last, the Appearance and the Reality. Whomsoever God elevates, none can degrade, and whomsoever God degrades no one can elevate. None can hide what He wants to reveal and nobody can conceal whatever He wants to reveal . . . May God bless Muhammad and his followers, his Companions and other saintly persons . . . After His praise I declare that the study of the knowledge and principle of the Traditions . . . gives light to him who pours water on burnt places through its knowledge. This path is, in fact, perilous and full of hazards and difficult in view of results. In this branch of knowledge the best book is the *Tamhid-u'l-Muhtadi* of Abu Shakur Salimi . . . This book has been studied under me, lesson after lesson, from the beginning to the end, minutely, attentively, carefully and thoroughly, by the dutiful son, the pious, the Imam of the Age and blessed, Nizam-u'l-Millat wa'd-Din Muhammad, son of Ahmad, who is an adornment of imams and scholars and the pride of the holy and the virtuous. May God bless him with the desire of submission to Him and be merciful to him and elevate his position . . . At the time of teaching him, I found him capable, able, meritorious, well-behaved, and good mannered. I now permit him to teach this book to students, provided he avoids mistakes in teaching, writing, and explaining it and utilizes his energy and knowledge in discussion, correction of manuscripts, and purification of the language. God is the real protector from errors of speech and a saviour from disruption and disease in religious work. This deed of permission was

drawn during the month of Ramadan, on a Wednesday. May God extend
the bounties of this blessed month. This document was drafted at the order
of the Shaikh of the Shaikhs of the World, may God ever protect his honour
and prestige, and was written by the humble slave of God, Ishaq son of Ali,
a resident of Delhi, in the presence of the Shaikh of the Shaikhs of this world.

I also permit Nizam-u'l-Millat wa'd-Din to narrate things which he has
learnt or heard from me and has collected and preserved.[1]

He should follow the right course and many blessings be on him. I also
permit him to adopt isolation in some mosque where the prayers are offered
in congregation. He should not disregard the conditions laid down about
seclusion. Progress [on the mystic path] lies in following them. The basis of
this seclusion is the Tradition of the Holy Prophet which runs: 'Live in the
world like a traveller or a wayfarer and count yourself among the dead.'
Consequently, the person who, in accordance with this precept has made
up his mind and summoned up his courage, is permitted to adopt seclusion,
provided he controls [the desires of] the flesh and thinks himself nonexistent
and weak, and renounces the world and its temptations. He must also be
aware of the harm that worldly ambitions and desires do [to the spiritual
personality]. The time of such a recluse becomes adorned with various devotions
when his material ego (*nafs*) is prevented from coming back to the ordinary
devotions from the higher devotions. When the struggle wears him out, he
should calm his passions either by religious devotions or by sleeping for a
while, for this pacification prevents the supremacy of the passions. One should
abstain from idle seclusion because this makes one's heart neglectful. May
God save Nizam-u'l-Haqq-wa'd-Din from such evils and guide him aright.
Nizam-u'd-din is really my deputy and successor in things worldly and religious,
and obedience to him is obedience to me. May God be kind to them who
show respect and honour to Nizam-u'd-din, whom I honour and for whom
I have great regard. If anyone does not respect him, may God disgrace him.
All these words are from *faqir* Mas'ud [*Siyar-u'l-Auliya*, pp. 166–20].

---

[1] It appears from *Fawa'id-u'l-Fu'ad* that the Shaikh had collected the sayings of his spiritual
mentor, Shaikh Farid, for personal reference and guidance. It was not made public, perhaps
because it contained confidential instructions on spiritual matters.

APPENDIX - V

CERTIFICATE GRANTED TO SHAIKH NIZAM-U'D-DIN
AULIYA BY MAULANA KAMAL-U'D-DIN ZAHID

The following is an abridged English translation of the Arabic certificate granted to Shaikh Nizam-u'd-din Auliya by his teacher Maulana Kamal-u'd-din Zahid, a renowned *muhaddith* of Delhi, in 679/1280.

This *Ijazat Namah* thus established the instructional *silsilah* of Shaikh Nizam-u'd-din Auliya with the author of *Mashariq-u'l-Anwar*.

Maulana Razi-u'd-din Hasan Saghani
Maulana Burhan-u'd-din Mahmud As'ad al-Balkhi
Maulana Kamal-u'd-din Zahid
Shaikh Nizam-u'd-din Auliya

In the name of God the most Beneficent and most Merciful.

All praise is for Him Whose quality is [providing] guidance and [bestowing] bounties [on His creatures]. At His order appear morning and evening . . . All bounties and His countless praises for [the Prophet] and blessings on him, as he possesses laudable qualities and is wise. His utterances are like a key [for unlocking the Divine mysteries] and his sayings (*ahadith*) are all true . . .

After praises of God and blessings on His Prophet, it may be known that God has blessed the saintly leader, wise, truthful, and devoted to God, Nizam-u'd-din Muhammad bin Ahmad bin 'Ali Bukhari, that despite his wide and erudite knowledge, eloquent speech, his being beloved of great saints and pious scholars—he studied this book—the *Mashariq-u'l-Anwar* which contains the gist of *Sahih Muslim* and *Sahih Bukhari*—from beginning to end from the writer of these lines with great dedication and effort. He assimilated its contents after careful discussion and made special efforts in deciphering the meaning and tracing the genesis of the Traditions.

The writer of these lines had learnt and heard this book [the *Mashariq-u'l-Anwar*] from two outstanding religious leaders, wise and perfect: one of them was the compiler of a commentary on *Athar-u'l-Nayyarain* and the other combined the knowledge of *Shari'ah* and *Tariqah* and was a great religious leader, Mahmud Abi al-Hasan As'ad Balkhi . . . May God confer many blessings on these two who narrated the book [to me] from its author.

It is my wish and will that [Nizam-u'd-din] should not ignore me and my progeny in his prayers while in seclusion.

He [Nizam-u'd-din] read this book from me in the Mosque of Najm-u'd-din Abi Bakr al-Tawasi in Delhi. May God protect this city from calamities!

This document is from the humble and insignificant Muhammad bin Ahmad bin Muhammad al-Marikalli known as Kamal Zahid. These lines were written on 22 Rabi'-u'l-Awwal 679/1280 while praising God and reciting *darud* on the Prophet. (*Siyar-u'l-Auliya*, pp. 104–5).

Appendix - VI

KHILAFAT NAMAH GRANTED BY SHAIKH NIZAM-U'D-DIN AULIYA TO MAULANA SHAMS-U'D-DIN YAHYA

The following is an abridged English translation of the Arabic *Khilafat Namah* granted by Shaikh Nizam-u'd-din Auliya to his disciple Maulana Shams-u'd-din Yahya, a renowned scholar of Delhi, in 724/1323. It throws valuable light on the aims and objects of the Shaikh in granting *Khilafat* to his disciples.

I begin in the name of Allah, the Merciful, and the Compassionate. God be praised and thanked who has protected His chosen ones from the temptations of the [material] world and the worldly people, because the world is a condemned place. God keeps the hearts of His chosen slaves directed towards Himself and it is on this account that such people are always inebriated with the wine of Divine love which is eternal. Their hearts are enlightened at night when their eyes shed tears. Such people (immersed as they are in Love of God) successfully narrate the secrets of their Friend . . . Some of them receive fresh enlightenment every moment and illuminate the world by their radiance. Their words are like the words of God because they invite the people towards God, so that the hearts of the people may become purified and they may become friends of God.

God's blessings on the Holy Prophet, who was sent to this world as guide and who was God's Messenger on earth. Blessings be on the Caliphs, who showed the right path, and on the descendants of the Holy Prophet who pray to God all the time.

To invite the people towards God is the most laudable function of Islam and the most necessary element of faith. A *hadith* says: 'I swear by God in Whose power is the life of Muhammad—and I swear because I want to convince you—that among the people of this world he is the friend of God who discloses the friendship of God to His creature and the friendship of His creature to Him, and he guides people on the path to God's love and affection and holds the people back from denying the existence of God and asks the people to do what has been permitted and what God wants His creatures to do.' It is due to this that the people pray to God for the safety of their women and children and for their own safety. God has made it obligatory on His creatures to follow the Prophet. God Himself says: 'Say Thou: This is my Way: I do invite unto God on evidence clear as the seeing with one's eyes I and whoever follows me. Glory to God and never will I join gods with God' [Qur'an 12.108]. This is what is meant by obedience to the Prophet, i.e. it consists in remembering the traditions of the Prophet and following his acts for the sake of God. A man should devote himself to God after severing all material contacts: 'He is really pure and can become the leader of the people because he knows God's qualities and believes in His Unity. Praises to God and to His chosen one! He is a leader of the followers of the Prophet and is like a shining sun of the faith of Muhammad. That man is Muhammad bin Yahya and may God bestow His lights and blessings through him on the faithful and the mystics. As Shams-u'd-din, son of Yahya, has become my disciple due to his pure faith and has received sufficient instructions from me, I permit him to offer the mystic-cloak (*khirqah*) to his disciples and to give leave to them (in their turn) just as my Shaikh gave the *khirqah* and *khilafah* to me, provided he does not deviate in the least from the path of the Prophet and devotes all his time in prayer and keeps himself aloof from the (material) world and its temptations. My own Shaikh was known all over the world for his saintliness, and his miracles were known everywhere, and in his meditations he reached the unseen world and was a lover of God. He was a noble follower of the Prophet's *Shari'ah* and was fearless in his devotion and faith. May God shower His blessings on his tomb and bestow His peace on him!

My Shaikh got the mystic-cloak from the king of the Shaikhs, the Sultan of *Tariqah* (mystic path), and one who was annihilated in the love of God, i.e. Qutb-u'l-Millat-wa'd-Din Bakhtiyar Aushi; who got it from the luminary of the gnostics, Mu'in-u'd-din Hasan Sijzi; who got it from the Proof of Truth for created beings, 'Usman Haruni; who got it from the righteous in speech, Haji Sharif Zindani; who got it from the shadow of God among the mortals, Maudud Chishti; who got it from the king of the Shaikhs . . . Nasir-u'l-Millat-wa'd-Din Yusuf Chishti; who got it from the refuge of devotees, Abu Muhammad Chishti; who got it from the pillar of the pious and the leader of the virtuous, Abi Ahmad Chishti; who got it from the lamp of the leaders, Abu Ishaq Chishti; who got it from the son of the *faqirs*, Mumshad Ulu Dinwari; who got it from the leader of the believers, Hubairat-u'l-Basri; who got it from the crown of rectitude and the proof of the lovers, Huzaifat al-Mar'ashi; who got it from the Sultan of the Shaikhs, the argument of the lovers and the forsaker of [earthly] domain and kingdom, Ibrahim bin Adham;

who got it from the pole-star of the country, master of virtues, excellences and sciences, Fuzail bin Ayaz; who got it from the pole-star of the universe and the great Shaikh Abd-u'l-Wahid bin Zaid; who got it from the commander of the Tabi'in and Imam of the world, Hasan al-Basri; who got it from the Amir-u'l Muminin, the successor of the Holy Prophet, the giver of the garment of succession and the receiver of the garment of *Khilafah* from the Holy Prophet, i.e. Hazrat Amir-u'l-Muminin, the last of the pious Caliphs and Imam of the East and the West, the most revered 'Ali Murtaza bin Abi Talib, may God bless him and shower peace and favour on him. May God make him honourable and purify the secret of all the saints, and maintain this light till the Day of Resurrection. He got the garment of successorship from the last of the apostles and of the Prophets, the prop of the world, who enjoyed the special favour of God, Hazrat Muhammad. May peace and blessings of Allah be upon him. May God bless those persons who are connected with the Holy Prophet.

Thus the man who could not come to me may accept the spiritual leadership of Shams-u'd-din bin Yahya as I have appointed him my successor and representative. He is my deputy both in religious and secular matters. To follow him in secular and religious matters is to follow me. May God elevate such persons. May God insult him who insults those whom I respect. God the Highest is the real helper and I seek help from Him and rely on Him.

These lines have been written at the direction of the Sultan of the Shaikhs, Nizam-u'd-din Muhammad bin Ahmad, May God maintain his saintliness and save his virtues from all calamities and evils. The writer of these lines, the seeker for divine favour is Husain bin Muhammad bin Mahmud Alavi al-Kirmani on the 10th Zu'l-Hijjah, 824 AH [*Siyar-u'l-Auliya*, pp. 229–36].

Appendix - VII

THE APOCRYPHAL *MALFUZ* LITERATURE

(A) The following collections of *malfuzat* are attributed to Shaikh Nizam-u'd-din Auliya as having been either edited or uttered by him:

  (i) *Rahat-u'l-Qulub*, conversations of Shaikh Farid, alleged to have been written by Shaikh Nizam-u'd-din Auliya.
  (ii) *Afzal-u'l-Fawa'id*, conversations of Shaikh Nizam-u'd-din Auliya, alleged to have been compiled by Amir Khusrau.
  (iii) *Rahat-u'l-Muhibbin*, conversations of Shaikh Nizam-u'd-din Auliya, alleged to have been compiled by Amir Khusrau.

(B) While assessing the authenticity of this literature one has to keep in mind the views expressed by Shaikh Nizam-u'd-din Auliya and Shaikh Nasir-u'd-din Chiragh-i-Delhi in this context:

  i) **Hasan Sijzi records:**
  A friend was present, he said, 'A man showed me a book in Awadh and said it was written by you.' The Shaikh replied: 'He spoke wrongly, I have not written any book' (*Fawa'id-u'l-Fu'ad*, p. 45).
  ii) **Hamid Qalandar records about Shaikh Nasir-u'd-din Chiragh:**
  . . . he said . . . Shaikh Nizam-u'd-din has said: 'I have written no book because neither Shaikh-u'l-Islam Farid-u'd-din, nor Shaikh-ul-Islam Qutb-u'd-din, nor the elder Chishti saints (*Khwajgan*), nor any of the preceding Shaikhs of my order wrote any book . . . '(*Khair-u'l-Majalis*, p. 52).

Shah 'Abd-u'l-'Aziz, the famous *muhaddith* of Delhi, is reported to have remarked: 'The book *Fawa'id-u'l-Fu'ad* is very reliable . . . but the authenticity of other *malfuzat* is doubtful' (*Malfuzat-i-'Azizi*, p. 81).

(C) Professor Mohammed Habib has examined very carefully the authenticity of this literature and has come to the conclusion that it has been wrongly attributed to Shaikh Nizam-u'd-din Auliya (*Politics and Society during the Early Medieval Period*, ed. K. A. Nizami, I, pp. 385–433).

(D) When was this literature fabricated? I think that when Sultan Muhammad bin Tughluq's removal of the capital to Deogir dispersed the circle of Shaikh Nizam-u'd-din Auliya's disciples and the living tradition of the Chishti *silsilah* was killed, a vacuum was created which these fabricated works tried to fill up. Professor Habib has also accepted this view (Ibid. pp. 429–30).

Maulana Rukn 'Imad has, perhaps for the first time, referred to *Rahat-u'l-Qulub* and *Rahat-u'l-Muhibin* in the list of sources consulted by him in the preparation of his *Shama'il-u'l-Atqiya* (MS pp. 14–15).

APPENDIX - VIII

———◆◆◆———

CONTEMPORARY RULERS

1.	'Ala-u'd-din Masud	639–644/1242–1246
2.	Nasir-u'd-din Mahmud	644–664/1246–1266
3.	Balban	664–686/1266–1287
4.	Kaiqubad	686–689/1287–1290
5.	Kaiymurth	689/1290
6.	Jalal-u'd-din Khalji	689–695/1290–1296
7.	Rukn-u'd-din Ibrahim	695/1296
8.	'Ala-u'd-din Khalji	695–715/1296–1316
9.	Shihab-u'd-din 'Umar	715/1316
10.	Mubarak Shah	716–720/1316–1320
11.	Nasir-u'd-din Khusrau	720/1320
12.	Ghiyas-u'd-din Tughluq	720–725/1320–1325
13.	Muhammad bin Tughluq	725–752/1325–1351

APPENDIX - IX

—•◦•—

THE SHAIKH'S TOMB AND THE BUILDINGS AROUND IT

1. Muhammad bin Tughluq (1325–51) constructed a dome over the grave of the Shaikh. Mir Khurd informs us:

بعد نقل سلطان المشايخ، سلطان محمد بن تغلق بر روضهء متبركهء سلطان المشايخ كنبد
عمارت كنانيد وحق جل وعلا برائے سلطان المشايخ حظيره با عمارتهائے رفيع بے نظير
وكنبدهائے فلك رفعت كه در لطافت وصفاى آں در اقصائے عالم كسے نشان ندارد، از غيب
مرتب گردانيد

(Siyar-u'l-Auliya, p. 154)
(After the death of Sultan-u'l-Masha'ikh, Sultan Muhammad bin Tughluq constructed a dome over his sanctified grave and God Almighty made mysterious arrangements for lofty buildings and imposing structures, unrivalled for their beauty and elegance in the whole world, to rise there.)

It is not clear why Mir Khurd has used the words از غيب مرتب گردانيد It may be that he just means that, without any effort on the part of the *khanqah* people, a complex of imposing structures rose up there!

2. Firuz Shah Tughluq (1351–88) thus refers to the additions made by him:

درهائے كنبد وجعفريهائے مقبرهء سلطان المشايخ حضرت نظام الحق والدين محبوب الهى
قدس الله سره العزيز از صندل ساخته وقنديلهائے زرين با زنجيرهائے زر در چهار
زاويهء كنج كنبد آويخته

(Futuhat-i-Firuz Shahi, p. 17)

(The doors of the domed chamber and the latticed screens of the mausoleum
of Sultan-u'l-Masha'ikh Nizam-u'l-Haqq wa'd-Din Mahbub-i-Ilahi
(may God hallow his holy grave) were also made from sandalwood. Golden
chandeliers were hung by gold chains in the four corners of the hall.)

3. The *Jama'at Khanah* Mosque near the tomb of the Shaikh has been
generally but erroneously considered to have been constructed by Khizr
Khan, son of Sultan 'Ala-u'd-din Khalji. The Archaeological Survey
of India was perhaps guided by a statement of Jamali who says:

این عمارت عالی که مقبرهٔ حضرت شیخ که در صحن وی واقع است، ساخت خضر خان
است

(*Siyar-u'l-'Arifin*, p. 74)
(The grand building in the courtyard of which the tomb of the Shaikh
stands was constructed by Khizr Khan.)

This is not correct. The *Jama'at Khanah* is hardly a few feet from the building
of the tomb. The author of *Siyar-u'l-Auliya* very clearly says (p. 154) that
the Shaikh was buried in *sahra* (jungle or desert).[1] Had the structure been
there at that time he would have said that the Shaikh was buried in the courtyard
(*sahn*) of the *Jama'at Khanah* Mosque. The *Qiwam-u'l-'Aqa'id* says that it
was in a jungle, where the Shaikh was buried near a tree under which he
used to sit and pray.

Firuz Shah Tughluq makes the position absolutely clear (*Futuhat*, p. 17)
when he says:

جماعت خانهٔ جدید بنا کرده که آنچنان پیش ازین آنجا نبوده

(a new *Jama'at Khanah*, such as had not existed there before, was built).

The façade of the *Jama'at Khanah* contains the following inscription which
could have been inscribed there after the death of the Shaikh:

---

[1] Sir Syed Ahmad Khan says:

موضع غیاث پور کی سرحد میں جہاں آپ کا مزار ہے آپ کو دفن کیا

Athar-u's-Sanadid, p. 39.

نظام دو گیتی شه ما وطـــین

سراج دو عالم شده بالیـــقین

چو تاریخ فوتش بجستم زغیب

ندا داد هاتف شهنشاه دیـــن

۷۲۵هـ

4. Syed-u'l-Hujjab Khwaja Ma'ruf,[2] a *nadim* and confidant of Firuz Shah
   Tughluq constructed a *chatta*[3] over the *baoli*.[4] An inscription on the
   southern gate, given below, shows his early association with the Shaikh.
   Soon after his birth, he was brought before the Shaikh who called him
   Ma'ruf and he became known as such.

خجستـــه خسرو اولاد آدم	بعهد دولت شاه معـظم
شه صاحبقران سلطان اعظم	مدار دین احمد شاه فیروز
اساس اینعمارت کرد محکم	موفق گشت از حق پند معروف
نظام الحق والدین قطب عالم	جــوار روضهء شیخ المشایخ
که با اهل ارادت بود همدم	وحید الدین قرشی والـد من
در اسرار ولي اللّه محــرم	بحسن اعتقاد وصدق اخلاص
بدست خود گرفت وکرد نامـم	مرا چون برد پیش شیخ عالم
درینعالم چوشیخ عیسوی دم	بلفظ خود مرا معروف خوانده
دران عالم بود معروف پرچم	رجا دارم کز انفاس مبارک
درین جا چوں بپای خیر مقدم	بخوان تاریخ اتمام عمارت
مرتب شد بنا واللّه أعلم	زهجرت هفت صدوهشتادویک بود

۷۸۱هـ

5. Inspired by feelings of love and devotion and anxious to seek Divine
   blessing, a large number of people throughout the centuries have added
   one thing or another to the tomb of the Shaikh and its building complex.

---

[2] For his account see, 'Afif, *Tarikh-i-Firuz Shahi*, pp. 445–51.

[3] Ceiling on a corridor.

[4] A large well into which people descend by steps to get water.

In this context the following persons are mentioned on different inscriptions:

(a)   Syed Faridun Khan who built a dome over twelve pillars and screens of marble in 970/1562.

ازپئے تعمیر شد خان فلک احـتشام   شکر که روضهٔ حضرت غـــوث الأنـام

سید عالی نسب مــیر فلک احـترام   مهر نسبت را شرف، اوج شرف را شهاب

آنکه بدوران شان هست سخن رانظام   بـانی او هـاشمـی، ساعی او هـاشمـی

کلک خرد زد رقم قبله گهی خاص وعام   ازپئے تـاریخ آں چـــوں متفکر شدم

شاید از الطاف پیر کار تو گردد نظام   روی بـــدرگـاه او آر فریـــدوں بـصدق

(b)   Nawab Murtaza Khan Shaikh Farid who built a *chappar khat* (a bedstead and curtains) of shells (*seep*) in 1017/1608. The *chappar khat* has the following verses inscribed in shell:

کار دنیا ودیں مهـــیا کرد   شیخ دهـلی نظام را دو فرید

یـک فریدش مقـام احـیا کرد   یـک فریـــدش مقام فانی داد

قبهٔ چوں سپهر بریـا کرد   مرتضی خاں فـــراز ترقـد او

در یک دانه در صدف جا کرد   ابر فیروزی از جهاں برخاست

چار در از چهار حـد وا کرد   هـر جهـاں کعبهٔ مربـــع او

بر زمین کار عرش اعلی کرد   عـرشهٔ مرقـــد مبارک او

چار تکبیر بے محابا کرد   عـرش در پای چهار قائمه اش

پشت بـر کعبهٔ معلـی کرد   هر کـــه رخ از مقام او تابید

رخ چو آئـینه مصفـا کرد   زانکـه رو در سـجود او آورد

می توان کار صد مسیحا کرد   خاک روب مقامش ار باشـی

"قبهٔ شیخ" عقل القـا کرد   سـال تـاریخ ایں بنا جستـم

١٠١٧ ھـ

آنکه ایں هفت سقف خضرا کرد   قـدر بـانی او رفـــــیـع کناد

(c)   Khalilullah Khan, governor of Shahjahanabad, built a *ghulam gardish*[5] in 1063/1653.

(*d*) In 1169/1755 'Aziz-u'd-din 'Alamgir II placed marble slabs, on which
there is the following inscription:

Excerpt 42

جو ہوئے خادم نظام الدین کا دل سے اے غریب

اس کے تئیں ہوتا ہے تاج خسروی جگ میں نصیب

خادمی کی تھی عزیز الدین نے با صدق ویقین

تاج شاہی ہند کا مجھ کو دیا ہے عنقریب

مرض دل افگار میرے کا وہ صحت بخش ہے

بے غذا وبے دعا وبے دوا وبے طبیب

بس پریشاں حال ہے اب خلق پر محبوب حق

فضل کر تقصیر داروں پر تم ہو حق کے حبیب

(*e*) Marble flooring of the entire area was done by Muhammad Shah.
(*f*) In 1236/1820 Nawab Faizullah Bangash covered the inner ceiling
of twenty-gate structure with copper plates and arranged ornamental
decoration.
(*g*) Akbar Shah II added a golden cupola in 1239/1823.
(*h*) Nawab Ahmad Bakhsh Khan Bahadur replaced the red-stone pillars
of *bara dari* with marble pillars in 1242/1826.
(*i*) In 1300/1882 Khurshid Jah of Hyderabad put up a marble railing.

Appendix - X

SELECT BIBLIOGRAPHY

A. Early Religious and Mystical Works

Asrar-u't-Tawhid fi Maqamat-i-Abi Sa'id, Muhammad bin Munawwar
Ed. Ahmad Bahmanyar (Tehran, 1934)

'Awarif-u'l-Ma'arif, Shaikh-u 'd-din Suhrawardi
Arabic text: (Beirut, 1966)
Urdu trans.: Maulvi Abu'l-Hasan (Nawal Kishore: Lucknow, 1926)

Persian version: *Misbah-u'l-Hidayah wa Miftah-u'l-Kifayah*, 'Izz-u 'd-din Mahmud
  Kashani, ed. Agha Jalal Huma'i (Tehran)
English trans.: Lt. Col. H. Wilberforce Clarke, Govt. of India Central Printing
  Office (Calcutta, 1891)

Ihya-u 'l-'Ulum, Imam Ghazzali

Arabic text: (Dar al-Fikr: Beirut, 1991)
Urdu trans.: *Mazaq-u 'l-'Arifin* (Nawal Kishore, 1875)

Kashf-u 'l-Mahjub, Shaikh 'Ali Hujweri

Persian text: (i) Matba'-i-Punjab (Lahore); (ii) (Lahore, 1968)
English trans.: R. A. Nicholson (London, 1936)
Urdu trans.:
    (i) Shah Zahir Ahmad (Lahore, 1925)
    (ii) Muhammad Ahmad Qadiri (Lahore, 1985)

Kimiya-i-Sa'adah: Imam Ghazzali Matba'-i-Hashimi (Meerut, 1377 AH)

Kitab-u 'l-Luma', Abu Nasr al-Saraj
Gibb Memorial Series (London, 1914)

Mirsad-u'l-'Ibad Min-al-Mabda ila al-Ma'ad, Najm-u 'd-din Daya Text (Tehran, 1336 Solar)

Qut-u'l-Qulub, Abu Talib Makki
2 vols. (Cairo, 1310/1892)

Risalah-i-Qushairi, Abu Qasim 'Abd-u'l-Karim Qushairi
Text: (Cairo, 1346/1927)

B. *Malfuzat*

Afzal-u'l-Fawa'id, conversations of Shaikh Nizam-u 'd-din Auliya, compilation attributed to Amir Khusrau
Text: (Rizvi Press: Delhi, 1304–1305 AH)
Urdu trans.: Latif Malik (Lahore, 1960)

Ahsan-u 'l-Aqwal, conversations of Shaikh Burhan-u 'd-din Gharib, compiled by Hammad bin Imad Kashani
MSS: (i) Personal collection
      (ii) Osmania Library (1478/1979)
Urdu trans.: (Matba' Jahangir Safari: Bombay, 1342 AH)

Anwar-u'l-A'yun, conversations of Shaikh Ahmad 'Abd-u'l-Haqq of Rudauli, compiled by Shaikh 'Abd-u'l-Quddus Gangohi (Ahsan-u'l-Mataba': Aligarh, 1905)

Asrar-u'l-Makhdumin, conversations of Khwaja Karak of Kara (Nasim-i-Hind Press: Fathpur-Haswa, 1893)

Durar-i-Nizami, conversations of Shaikh Nizam-u'd-din Auliya, compiled by Maulana 'Ali Jandar
MSS: (i) Buhar Collection, Asian Society of Bengal (183)
      (ii) Salar Jang Museum, Hyderabad (61/5–99)
      (iii) Personal collection

Fawa'id-u'l-Fu'ad, conversations of Shaikh Nizam-u'd-din Auliya compiled by Amir Hasan Sijzi
MSS: (i) MS Personal Collection
      (ii) MS Personal Collection—prepared for Rai of Kuchesar on 30 July 1863
Texts: (i) Nawal Kishore (Lucknow, 1302/1884)
        (ii) Ed. M. Latif Malik (Lahore, 1966)
Urdu trans.: Shams Barelvi (Karachi, 1978)
            Khwaja Hasan Sani Nizami (Delhi, 1990)

Fihi-ma-Fihi, conversations of Maulana Jalal-u'd-din Rumi, compiled by his son Sultan Baha-u'd-din
Ed.: Maulana 'Abd-u'l-Majid Daryabadi (Azamgarh, 1928)

Ghara'ib-u'l-Karamat, conversations of Shaikh Burhan u'd-din Gharib, compiled by Majd-u 'd-din
MS: Salar Jang Museum 43/876

Jami'-u'l-Ulum, conversations of Syed Jalal-u'd-din Bukhari
Ed.: Qazi Sajjad Husain (Delhi, 1982)

Jawami'-u'l-Kalim, conversations of Syed Muhammad Gisu Daraz, compiled by Syed Muhammad Akbar Husaini
Lith: (Intizami Press: Kanpur, 1936)

Khair-u'l-Majalis, conversations of Shaikh Nasir-u'd-din Chiragh of Delhi, compiled by Hamid Qalandar
Text: Ed. K. A. Nizami, A. M. U. (Aligarh, 1959)
Urdu trans.: *Siraj-u'l-Majalis* (Delhi, 1315 AH)

Lata'if-i-Quddusi, conversations of Shaikh 'Abd-u'l-Quddus Gangohi, compiled by Shaikh Rukn-u'd-din
Matba'-i-Mujtaba'i (Delhi, 1311 AH)

Ma'din-u'l-Ma'ani, conversations of Shaikh Sharaf-u'd-din Yahya Maneri, compiled by Zain Badr 'Arabi
2 vols. Sharaf-u'l-Akhbar (Bihar, 1301–1303 AH)

Malfuzat-i-Shah 'Abd-u'l-'Aziz,
Ed.: Qazi Bashir-u'd-din
Lith.: (Mujtaba'i Press: Meerut, 1314 AH)

Nafa'is-u'l-Anfas, conversations of Shaikh Burhan-u'd-din Gharib, compiled by Rukn-u'd-din bin Imad Kashani
MSS: (i) Nadwat-u'l-'Ulama Library (Lucknow, 1366)
       (ii) Personal Collection

Rahat-u'l-Muhibbin, conversations of Shaikh Nizam-u'd-din Auliya; compilation attributed to Amir Khusrau
MS: Personal Collection

Rahat-u'l-Qulub, conversations of Shaikh Farid Ganj-i-Shakar, compilation attributed to Shaikh Nizam-u'd-din Auliya
MS: Personal Collection
Lith.: (Qadiri Press: Lucknow, 1311 AH)

Sarur-u's-Sudur, conversations of Shaikh Hamid-u'd-din Nagauri, compiled
   by his grandson, Shaikh Aziz
MSS: (i) Habibganj collection, Aligarh Muslim University Library
        (ii) Photostat of MS in Pakistan Historical Society, Karachi
        (iii) Personal Collection

Shama'il-u'l-Atqiya, conversation of Shaikh Burhan-u'd-din Gharib, compiled
   by Rukn-u'd-din bin 'Imad-u'd-din
MS: Personal Collection
Lith.: (Ashraf Press: Hyderabad, 1347 AH)

Shawamil-u'l-Jumal dar Shama'il-Kumal, by Abu'l-Faiz Minallah
MS: Rauza-i-Shaikh Collection, Gulbarga

Siraj-u'l-Hidaya, conversations of Syed Jalal-u'd-din Bukhari, compiled by
   Makhdumzada Abdullah
MS: Personal Collection
Ed.: Qadi Sajjad Husain (Delhi, 1983)

Tuhfat-u'l-Majalis, conversations of Shaikh Ahmad Maghribi, compiled by
   Mahmud bin Sa'd Irjii
MS: India Office Pers. Collection DP. 979
Urdu trans: Syed Abu Zafar Nadwi (Ma'arif Press: Azamgarh, 1939)

C. Early *Tazkirah*s and Biographical Accounts

Nafahat-u'l-Uns, 'Abd-u'r-Rahman Jami (Nawal Kishore: Lucknow, 1915)

Qiwam-u'l-'Aqa'id, Muhammad Jamal Qiwam-u'd-din
MS: Osmania University Library, Hyderabad

Siyar-u'l-'Arifin, Fazlullah known as Durwesh Jamali
  (i) Photostat copy of MS in John Rylands Library (earliest known MS)
  (ii) MS: Personal Collection
  (iii) Lith.: (Rizwi Press: Delhi, 1311 AH)
  (iv) Urdu trans.:
        (*a*) Ghulam Ahmad, Shams-u'd-Mataba' (Moradabad, 1901)
        (*b*) Ayyub Qadiri (Lahore, 1976)

Siyar-u'l-Auliya, Syed Muhammad bin Mubarak Kirmani, known as Amir
   Khurd
  (i)   MS: Personal collection, collated and compared by Diwan Allah Jiwaya
         of Pakpattan

(ii)   Lith: Chirangi Lal (Muhibb-i-Hind Press: Delhi, 1302/1885)
(iii) Urdu trans:
    (*a*) Ghulam Ahmad Biryan (Muslim Press: Delhi, 1320)
    (*b*) I'jaz-u'l-Haqq Quddusi (Lahore, 1980)

D. Early Historical Works

Babur Namah, Babur
  (i)   Persian trans.: 'Abd-u'r-Rahim Khan-i-Khanan (Bombay, 1308 AH)
  (ii) English trans.: Mrs. A. S. Beveridge (London, 1921)

Futuhat-i-Firuz Shahi, Firuz Shah Tughluq
  (i)   Lith: (Rizvi Press: Delhi, 1885)
  (ii)   Sh. Abd-u'r-Rashid, M. A. Makhdoomi, Aligarh (with English trans.)
  (iii) M. A. Chaghatai with Urdu trans. (Poona, 1941)

Futuh-u's-Salatin, 'Isami
Ed.: A. S. Usha (Madras, 1948)
English trans.: 3 vols. A. Mahdi Husain (Asia Publishing House, 1967–77)

Khaza'in-u'l-Futuh, Amir Khusrau
Ed.: M. Wahid Mirza (Asiatic Society of Bengal: Calcutta, 1953)
English trans.: M. Habib, *The Campaigns of Sultan Ala-ud-Din Khalji*, (Madras, 1931)

Mukatabat-i-Rashidi, Rashid-u'd-din Fazlullah
Ed.: Mohd. Shafi' (Educational Press: Lahore, 1947)

Rihla, Ibn Battuta
Arabic text: (Cairo, 1928)
Urdu trans.: K. B. Muhammad Husain (Delhi, 1345 AH)
English trans.: (*a*) (abridged): H. A. R. Gibb (London, 1929)
            (*b*) A. Mahdi Husain (Baroda, 1953)

Sirat-i-Firuz Shahi, anonymous
MS: Bankipur Library

Tabaqat-i-Nasiri, Minhaj-u's-Siraj
Ed.: (*a*) Nassau Lees, Khadim Husain and 'Abd-u'l-Hayy (Calcutta, 1864)
     (*b*) 'Abd-u 'l-Hayy Habibi, Kabul
English trans.: M. G. Reverty (Bib. Indica, 1897)

Tarikh-i-Firuz Shahi, Zia-u 'd-din Barani
Ed.: Sir Syed Ahmad Khan (Asiatic Society of Bengal: Calcutta, 1860)

Tarikh-i-Firuz Shahi, Shams-i-Siraj 'Afif
Ed.: Vilayat Hosain (Asiatic Society of Bengal: Calcutta, 1889–91)

Tarikh-i-Mubarak Shahi, Yahya bin Ahmad Sirhindi
Ed.: K. B. Hidayat Hosain (Asiatic Society of Bengal: Calcutta, 1931)
English trans: K. K. Basu, Gaekwad Oriental Series, 1932

E. Early Literary and Religious Works

Dibacha Ghurrat-u'l-Kamal, Amir Khusrau
Yasin 'Ali Dihlawi, Matba'-i-Qaisariya (Delhi)

I'jaz-i-Khusrawi, Amir Khusrau (Nawal Kishore, 1865)

Insha-i-Mahru, 'Ain-u'l-Mulk Mahru
Ed.: S. A. Rashid (Lahore, 1965)

Mukh-u'l-Ma'ani, Hasan Sijzi
MS: Aligarh Muslim University Library

Mulhimat, Jamal-u'd-din Hanswi
Text: (*a*) (Alwar, 1306 AH)
       (*b*) (Delhi, 1891)
English trans: Sardar 'Ali Ahmad Khan (ed.), with English trans. (Lahore, 1985)

Tuhfat-u 'l-Mahbub,
Urdu trans. of Shaikh Nizam-u'd-din Auliya's mystic treatise, by M. Abu 'l-
   Muhiy-u 'd-din Khan (Agra, 1902)

Usul-u 's-Sama, Maulana Fakhr-u'd-din Zarradi
Lith: (Muslim Press: Jhajjar, 1311 AH)

F. Early Poetical Works

A'ina-i-Sikandari, Amir Khusrau
Ed.: Sa'id Ahmad Faruqi (Aligarh, 1917)

Bahr-u'l-Ma'ani, Letters of Ja'far Makki al-Husaini (Ahtashamiya Press:
   Moradabad, 1889)

Dawawin-i-Khusrau, Amir Khusrau (Nawal Kishore, 1871)

Diwan-i-Hasan Dihlawi
Ed.: Mas'ud 'Ali Mahwi (Ibrahimiya Machine Press: Hyderabad, 1352 AH)

Diwan-i-Jamal u'd-din Hanswi
Pirji Rafi'-u'd-din Tehsildar (Chashma-i Faiz Press: Delhi, 1889)

Diwan-i-Mutahhar
Oriental College Magazine (May–August 1935)
Ma'arif (May–July 1935)

Duwal Rani Khizr Khan, Amir Khusrau
Ed.: (i) Rashid Ahmad Salim (Aligarh, 1917)
    (ii) With English Introduction and notes by K. A. Nizami (Aligarh, 1988)

Fragments of Hamid Qalandar's Poetical Compositions particularly verses in
    praise of Shaikh Nizam-u'd-din Auliya (fos. 130^a, 137^a)
MS: British Museum Supp. Catalogue p. 232

Hasht Bihisht, Amir Khusrau
Ed.: Maulana Sulaiyman Ashraf (Aligarh, 1918)

Majnun Laila, Amir Khusrau
Ed.: Habibur Rahman Khan Sherwani (Aligarh, 1917)

Matla'-u'l-Anwar, Amir Khusrau
Ed.: M. Muqtada Khan Sherwani (Aligarh, 1926)

Nuh-Sipihr, Amir Khusrau
Ed.: M. Wahid Mirza (Calcutta, 1948)

Qir'an-u'd-Sa'dain. Amir Khusrau
Ed.: Maulvi Muhammad Isma'il (Aligarh, 1918)

Shirin-o-Khusrau, Amir Khusrau
Ed.: 'Ali Ahmad Khan Asir (Aligarh, 1927)

Tughluq Namah, Amir Khusrau
Ed.: S. Hashmi Faridabadi (Aurangabad, 1933)

Wast-u'l-Hayat, Amir Khusrau
Ed.: Fazl Ahmad Hafiz (Aligarh, 1920)

F. Later Biographical Accounts, *Tazkirah*s, etc.

Akhbar-u'l-Akhyar, Shaikh 'Abd-u'l-Haqq Muhaddith Dihlawi
MS: Personal Collection
Text: (Mujtaba 'i Press: Delhi 1309 AH)
Trans.: (i) Syed Yasin Ali (Muslim Press: Delhi, 1328 AH)
    (ii) Subhan Mahmud and Muhammad Fazil (Karachi, n.d.)

Akhbar-u'l-Asfiya, 'Abd-u'l-Samad bin Afzal Muhammad
MSS: (i) India Office Library
    (ii) Bankipur

Anwar-u'l-'Arifin, Hafiz Muhammad Husain Moradabadi
Nawal Kishore (Lucknow, 1876)

Gulzar-i-Abrar, Muhammad Ghauthi Shattari
MS: Personal Collection
Urdu trans.: *Azkar-u'l-Abrar*, by Maulvi Fazl Ahmad (Agra, 1326 AH)

Hada'iq-u'l-Hanafiya, Faqir Muhammad Jihlami
 (i)   Nawal Kishore (Lucknow, 1906)
 (ii)   Ed. Khurshid Ahmad Khan (Lahore, n.d.)

Hasanat-u'l-'Arifin, Dara Shukoh
MS: Nadwat-u'l-'Ulama Library, Lucknow
Urdu trans.: Muhammad 'Umar Khan (Kapoor Art Press: Lahore, n.d.)

Iqtibas-u'l-Anwar, Muhammad Akram Baraswi
(Lahore, 1895–1896)

Jawahir-i-Faridi, 'Ali Asghar Chishti
MS: Personal Collection
Lith.: Lahore 1301/1884
Urdu trans.: (Karimi Press: Lahore)

Khazinat-u'l-Asfiya, Ghulam Sarwar
2 vols (Thamar-i-Hind Press: Lucknow, 1873)

Lata'if-i-Ashrafi, Nizam-u'd-din Yamani
(Nusrat-u'l-Mataba': Delhi, 1295 AH)

Ma'arij-u'l-Walayat, Ghulam Mu'in-u'd-din Abdullah
MS: 2 vols. Personal Collection

Majma'-u'l-Auliya, Mir 'Ali Akbar Husaini Ardistani
MS: India Office Library

Manaqib-u'l-Mahbubin, Maulana Najm-u'd-din
(Thamar-i-Hind Press: Lucknow, 1875)

Matub-u't-Talibin, Syed Muhammad Bulaq Chishti
MS: Personal Collection

Mir'at-u'l-Asrar, 'Abd-u'r-Rahman Chishti
MS: Personal Collection

Munis-u'l-Arwah, Jahan Ara Begum
MS: Personal Collection
Urdu trans.: *Anis-u'l-Ashbah*, Muhammad Fazl-i-Haqq,
(Matba'-i-Nami: Lucknow, 1315 AH)

Nuzhat-u'l-Khawatir, Hakim Syed 'Abd-u'l-Hayy,
(Da'irat-u'l-Ma'arif: Hyderabad, 1956–62)

Rauzah-i-Aqtab, Muhammad Bulaq Chishti
Chirangi Lal (Muhibb-i-Hind Press: Delhi, 1887)

Rauza-i-Auliya, Azad Bilgrami
(Matba'-i- Eijaz Safdari, 1310 AH)

Risalah Hal Khanwadah-i-Chisht
Maulana Taj-u'd-din, a descendant of Mauiana Shihab-u'd-din Imam
MS: Personal Collection

Saba' Sanabil, 'Abd-u'l-Wahid Bilgrami
(Nizami Press: Kanpur, 1299 AH)

Safinat-u'l-Auliya, Dara Shukoh
MS: Personal Collection
Lith.: (Nawal Kishore: Kanpur, 1900)
Arabic trans.: Shaikh Ja'far Sadiq of Gujarat,
MS: Personal Collection
Urdu trans.: Muhammad 'Ali Lutfi (Karachi, 1982)

Shajrat-u'l-Anwar, Rahim Bakhsh Fakhri
MS: Personal Collection

Subhat-u'!-Marjan, Ghulam 'Ali Azad Bilgrami
Ed.: M. Fazlur Rahman Nadwi, vol. i (Aligarh, 1976)

Tazkirah 'Ulama-i-Hind, Rahman 'Ali
Lith.: (Nawal Kishore: Lucknow, 1914)
Urdu trans.: Ayyub Qadiri (Pakistan Historical Society: Karachi, 1961)

Tiqsar al-Ahrar min Tizkar Junud al-Abrar, Siddiq Hasan Khan (Bhopal, 1878)

Zikr-i-Jami' Auliya-i-Dehli, Muhammad Habibullah
MS: British Museum, Oriental 1746

G. Later Historical Works

'Ain-i-Akbari, Abu'l-Fazl
Text: Ed. Sir Syed Ahmad Khan (Delhi, 1272 AH)
English trans.: vol. i: H. Blochmann, reprint (Delhi, 1977)
            vol. ii: H. S. Jarrett, reprint (Delhi, 1978)
            vol. iii: H. S. Jarrett, reprint (Delhi, 1978)
Urdu trans.: 3 vols. M. Fida 'Ali Talib (Lahore, n.d.)

Akbar Namah, Abu'l-Fazl
Text: Ed. Agha Ahmad 'Ali and Abd-u'r-Rahim (Calcutta, 1873–87)
English trans: H. Beveridge, 3 vols. (Calcutta, 1897–1921)

Burhan-u'l-Ma'asir, Syed 'Ali Tabataba'i
Ed.: Ghulam Yazdani (Hyderabad, 1355 AH)

Muntakhab-u't-Tawarikh, 'Abd-u'l-Qadir Badaoni
Text: Ed. Ahmad 'Ali, Kabir-u 'd-din and W. Nassau Lees. Bib Indica (Calcutta, 1864–9)
English trans.: vol i: G. S. A. Ranking (Calcutta, 1895)

Tabaqat-i-Akbari, Nizam-u 'd-din Ahmad Bakhshi
Ed.: B. De and Hidayat Husain, Bib. Indica (Calcutta, 1913–40)

Tarikh-i-Ferishta, Muhammad Qasim Hindu Shah
 (i)   Nawal Kishore 1281 AH
 (ii) Chapter XII dealing with Sufi-saints, Matba'-i Majidi (Kanpur, 1926)
Urdu trans.: M. Fida 'Ali Talib (Hyderabad, 1926–32)

Tazkirah-i-Humayun-wa-Akbar, Bayazid Bayat
Text: Ed. Hidayat Husain, Bib. Indica (Calcutta, 1941)

WORKS IN ENGLISH

Afifi, A. H., *The Mystical Philosophy of Muhiyuddin Ibn-ul-Arabi* (Cambridge, 1939)
Ahmad, Aziz, *An Intellectual History of Islam in India* (Edinburgh, 1969)
——— *Studies in Islamic Culture in the Indian Environment* (Oxford, 1964)
Ahmad, M. G. Zubaid, *The Contribution of India to Arabic Literature* (Allahabad, 1946)
Arberry, A. H. *Sufism* (London, 1956)
Blackie, J. S., *Self-Culture* (Edinburgh, 1886)
Chaghatai, Abdullah, *Pakpattan and Baba Farid* (Lahore, 1968)
Faruqi, Burhan Ahmad, *The Mujaddid's Conception of Tawhid* (Lahore, 1940; reprint Delhi, 1977)
Gibb, H. A. R., *Mohammadanism* (London, 1951)
Habib, Muhammad, *Life and Works of Hazrat Amir Khusrau of Delhi* (Aligarh, 1927)
——— *Politics and Society during the early Medieval Period*, collected works, ed. K. A. Nizami, vols. (P. P. House, 1974–81)

Habib, M., and Nizami, K. A. (eds), *The Comprehensive History of India*, vol. v, (Delhi, 1970)

Habibullah, A. B. M., *The Foundation of Muslim Rule in India* (Lahore, 1945)

Haq, S. Moinul, *Islamic Thought and Movements in the Subcontinent (711–1947)* (Karachi, 1979)

Husain, A. M., *Tughluq Dynasty* (Thacker Spink: Calcutta, 1963)

——— *The Rise and Fall of Muhammad bin Tughluq* (Luzac, 1938)

Iqbal, Mohd., *The Reconstruction of Religious Thought in Islam* (Lahore, 1944)

——— *Islam and Ahmadism* (Lahore, 1936)

Lal, K. S., *History of the Khaljis* (Munshiram Manoharlal: Delhi, 1980)

Mirza, Muhammad Wahid, *Life and Works of Amir Khusrau* (Calcutta, 1935)

Nizami, K. A., *The Life and Times of Shaikh Farid-u'd-din Masud Ganj-i-Shakar* (Aligarh, 1955)

——— *Studies in Medieval Indian History and Culture* (Kitab Mahal: Allahabad, 1966)

——— *Some Aspects of Religion and Politics in India during the Thirteenth Century*, 3rd edn (Delhi, 1978)

——— *On History and Historians of Medieval India* (Delhi, 1983)

Prasad, Ishwari, *History of the Qaraunah Turks* (Indian Press: Allahabad, 1936)

Qureshi, I. H., *The Administration of the Sultanate of Delhi*, 1st edn (Lahore, 1942; 4th rev'd edn, Karachi, 1958)

Schimmel, Annemarie *Mystical Dimensions of Islam* (University of North Carolina Press, 1975)

——— *Islam in the Indian Sub-Continent* (Leiden, 1980)

Stephen, Carr, *The Archaeology and Monumental Remains of Delhi* (Ludhiana, 1876)

Toynbee, Arnold, 'An Historian's Approach to Religion', Gifford Lectures delivered in the University of Edinburgh, 1952–3

Tripathi, R. P., *Some Aspects of Muslim Administration in India* (Allahabad, 1936)

Vambery, Arminius, *History of Bokhara* (London, 1873)

Williams, John Alden, *Themes of Islamic Civilization* (Berkeley, 1973)

Yamamoto, Tatsura, 'Delhi: Architectural Remains of Delhi', in Matsuo Ara and Takinowo, *Sultanate*, 3 vols (Tokyo, 1970)

WORKS IN URDU

'Abd-u'l-Haqq, *The Sufis' Work in the Early Development of the Urdu Language* (Aurangabad ,1933)

Abd-u'r-Rahman Sabah-u'd-din, *Bazm-i-Sufiyah* (Azamgarh, n.d.)

Ahmad Khan, Sir Syed, *Asar-u'd-Sanadad* (Karachi, 1966)

——— *Lakchuron Ka Majmu'a* (Lahore, 1890)

Ali, Syed Yasin, *Sirat-i-Nizami* (Delhi, 1332 AH)

Ambethavi, Mushtaq Ahmad, *Anwar-u'l-'Ashiqin* (Osman Press: Hyderabad, 1332 AH)

Bashir-u 'd-din, *Waqi'at-i-Dar-ul-Hukumat Delhi* (Agra, 1916)

Bismil, Razi-u'd-din, *Tazkirat-u'l-Wasilin* (Lahore, 1318 AH)

——— *Kanz-u't-Tawarikh* (Nizami Press: Badaun, 1907)

Dihlawi, Akhlaq Husain, *Hazrat Mahbub-i-Ilahi* (Delhi, 1964)

Dihlawi, Mirza Muhammad Akhtar, *Tazkirah-i-Auliya-i-Hind* (Munir Press: Delhi, 1928)

Faridi, Muhammad Alam Shah, *Mazarat-I-Auliya-i-Delhi* (Jan-i Jahan Press: Delhi, 1330 AH)

Farrukhi, Aslam, *Sahibji Sultanji* (Karachi, 1989)

——— *Nizam Rang* (Karachi, 1988)

Habib, Muhammad, *Hazrat Nizam-ud-din Auliya-Hayat Aur Ta'limat* (Delhi, 1972)

Ikram, M. *Mauj-i-Kausar* (Lahore, 1952)

Lahori, Ghulam Sarwar, *Hadiqat-u'l-Auliya*, Lith.: (i) Matba'-i- Khurshid 'Alam (Lahore, 1293 ah) (ii), Ed., M. Iqbal Mujaddidi (Lahore, 1875)

Mahrahravi, Sa'id Ahmad, *Hayat-i-Khusrau* (Lahore, 1909)

Nadwi, Syed Abu 'l- Hasan 'Ali, *Tarikh-i-Da'wat-o-'Azimat*, vol. iii (Lucknow, 1963)

Nizami, Khwaja Hasan, *Tarikh-i-Auliya* (*Nizami Ban Sari*) (Delhi 1945, 4th edn, Delhi, 1984)

Nizami, Khwaja Hasan Sani, *Tazkirah-i-Nizami* (Delhi, 1971)

Nizami, K. A., *Salatin-i-Dehli Kay Mazhabi Rujhanat* (Delhi, 1958)

——— *Tarikh-i-Masha'ikh-i-Chisht*, vol. i (revised edn, Delhi, n.d.)

——— *Shaikh Nizam-u'd-di Auliya* (National Book Trust: India, 1985)

——— *Tarikhi Maqalat* (Delhi, 1965)

Zahir-u'd-din, *Ikhbar-u'l-Akhbar* (Nami Press: Lucknow, 1305 AH)

WORK IN JAPANESE

Matsuo Ara, *Dargahs in Medieval India* (Institute of Oriental Culture, University of Tokyo: Tokyo, 1977)

GENERAL

Encyclopaedia of Islam, new edn

Encyclopaedia of Religion and Ethics, James Hastings (ed.) (Edinburgh, 1914)

Epigraphia Indo-Moslemica

Islamic Culture, Hyderabad

Journal of Islamic Studies (Oxford University Press, 1990–1)

Journal of the Pakistan Historical Society, Karachi

Memoirs of the Archaeological Survey of India

Pearson, J. D., *Index Islamicus*

Storey, C. A., *Persian Literature: A Bio-Bibliographical Survey* (London, 1935–53)

INDEX